BETWEEN
TWO FLAGS

This book is dedicated to my father who first told me the story of John Mitchel and Jenny Verner and to Diane, Julie, Hannah and Eve who have lived with it.

BETWEEN TWO FLAGS

JOHN MITCHEL & JENNY VERNER

ANTHONY G. RUSSELL

MERRION
PRESS

First published in 2015 by Merrion Press
8 Chapel Lane
Sallins
Co. Kildare

British Library Cataloguing in Publication Data
An entry can be found on request

978-1- 78537-000-7(paper)
978-1- 78537-001-4(cloth)
978-1- 78537-002-1(PDF)

Library of Congress Cataloging in Publication Data
An entry can be found on request

Printed in Ireland by SPRINT-print Ltd

CONTENTS

Acknowledgements

The writer wishes to express his appreciation to the following people and organizations:

Dr James Quinn of the Royal Irish Academy for his consistent insight and advice;

Dr John Nelson of the Non-Subscribing Presbyterian Church for providing much material on, and an interview about, the Revd John Mitchel;

Mrs Pat Brown, descendant of Matilda Mitchel, for many sources and photographs;

The staff of the National Library of Ireland for their kind, helpful efficiency;

Lisa Hyde and Conor Graham of Merrion Press for recognising an incredible story.

List of Plates

1. The plaque on the pavement in Dawson Street, Dublin, commemorating the first meeting of the Grand Orange Order.
2. Jenny Verner: 'Jenny was a masterpiece in miniature'. (Courtesy Pat Brown)
3. Revd John Mitchel: He 'fairly observed the legitimate distinction between persons and opinions…' observed Revd Bagot. (Courtesy Non-Subscribing Presbyterian Church, Newry)
4. Mrs Mitchel, John's mother: 'There was a clearness, and energy and a decisiveness about her modes of thought and action which powerfully impressed and fascinated those who had the advantage of her friendship'. (Courtesy Pat Brown)
5. John Mitchel: the rebel with the cultivated looks of Byron. He loved walking, talking and smoking. (Courtesy of Pat Brown)
6. Jenny's home, 52 Queen Street (now Dominic Street) Newry. Jenny eloped through the middle door. The end house below the chimney was the boyhood home of Lord Russell of Killowen, a nationalist who defended Parnell and became Chief Justice of England.
7. Drumcree Church, near Portadown, where John and Jenny were married in the tower. The rest of the building did not exist in 1836.
8. Apprentice Solicitor: John Mitchel's Certificate of Legal Apprenticeship dated 20 March 1836. (O'Connor Papers)
9. Thomas Davis invited Mitchel to join the council of the '82 Club. When Davis died on 16 September 1845 John Mitchel replaced him at the *Nation,* with a very different pen.

10. 1 Upper Leeson Street: the Mitchels' first home in Dublin, with the white doorway nearest the bridge over the Grand Canal. Here there were 'nights and suppers of the Gods, when the reckless gaiety of Irish temperament held fullest sway…'.
11. Thomas Francis Meagher in 1848: 'How fresh and clear and strong! What wealth of imagination and princely generosity of feeling! To me it was the revelation of a new and great nature, and, I reveled in it…'. John Mitchel on Meagher.
12. Rotunda, Sackville Street (now O'Connell Street, Dublin). Here the Confederation was to have a more practical and serious intent than the '82 Club.
13. Charles Gavan Duffy: It was Duffy who invited Mitchel to Dublin but he was more cautious than Mitchel and became a lifelong enemy.
14. The Tricolour: when Meagher introduced it in the Music Hall, Lower Abbey Street, Mitchel proclaimed: 'I hope to see that flag one day waving, as our national banner, over a forest of Irish pikes'.
15. William Smith O'Brien: Smith O'Brien, the Anglo-Irish landowner and Mitchel, the son of the manse, often disagreed but, unlike Gavan Duffy, O'Brien remained a favourite family friend.
16. Judges Dunne, Lefroy and Moore at Mitchel's trial: if there was to be another trial, Jenny suggested, '…the moment the Judge passes sentence he should be shot…'.
17. 8 Ontario Terrace was John and Jenny's second canal-side home in Dublin. From these steps an elegant Jenny urged the crowd not to allow John Mitchel to be transported.
18. Plaque on 8 Ontario Terrace.
19. Prison hulks in Bermuda: the *Dromedary* is to the right and is where Mitchel contemplated suicide. 'I hope to do my children some good before I die.'

30. Edmund Ruffin was an extreme Confederate who liked Mitchel but thought his *Southern Citizen* newspaper so extreme that it could harm the southern cause. (Library of Congress)

31. Naturalisation Certificate: in May 1860, before he returned to Paris with Jenny and the younger children, John Mitchel became a citizen of the United States. (O'Connor Papers)

32. Captain John Dooley was an Irish Catholic who recorded the death of his friend, Private Willie Mitchel. His father, the retired Major Dooley and John Mitchel, went into the Confederate camps to visit their sons. It was Major Dooley who finally broke the bad news of Willie's death to John Mitchel.

33. The plaque to Captain C. Mitchel, outside his grandfather's home, is surrounded by the laurels mentioned by his father in *Jail Journal*. It was erected to commemorate the 150th anniversary of the young captain's death.

34. Captain C. Mitchel: in 1896 Jenny presented her eldest son's sword, and the flag that flew over Sumter on the day he was killed, to Charleston Museum.

35. The plaque commemorating John Mitchel's imprisonment in Fortress Monroe. (Courtesy Kelly J. O'Grady)

36. Three Old Friends: John Martin, John Mitchel and Father Kenyon. 'Over these pleasant days in Paris impends a kind of a shadow. We three old friends, when we part this time, will probably never meet again, altogether.' (Courtesy Pat Brown)

37. Dromalane houses: in his absence, John Mitchel's brother-in-law Hill Irvine added the dressed granite house to the back of the Revd John Mitchel's older house. John Mitchel died in the room to the left of the laurels. (Courtesy Hannah Russell)

38. John Mitchel's graveyard, High Street, Newry: Mitchel lies with his parents in the tomb to the left of the obelisk. Jenny's tribute is to the far left. (Courtesy Hannah Russell)

39. Jenny's tribute: it is not the Celtic cross she originally wanted.

40. A 1970s political protest at Mitchel's statue, but not against his involvement in slavery. Few people were aware of that aspect of his politics. They were protesting against Ireland's membership of the Common Market.

41. The statue of John Mitchel: he stands, confident with his books, demanding to be heard. It is a statue to a man who was heroic; to a man who, more than any other writer or politician, defined the nationalist perception of the Great Famine. It is a statue to a rebel. It is not a statue to a great revolutionary. (Courtesy Hannah Russell)

CHAPTER ONE

Background – Before and After Drumcree

The story of John Mitchel and Jenny Verner is remarkable. Set amidst the mid-nineteenth century politics of both Ireland and the United States, theirs is the story of two unusual, handsome, committed and flawed people. They repeatedly sacrificed both their own happiness and the lives of their children, not for one cause but two. They were both ardent physical force Irish Republicans. They were both American Confederates. Their story, heroic in both geography and deed, is tainted for many, by their support of violence for political ends and, for most, by their support of slavery. Yet they were also passionate, compassionate and tolerant; they loved and cared for family and friends and had no time for ethnic and religious animosity. Their story is fascinating, complex and tragic. It originated in the landscape of Ulster, a landscape of low volcanic hills, rolling drumlins and sectarian violence. A landscape dominated by Church of Ireland Ascendancy landlords like the Verners; landlords who depended mainly upon the rents from tenant farmers and the cottage-based spinners and weavers of flax into linen. In contrast John Mitchel's father was a Presbyterian minister from tenant farming stock.

Although, following the Plantation of Ulster, both families had entered Ulster seeking land, by the 1830s they were from different classes. The Verners had become major landowners and landlords, a political force, but, as yet, lacking in 'heritable honours'.[1] In the 1830s, Irish landlords like the Verners, although politically weakened by the 1801 Act of Union and the loss of their parliament in Dublin, still sat astride their hunters surveying a fatally flawed economic system and an increasingly dysfunctional rural Irish landscape. They were unaware of the impact of a collapsing rural linen industry, unaware of approaching famine.

Jenny's father, James Verner, was the older brother of Sir William, First Baronet of Churchill, County Armagh who had 'succeeded to the estates of his paternal grand uncle, Thomas Verner Esq. in 1788'.[2] The Verners owned land in Armagh, Tyrone and Monaghan. In 1828, the *Newry Commercial Telegraph* praised Churchill, their house and grounds, near Loughall: '... a more chastely, beautiful and classic building, or more tastefully laid out pleasure grounds we have never beheld'.[3]

Dating back to the days before the Act of Union, the Verners, like most landlords, also had a townhouse in Dublin, so that they could attend sessions of the Irish parliament and enjoy a vibrant social life in the capital. A plaque on the pavement in Dawson Street, Dublin, close to the site of the Verners' townhouse, still records: 'The first meeting of the Grand Orange Lodge of Ireland was held on premises on this site on 9 April 1798.' The date 1798 is significant. It was the year of the United Irish Rebellion. In Ulster it was mainly a liberal, Presbyterian, merchant rebellion. It was preceded in 1795 by the agrarian Battle of the Diamond at Loughall, close to Churchill. This was a sectarian fight between the Defenders, a rural Catholic defence organization of peasants and artisans, and the Presbyterian and Church of Ireland Break o' Day Boys, who early in the morning attacked Catholic homes.

Afraid of a threat to their power and position from an alliance of liberal Presbyterians within the United Irish and the Catholic Defenders, the Verners identified with, and led, the Orange response; hence the plaque on Dawson Street, Dublin.

Following the Catholic Relief Acts of 1778 and 1792, which allowed Catholics increased rights of land tenure, sectarian conflict in north Armagh became especially violent. With almost equal numbers tolerance was a luxury neither side thought it could afford. In addition spade cultivation of the potato had increased the food supply for all and cut the death rate; but the proportion of Catholics was rising faster. With an increasing population, with increased rights of land tenure and with increasing political confidence, Catholics also began to participate in the rural linen industry. Thus competition for land and trade was increasing sectarian tension, especially in north Armagh. Magistrate John Ogle, in a letter dated 15 July 1796, described the ongoing spiral of violence in north Armagh between the Defenders and the Break o' Day Boys:

> They began about the year 1786 their outrages under the title of Break o' Day Boys ransacking the houses of Papists and taking not only arms but other valuables and thereby rendered the others more resolute to foresee the means of defence in their [own] hands and oppose force to force.[4]

Thus, it was this spiral of rustic violence that resulted in the 1795 Battle of the Diamond, near the Verner's home and led to the setting up of the Orange Order. Given the Verner's close identification with the Orange Order it is ironic that Jenny, through her marriage to John Mitchel and through her own convictions, meant that the name is also associated with extreme physical force republicanism. Jenny's father James was the grand-nephew of Thomas Verner. Initially James was to succeed to the Churchill estates but perhaps because of an unknown quarrel[5] he was replaced by his younger brother William. In 1788, the year he died, Thomas decreed that in the event of William's death the estate could pass through the family but was to avoid the 'unfortunate' James. By the 1830s, after two limited army careers, one in India and one in Dublin, the 'unfortunate James' lived in retirement in 52 Queen Street, now Dominic Street, Newry. He had an allowance of £400 from his younger brother, William.[6] James lived with Mary Ward and her two children Jenny and Richard. Although they lived as a married couple *Burke's Peerage* records that James Verner, 1777–1847, died unmarried.[7] However, despite the ill-defined relationship with her mother James loved Jenny and treated her as his natural daughter, sending her to Miss Bryden's School for young ladies in Marcus Square, Newry.

In Newry, Captain James and Mary Ward Verner lived beside, and were tenants of, the brewer Arthur Russell, the father of the future Lord Charles Russell of Killowen. Charles Russell would defend Parnell and become the first Catholic Lord Chief Justice of England since the Reformation. The two families were very friendly and, towards the end of her life when she was a widow in New York, Charles Russell would visit Jenny, remembering a 'weak and fragile' young woman.[8] Jenny Verner was a fifteen-year-old beauty when she first caught the eye of John Mitchel.

The Mitchels were originally tenant farmers in County Derry. Unlike the rest of Ireland, the mainly Presbyterian farmers of Ulster enjoyed Tenant Right. This unwritten agreement allowed a departing, or even an evicted tenant, to have the value of any improvements he had made and to sell his tenancy to someone else – provided of course it was someone the landlord approved of. The security offered by Tenant Right, allied to participation in the rural linen industry, encouraged investment in the farm. John Mitchel's paternal grandfather was one such tenant farmer near Cumber, Claudy, County Derry. His mother's people, the Hasletts in Derry, were merchants and bankers of English origin.

However, despite Tenant Right, Presbyterians, like Catholics, suffered under the Penal Laws, passed by the Ascendancy parliament in Dublin. For example, marriages performed by a Presbyterian minister were not recognized. Thus, the children of such marriages were deemed illegitimate, with implications for wills and land tenure. Denied access to Trinity College in Dublin, Presbyterian ministers, often the sons of tenant farmers, were educated at Glasgow University because, as Nancy Curtin observed, they 'made their way to the more congenial universities of Scotland',[9] where their church was the Established Church. As their wealth increased Presbyterians sought commensurate political power. In the late eighteenth century they did so through participation in the Volunteer movement. With the government weakened by the revolutionary war in North America, Presbyterian merchants and sympathetic members of the Ascendency parliament in Dublin raised the Volunteers, essentially a private army, to repel a feared French invasion. Although raised to support the government the Volunteers remained outside their control and in 1782 were able to use a limited parliamentary franchise in one hand and a musket in the other to force reform; to achieve free trade, for Ireland, and the short lived, legislative independence of the Irish parliament. Although the Irish parliament could now pass laws, without needing the approval of the Westminister parliament, it had no control over the Irish executive, which along with the Lord Lieutenant continued to be appointed by the government in London. It therefore remained a weak parliament.

Initially the Volunteers were heartened by, and were supporters of, the 1789 storming of the Bastille and the French Revolution.

However, later violent and ungodly events in revolutionary France moved many towards supporting the government. This was especially the case in north Armagh, and Churchill, where Catholic competition for resources was greatest. By the 1790s many radical Presbyterians had also become disillusioned with their great hero, Thomas Paine, the author of the 1791 *Rights of Man*. In 1794 Thomas Paine followed the *Rights of Man* with the *Age of Reason*. Presbyterians had readily agreed with the idea that the individual had inherent rights but when, in the *Age of Reason*, Paine attacked parts of the Bible it did not sit well with stern Presbyterians. Many preferred a bad Protestant government that believed in God to French radicals who might reject the Bible.

A.T.Q. Stewart in *The Narrow Ground* succinctly summed up their dilemma:

> The Presbyterian is happiest when he is being radical. The austere doctrines of Calvinism, the simplicity of his worship, the democratic government of his Church, the memory of the martyred Covenanters, and the Scottish refusal to yield or dissemble – all these incline him to that difficult and cantankerous disposition which is characteristic of a certain kind of political radicalism. His natural instinct is to distrust the outward forms of civil government, unless they are consonant with his religious principles.[10]

Although democratic and radical, Thomas Paine's later writing in *Age of Reason* was not consonant with the 'austere doctrines of Calvinism' and many who had formerly admired him rejected him. The Revd John Nelson, historian of the Non-Subscribing

Presbyterian Church, in an interview with the writer, agreed with A.T.Q. Stewart. He too referred to the democratic tradition of the prospering Presbyterian tenant farmers. Democracy was part of their psyche and in Presbyterian churches all heads of family had an equal vote. The Revd Nelson also referred to the Presbyterian resistance to being governed and their love of freedom of thought: 'within Presbyterianism, there was an ingrained dislike of government, of being told what to do, of being told what to think'.[11] However, having a vote was not the same as having power and as the Revd Nelson pointed out 'the usual social distinctions applied and the tenant farmer was unlikely to talk down the landlord, but the farmer was very proud of his vote'.[12] The dislike of government, of being told what to do was amplified by historical resentment. Presbyterians, who had held the Walls of Derry, helped William defeat King James and protected the Crown for Protestantism 'thought they had they received little credit or reward for their sacrifice'. [13]

Thus, in the 1790s there were tensions within the Presbyterian mind, within the Presbyterian community, especially in and around the Verners' Churchill. Here, especially for demographic reasons, Presbyterians were more likely to support the landlord and Orangeism. By 1793, the government had suppressed the Volunteers, and in 1796 replaced them, for the defence of the realm, with the government controlled Irish Yeomanry. Reflecting the tensions between a dislike of being told what to do, a pride in freedom of thought, a love of the Bible and fear of a Catholic takeover, Presbyterians in Ulster split into radical United Irish rebels and 'austere' loyalists, who were more likely to join the Irish Yeomanry. Thus, on the 1798 battlefields of Ulster the mainly Presbyterian United Irish and the mainly Presbyterian Yeomanry confronted each other. The Crown forces also comprised of other auxiliaries including the Irish-speaking Monaghan militia. As in Wexford and the rest of Ireland the United Irish were routed.

However, following the failure of the 1798 Rebellion, when they felt let down by the Catholic Defenders and were appalled by stories from Wexford of sectarian massacres during the rebellion, many radical Presbyterians, belatedly, embraced the 1801 Act of Union, which abolished the Irish Parliament in Dublin. With the relaxation of the Penal Laws, especially against Presbyterians, they participated fully in the emergent Industrial Revolution. First in supplying and working in increasingly large rural, water-powered mills and then being part of the rapid steam-powered, mechanized manufacturing growth of Belfast. Economically they increasingly looked to the coalfields of central Scotland and Lancashire for power and markets while politically they were enjoying their new rights and looking away from the neutered Irish capital towards the real centre of power – Westminster. Even many Presbyterians whose families had been liberal rebels in 1798 were now unionists. They perceived themselves as a new 'enlightened generation'. Such was the case with William Drennan and John Swanwick Drennan who proudly recognized that their father, William, had been the founding philosopher of the United Irish, even before Wolfe Tone,[14] whose grave at Bodenstown, County. Kildare is revered as the resting place of the father of Irish Republicanism.

However, John Mitchel's father, the Revd John Mitchel, was not from increasingly conservative and industrializing Belfast. He was from the periphery of industrial Ulster, from Derry and later Newry. Unlike the majority of Presbyterians, he was from, and remained on, the liberal edge of Presbyterianism. In a speech in Conciliation Hall on 13 July 1846, with reference to his pride in his father's radical views, John Mitchel claimed that in 1798 his father had been a rebel with men who 'thought liberty worth some blood letting'.[15] If true, the future Revd John Michel would have been a seventeen-year-old rebel.

Born on 11 November 1781, the Revd John Mitchel was the son of a tenant farmer, James Mitchel of Ballyarton, near Dungiven, County Derry.[16] Unlike his own son, who was later able to attend Trinity College, Dublin the Revd Mitchel graduated from Glasgow University where, unlike his son in Dublin,[17] he was remembered as a diligent student. He received his licence to teach on 7 August 1804 and returned to Dungiven, as a minister, on 19 March 1805. On 1 August 1819 he was installed in First Derry.[18] This was a collegiate appointment meaning that, unusually within Presbyterianism, he shared the ministry with the Revd George Hay, who was tolerant of the views of others and disliked sectarianism. There were only two collegiates in Ulster. The other was First Belfast. First Derry was a very significant and prestigious congregation that increased the perception of the Revd Mitchel as a minister of renown, and as a man who could cooperate and work with others, a skill later lacking in his son. In 1822 the Great Synod of Ulster was held in Newry and the Revd John Mitchel was elected Moderator of the Presbyterian Church. Following this, Newry Presbyterians, 'having received favourable accounts of Mr. Mitchel's clerical conduct and character', 'invited him to be their minister and he 'entered the care of the Newry Congregation on 2 September, 1823'.[19] It was in Newry that 'the rays of divine truth began to dissipate the murky gloom of Calvinism; and his innate candour would not allow him to close his eyes against the perception of the light'.[20] The Revd Mitchel became a 'New Light' Unitarian, although he disliked the appellation. He wrote, 'I firmly believe, what Christ himself has taught me, that the Father is "the only true God" and yet I equally repudiate the unscriptural denomination of Unitarian, as that term is usually understood.'[21] Even in rebellion he was in favour of 'moderate Unitarianism'. Moderation in rebellion was not to be a trait associated with his son.

Although the Revd John Mitchel engaged his opponents in strong written argument, about 'the oneness of God', the Revd Daniel Bagot, who led the arguement for the Deity of Christ, noted that the Revd Mitchel wrote with 'a greater amount of liberal and conciliating charity than any other... he has well and fairly observed the legitimate distinction between persons and opinions'.[22] In arguments with political opponents the Revd Mitchel's son would make little attempt to distinguish between person and principle.

Having led the split in the Presbyterian Church in Newry, the Revd John Mitchel's independence of thought was further demonstrated when he defied his own congregation by supporting the Catholic candidate in a local election. It earned him the title 'Papist Mitchel'.[23] Equally tolerant of other faiths, but unlike his father in his lack of belief, John Mitchel was to take the Revd Mitchel's rebellious tendencies to the extreme.

Thus, the young John Mitchel, aged eight when he moved to Newry, would have been aware of his father's liberal philosophy, aware of his theological anguish and aware of the1828 schism. He would also have been aware of his father's kindness and toleration of conflicting ideas. Alas, toleration of others' ideas would not be identifiable in the son.

Born in 1786, much less is known about John Mitchel's mother, Mary Haslett, whose merchant family was involved in the 1798 Rebellion. William Dillon, the son of a close political and family friend, who was asked by Jenny to write a posthumous

1888 biography of her husband, reflecting on family testimonies, described the older Mrs Mitchel as small, 'full of intelligence, wit and fire … There was a clearness, and energy and a decisiveness about her modes of thought and action which powerfully impressed and fascinated those who had the advantage of her friendship.'[24] These are attributes identified by both friend and foe in her elder son. Although devoted to the memory of the Revd John Mitchel, her reaction to their granddaughter Henrietta's conversion to Catholicism would suggest that, at least in later life, she was less tolerant of Catholicism than her late husband had been.

However, one feature of John Mitchel's upbringing that was common to both father and mother was a very strong sense of being Irish. Their house on the Dromalane Road in Newry was an Irish home. Presbyterians, both radical and unionist, embraced Irish culture and language. They were happy to drop a few words into a conversation. Up until the Home Rule movement of the 1880s Presbyterians perceived themselves as being Irish. For example, until 1878 the Revd Classen Porter was the Non-Subscribing Presbyterian Minister in Larne. He was pro-Union yet his young son wrote:

> R.W. Porter is my name
> Ireland is my nation
> Larne is my dwelling place
> And Christ my expectation.

This verse was copied into hundreds of Presbyterian schoolbooks.[25] Perhaps the Revd John Mitchel's elder son's sense of being Irish was extreme, but it was an extreme version of how Presbyterians perceived themselves for most of the nineteenth century. They looked to Scotland for their education but thought themselves Irish.

Thus as the nineteenth century progressed, as relatively secure tenant farmers, as rural spinners and weavers of flax, and later as workers, merchants and industrialists in Belfast the Presbyterians of Ulster were prospering. They were more conservative than the previous generation and generally satisfied with the political status of Ireland, within the Union, within the expanding British Empire. In contrast however, the Catholics of Ireland, despite initially supporting the 1801 Act of Union, soon turned against it. The hierarchy of the Catholic Church had originally supported union with Britain in the hope of being granted emancipation. When it did not happen Catholics felt both betrayed and isolated. It was then the Catholic landowner, and lawyer from Derrynane, County Kerry, Daniel O'Connell, with the backing of the priests, emerged to lead a successful campaign that culminated in 1829 with the granting of Catholic Emancipation. However, within the Union, Emancipation did not bring improved living standards. Without Tenant Right, Catholics were still mainly rural peasants paying increasing rents. O'Connell, therefore, began his second great campaign for the restoration of an Irish parliament and the Repeal of the Act of Union.

The Revd John Mitchel had strongly supported O'Connell's campaign for Catholic Emancipation. However, like many other Presbyterians, this support for Emancipation did not extend to support for O'Connell's Repeal Association. As noted above, although there was a small Protestant Repeal Association, Presbyterians were increasingly content within the Union and Repeal of the Union was perceived as an unnecessary Catholic wish. It was opposed, not only by the theologically and politically conservative Henry Cooke but also, by the more liberal Henry Montgomery. Cooke was an evangelical Presbyterian minister who successfully united Protestant

Christianity against O'Connell's Catholicism and is recognized as the father of Ulster Unionism. In contrast, the Unitarian Montgomery was Cooke's great theological opponent and had supported Catholic Emancipation. However, Montgomery wrote to a disappointed Daniel O'Connell expressing his opposition to the repeal of the Act of Union. In turn, on 22 February 1831, the Revd John Mitchel wrote to Montgomery supporting his anti-repeal stance:

> My Dear Montgomery, Your letter to O'Connell has been of essential service in many ways, and the virulence it has called forth from the O'Connellites will do you no harm. You have with you all the virtue and intelligence of the country…You stand upon unassailable ground; you are well able to maintain it.[26]

In contrast, the Revd Mitchel's elder son would strongly support repeal and initially supported O'Connell. However, for very different reasons John Mitchel was to become one of O'Connell's most bitter opponents.

One of eight children, five of whom survived childhood – John, Matilda, Margaret, Mary and Henrietta – John Mitchel, five feet ten inches tall with the cultivated looks of a romantic rebel, was part of a loving, close-knit family. Born in Cammish, County Derry on 3 November 1815 he was eight when the family moved to Newry. They lived on the Dromalane Road, at the edge of the nineteenth-century town. John was a solitary child who loved walking the hills but when attending Dr Henderson's Classical School, in Needham Place, now John Mitchel Place, he met and formed a lifelong friendship with John Martin. Both suffered from asthma. John Martin loved and remained loyal to John Mitchel even as their political thoughts matured in different directions. John Martin would become a leading non-violent Home Ruler.

After school, on 4 July 1831 John entered Trinity College, Dublin. He graduated but turned away from following his father into the church. He was sent to his mother's people, the Hasletts, in Derry, to be trained as a banker – a position he hated. In a letter to his father he pleaded to be allowed to return to Newry. He wrote, '...I have come to the conclusion that the thing is really not fit for me, nor I for it...such intermittent slavery is intolerable.'[27] Given his enthusiastic support of slavery in later life there is an unintended irony in the young Mitchel describing slavery as intermittent. Perhaps because John suggested in the letter his work was affecting his health his father relented, and allowed him to return to Newry.

However, the handsome young John was also enjoying a vibrant social life. In a letter to his sister Matilda, from Belfast in 1834, he described meeting 'dashing' young ladies and 'clerical, medical and philosophical lions'. [28] He fell in love with one of the 'older' young ladies and in the winter of 1834 he walked from Newry to Belfast to be with her. To his regret he was not allowed to meet with his love and was taken back to Newry, where he became very ill. Although he recovered from both the emotional and physical trauma, bronchial problems were a feature for the rest of his life. In March 1836 he was apprenticed to the Newry solicitor John Henry Quinn, a friend of the family.[29]

John Mitchel and Jenny Verner were from different religions and different classes. The Mitchels were of the manse, Dissenters and middle-class Presbyterians. The Verners were Protestants, Church of Ireland, landed minor aristocracy. Despite this wealthy connection, Captain James Verner, a retired army officer, lived a relatively modest life in Queen Street, Newry. The moment the twenty-one-year-old

John Mitchel met the fifteen-year-old Jenny Verner, on a street in Newry, is imagined, with a 'Mills and Boon' intensity, by Rebecca O'Connor, who wrote an admiring biography of Jenny Verner Mitchel.

> Her life is open and clear from her fifteenth year and the moment her eyes met those of John Mitchel, for the first time and with the shock of love, so strong as to be a commitment. They were walking on opposite sides of the Glanrye [Clanrye] River... The small stream would not long divide them.[30]

With the suggestion that Jenny's father might move to France for the sake of his health, John and Jenny decided to elope. In November 1836 the young lovers planned that Mitchel would make to go to Dublin on legal business, as usual, but would double back and wait for Jenny, with a carriage, at the foot of the Dublin Road. However, a clerk in Quinn's office, an informer, told Revd Mitchel who then told Captain Verner. A watch was kept on Jenny and on the Dublin Road, but since the elopement was not planned until the following day nothing happened and the watch was withdrawn. The next day Jenny left her house at 52 Queen Street, by the front door. William Dillon tells of the young couple galloping in a carriage to Warrenpoint and rowing out from the beach to stop and board the Liverpool steamer, in the middle of Carlingford Lough.[31] Less romantic, but perhaps more realistic for a winter's night, the *Dublin Mail* of 16 November 1836 reported that they fled through Dundalk, Drogheda and Dublin and then on to Liverpool. Here John learned that a marriage licence might be issued more quickly in Chester. There the 'unfortunate' James Verner caught 'Lieutenant and Miss Johnson' in lodgings, chastely reading to each other from

Disraeli's *Young Duke*. Jenny, whose age was given as fourteen by the *Mail*, was sent away to the country and since she was a minor John was put in Kilmainham Jail to await trial at Armagh Assizes. Eighteen days later, on 29 November 1836, he was discharged on bail.[32] John 'succeeded in finding out where the lady of his love was concealed,'[33] and he persuaded Jenny to go through with their plans. John Mitchel married Jenny Verner in the Church of Ireland, Drumcree on 3 February 1837.

The Revd David Babbington, who married them, was to labour 'tirelessly to relieve widespread destitution' during the Great Famine.[34] His church was undergoing renovations at the time and weddings took place in the porch, which still exists today. Upon their return to Newry Jenny was reconciled with her mother and father but not with the Churchill Verners. Jenny had not just married a man. She had married a one-man 'revolutionary' movement. John Mitchel was a natural rebel. He had already rebelled against a father whom he loved dearly. He was to rebel against the British, against Daniel O'Connell, against his colleagues in Young Ireland, against his newspaper the *Nation*, against the Australian authorities, against the USA, against the Confederate States Government and finally against the Fenians. It was to be a most interesting and tragic life for both John and Jenny.

After their wedding the young Mitchels moved first into his father's house in Dromalane, and then to a cottage on the same road. Jenny was warmly accepted as a Mitchel and throughout her life received and returned kindness. On 3 June 1839 John qualified as a solicitor[35] and formed a partnership with Samuel Livingstone Frazer at 8, Trevor Hill. Frazer, who was ten years older than Mitchel, had qualified in 1832 and was already a successful attorney in Newry. He was a Freemason and a member of the Revd Mitchel's Non-Subscribing Presbyterian Church. These were happy days: days of

parties, dancing and earnest conversations – especially around the
fireplace of their good friend John Martin, whom they often visited
at Loughorne, north of Newry. John and Jenny had four children,
John, James, Henrietta and Willie. Jenny was enjoying the life of
a young, beautiful middle-class wife. John was enjoying smoking,
walking and talking, his three favourite pastimes. Years later, John
Martin's sister, in a letter to Jenny, recalled those days in the County
Down countryside: 'And when you and he and the children would
come to Loughorne, it was a sight to see him under the shadow of
a big tree, with his boys tumbling over him…he was the very type
of a happy man.'[36]

However, Mitchel the Attorney was not such a happy man. In a
letter to John Martin he envied Martin his farm:

> You will think this all extravagant because your ordinary
> employments are not of the tormenting character that
> mine are. But if you want to understand me quite well,
> spend seven years quarrelling for other people about
> matters that you would see at the devil…guarding
> and fencing your client…arguing eternally with 'shrill
> attorney logic' about less than nothing…[37]

Despite these frustrated comments about the trivial nature of his
professional practice, the treatment and insecurity, especially of
Catholic tenant farmers, unsettled the young lawyer. Following
sectarian disturbances and 'in the legal proceedings arising out
of these affrays John Mitchel sympathized with and was often
employed by the Catholics'.[38] Like Magistrate Ogle, forty years
before, Mitchel recognized the injustice of Orangemen sitting as
magistrates in cases involving fellow Orangemen. Indeed, Jenny's

uncle Sir William Verner, who was to be elevated to the peerage in 1846 and was a member of Dublin Orange Lodge 176, was removed as a magistrate in 1837 because of his 'partisan behaviour'[39] in neighbouring County Armagh.

His experience in the County Down countryside was to have a profound impact upon John Mitchel, and was to mark him as different from many of his more urban, future colleagues in Young Ireland; and since the nature of the pre-Famine rural economy helps us to understand both John Mitchel's thinking and the selective severity of the Great Famine, then it is worth examining the social economy of the pre-Famine landscape in Mitchel's County Down.

Mainly due to Tenant Right, pre-Famine County Down was described as 'the best conditioned quarter of Ireland'.[40] However, below and employed by tenant farmers were the cottiers and labourers who existed either outside or on the fringe of the money economy. They could not afford to hire the services of John Mitchel. Cottiers and labourers rented a small area of land from a tenant farmer. On it they could only afford to grow potatoes. Often for the cottier no money changed hands. Their rent was their labour (although it was nominally fixed for an amount of £.s.d.). Cottiers had a long-standing agreement with tenant farmers for year-round work, and a certain security. Labourers were casual and without security. If they were not granted a plot of land they queued in market squares hoping for short-term employment at 4s per week. Often, not being able to write, they recorded each day's work as a notch on a stick.

The *Belfast Penny Journal* highlighted the vertical dichotomy between the better off tenant farmers and their cottiers and labourers. On conditions for cottiers and labourers the *Belfast*

Penny Journal commented: 'Many of the dwellings I saw upon the road looked to me like abodes of extinguished hope ... grovelling, despairing almost idiotic wretchedness. I did not know that men and women, upright and made in the likeness of God could live in styes, like swine, with swine.'[41] Ironically, despite being badly clothed and poorly housed in mud cabins, the potato diet meant the cottiers and labourers were well fed and generally taller than the English proletariat. In the absence of pasture, feeding potato slops and skins to fatten a pig was a way of gaining some cash. The pig was an asset that needed to be taken into the cabin at night.

This local, pre-Famine, rural economy was also described by witnesses to the 1833-34 *Commission to Enquire into the Conditions of the Poorer Classes in Ireland* and to the *1843-45* Devon Commission, the 'Commission on Occupation of Land (Ireland)'. Three Church of Ireland clergymen from the Newry area (Clonallan parish) described housing conditions to the enquiry:

> The cabins of the poorer classes are generally of clay, roofed with sods and thatch; they seldom contain any furniture, except, perhaps, a table, and a chair or stool. The bedsteads are mostly filled with straw...they seldom have sheets, and frequently their only covering is the clothes they wear throughout the day.[42]

The Devon Commission, set up by Sir Robert Peel to report on conditions in the Irish countryside, confirmed the evidence from the earlier report. Its witnesses – better-off farmers, clergymen and land agents – gave evidence showing average farm size around Newry to be seven acres; a significant number for the Commission. It was the number it identified for holdings being 'inadequate to support the families residing upon them'. In Ireland there were 326,084 farms of seven acres or fewer.[43] Their tenants, cottiers and labourers would bear the brunt of the Great Famine. George William Bradell, an agent, told the Devon Commission that in Clonduff (to the east of Newry) farm size ranged from three to thirty acres, that there was frequent recourse to usurers to pay the rent and that many relied on money from children who had already emigrated to England. For Donaghmore parish (to the north of the town) John Martin's uncle, James Harshaw, a farmer of eighty acres, reported increasing population and therefore severe subdivision of holdings, with the majority under fifteen acres. The larger farms, like his own eighty-acre farm, practiced a five or six-year rotation with fertiliser and were therefore not dependent upon the potato. When asked about the smaller tenantry he replied with understatement, 'I think their comforts are not improving.'[44] The condition of the labourers he thought had changed little.

Even before the Great Famine, this was the rural environment that fuelled John Mitchel's sense of injustice and opposition to England's direct rule of Ireland. Mitchel was scornful of the work of the Devon Commission. He quoted Daniel O'Connell: it was 'a jury of butchers trying a sheep for its life'. It was the 'Gospel of Irish Landlords'. Its main aim was to argue for consolidation of small farms which 'would require the removal of about 196,368 families' or the one million people at the base of the social hierarchy. For Mitchel, with hindsight from the Great Famine, this represented 'the killing of a million of persons'.[45]

Fired by his legal work and his observations of the landscape described above, John Mitchel's public political journey began in 1839 when he helped organize the visit of Daniel O'Connell to Newry. Thousands lined the streets and O'Connell, after being received by the

Catholic Bishop of Dromore, Dr Blake, in his cathedral, sat down in a local hotel to a dinner with 400 reformers, including John Mitchel. In February 1840 the family moved to Banbridge to further develop Fraser and Mitchel Solicitors. Following the death of his beloved father on 28 February 1840 John Mitchel, who as the eldest son had inherited the family home, made the (Dromalane) house over to his mother. Despite this act of filial kindness, in *Jail Journal,* he was to express sorrow at the grief he had caused his father: 'I wish the mild shade of my father wore a less reproachful aspect. I wish he had less reason.'[46]

In June 1844, at Tullyish, County Down, John Mitchel attended his first Repeal Association public meeting.[47] His intimate knowledge of the Ulster landscape and of the poverty of small tenants, cottiers and labourers was to mark him out from the other, more urban members of the Repeal movement, and later Young Ireland. His father had rejected O'Connell's bid for repeal of the 1801 Act of Union. John Mitchel was now actively seeking it. As a solicitor John Mitchel had to make trips to Dublin, but increasingly less for legal and more for political reasons. On such a trip, at Turner's Glen, on the outskirts of Newry (it was Samuel Turner who betrayed the United Irish Directory to Lord Downshire)[48], he met Jenny's old Queen Street neighbour, the future Lord Charles Russell of Killowen. Years later, Russell recalled the meeting in his diary:

> The only time I ever recollect seeing John Mitchel was when the railway from Dublin reached no further than Drogheda. We were going to Dublin and both got on the coach together on the Ballybot side of the town, close to Turner's Glen (Bottom of the Dublin Road) …I still think of him as the most brilliant journalistic writer I have ever known.

This was high praise for Mitchel, from a man who would take a very different path, and would hold an office of state in a regime hated by Mitchel. Russell described John Mitchel as having 'a certain sharpness of feature and nobility of brow that gave him a peculiarly intellectual appearance. His dark grey eyes seemed full of dreams and melancholy.'[49]

John Mitchel's career in journalism began with a review, letter and article in the *Nation*.[50] His vivid, imaginative writing gained the attention and admiration of Thomas Davis, Charles Gavan Duffy and John Blake Dillon who, in 1842, founded the *Nation*. Dillon's son William would write Mitchel's first biography. For T.F.O. O'Sullivan, author of the 1944 *Young Irelanders*, there never was 'published...a journal which was imbued with higher ideals of nationality, which attracted such a brilliant band of writers in prose and verse...or which exercised a greater influence over all classes'.[51] It appealed to all classes and was read to those who could not read, or afford to buy it, by friends, clergy and schoolmasters. T.F.O. O'Sullivan especially admired the *Nation*'s editor, the young Protestant lawyer Thomas Davis, born in Mallow in 1814. Thomas Davis was:

> ...indefatigable in searching out efficient recruits amongst the young men of his acquaintance, kindling their ambition and filling them with the same generous spirit of mutual forgiveness for the past, and a common hope for the future, by which he designed to obliterate the religious feuds of ages and raise up a new Irish nation.[52]

This 'gifted circle of young Irishmen, of all religions and none' became known as Young Ireland. For Mitchel they were very different from the 'obscure people, generally very humble servants of O'Connell'. [53]

In April 1845, Davis began to create an identity separate from O'Connell's Repeal Movement. He formed the '82 Club with a view to it providing an officer corps for any future national guard.[54] 1782, mainly due to the implied threat from the armed Volunteer Movement, was the year the Irish parliament had gained a limited independence from Westminster. In reality, like the officer corps of the original Volunteers from the 1780s, whom it sought to honour, the '82 Club was mostly an elitist, splendidly uniformed social and debating society. Davis asked Mitchel to join its council and it was as an '82 Club delegate that he went to London in support of William Smith O'Brien, who had been imprisoned, by the House of Commons, in the basement, because he would only participate in parliamentary debates on Ireland.[55] Smith O'Brien, born in 1803 in Dromoland, County Clare, was an Irish aristocrat who began his political career as a Unionist but one who supported Catholic Emancipation. He then joined O'Connell's Repeal Association and would become both leader of Young Ireland and a lifelong friend of the Mitchel family. In contrast, Gavan Duffy, born in 1816, was the son of a Monaghan shopkeeper and although an able journalist and fellow Young Irelander he would become John Mitchel's most enduring personal and political enemy.

On his visit to the imprisoned Smith O'Brien Mitchel met Thomas Carlyle, famous for his anti-Irish views yet, ironically, a kindred economic and philosophical spirit.[56]

A strong relationship was developing between the founders of the *Nation* and John Mitchel. So much so that in August 1845 John Mitchel invited Charles Gavan Duffy to join himself, John Martin and Newry man John O'Hagan, born 1822, on a walking tour from Rostrevor to

Donegal. O'Hagan, a lawyer and contributor to the *Nation,* was already a staunch friend to Duffy. Looking back on that journey, over three decades later, when they were personal enemies, Duffy remembered a cultured, suave and 'happily married' Mitchel who 'lived contentedly among his books.'[57] He had been so content that on 23 June 1844 he had even refused to go to Dublin on a Repeal delegation. Mitchel wrote, 'A deputation goes this night to Dublin with address and rent, of which deputation I was named one, but totally refused to go, as I could not leave my business.'[58] And almost a year earlier in September 1843 Mitchel had written to Duffy refusing an invitation to become more closely involved in the governance of the Repeal movement:

> …the project of this council is a noble one, the plot a good plot, the service an honourable one…not to have been a member will hereafter be a source of regret; but in short, I cannot afford to neglect my business. I have a wife and children. To devote myself to this cause would simply ruin me, and I cannot sacrifice my family.[59]

The last sentence was to become prophetically ironic, given the sacrifices Jenny and, especially his children, would have to make when Mitchel crossed 'the path of the British car of conquest'. Two of his children would be 'crushed to atoms'.[60] The council referred to in the letter was probably O'Connell's Council of Three Hundred, which never met, and will be referred to in the following chapter.

Duffy also commented on meeting John Martin: 'Mr. Martin – the eldest of the party – a gentleman farmer of unusual culture, but whose gentle manners and feeble health gave little promise of political action. He had been Mitchel's schoolfellow, and his life then and thereafter was undoubtedly ruled by this fact.'[61]

Although with the benefit of hindsight Gavan Duffy was suggesting an asymmetrical relationship between Martin and Mitchel, he was also recognizing Martin's qualities as a peacemaker. For example, when visiting Bryansford the four young men stayed in a lodge owned by Lord Roden, who left a Bible on every toilet table. Mitchel, the son of the Manse, objected; he would not let the Bible be thrust upon them and he fumed 'I'll ring the bell and order the waiter to carry them off forthwith'. In contrast to Mitchel's reaction, John Martin, 'who acted as general peacemaker insisted that the Bibles were doing us no hurt, that we were not forced to read them, that Lord Roden meant well...'[62] The disparity in their reactions and difference in character illuminated by this incident would be a constant during the lives of John Mitchel and John Martin. Mitchel would fume; Martin would reflect and reason.

As the four 'Ulstermen bred among flax and linen'[63] travelled towards Enniskillen, hoping to experience an Orange demonstration, they discussed politics. O'Hagan, whom Duffy thought, 'brought a rare insight and sagacity',[64] summarized the opinions of his walking companions towards the Union, when he wrote the following often quoted, simple but bitter, verse:

How did they pass the Union?
By perjury and fraud;
By slaves who sold their land for gold
As Judas sold his God...[65]

O'Hagan's doggerel was taught in the Republic of Ireland's National Schools until the 1960s. However, like many of the Young Irelanders, he was later absorbed into the establishment. When the Land Law (Ireland) Act of 1881 was passed John O'Hagan 'was appointed a

Judicial Commissioner with the rank of Justice of the High Court of Justice'.[66]

Mitchel's contentment with a legal and bucolic life, as suggested in the above letter to John Martin, was not as content as Duffy thought. In June 1845 Thomas Davis, described by Mitchel as 'the foremost and best, the gentlest and bravest'[67] of the Young Irelanders, died from scarlet fever. In the autumn John Mitchel overcame his earlier reservations and, after considering returning to Newry, accepted an invitation, from Gavan Duffy, to join the staff of the *Nation* full time. At this stage Mitchel's *Life of Aodh O'Neil* 'was still unpublished, and few suspected the remarkable powers as a writer and speaker he was destined to develop.'[68]

In October 1845, Jenny, John and their four children left 'a little village on the pastoral Bann'[69] to take centre stage in national and political life, first at 1 Heathfield, Upper Lesson Street and then at 8 Ontario Terrace, Dublin. The John Mitchel who arrived in Dublin was in the moderate mainstream of Repeal thought. John Mitchel, in supporting Repeal, had not gone the way of most of his fellow northern Presbyterians who were enjoying a fast-developing urban prosperity associated with the Union and commerce with Britain. Mitchel, through his walking and legal work, knew of the plight of the rural poor. He believed Repeal was part of the answer to their conditions. However, at this stage he thought Ireland could win Repeal using constitutional methods. On 13 July 1846, in repudiating O'Connell's accusation that 'juvenile members'[70] were trying to split the Association by opposing a parliamentary compromise with the Whigs, he declared:

> This is a legally organized and constitutional society,
> seeking to attain its object, as all the world knows,
> by peaceable means and none other. Constitutional

agitation is the very basis of it; and nobody who contemplates any other mode of bringing about the independence of the country has a right to be here...I believe that the legislative independence of Ireland can be won by these peaceful means if boldly, honestly and steadfastly carried out.[71]

Peaceful means and constitutional agitation were not to remain John Mitchel's way.

At the same time as John was becoming more and more involved in the affairs of Ireland family life continued and Mary (Minnie), John and Jenny's fifth child, was born in Dublin on 16 August 1846.

CHAPTER TWO

Nights and Suppers of the Gods

As John Mitchel settled into his new career he used his position 'to scowl on the engine of foreign rule'.[1] His home became a centre of political discussion where ironically, given Mitchel's views on 'the foul fiend of English imperialism',[2] Thomas Carlyle was an admired visitor. Carlyle repaid the compliment and thought Mitchel to be 'a noble, chivalrous fellow, full of talent and manful temper of every kind'.[3] Of his visit Carlyle wrote, 'Mitchel's wife, especially his mother (Presbyterian parson's widow of the best Scotch type), his frugally elegant small house and table pleased me much, as did the man himself...' However, he grieved to see Mitchel 'rushing on destruction, palpable, by attack of windmills'.[4]

Despite a mutual admiration, Mitchel strongly disagreed with Carlyle's view of Oliver Cromwell, as the yet unrecognized face of Ireland's 'first friend'. Mitchel countered:

> We, being Irish and not English, do hold to the opinion that Oliver Cromwell was strictly and literally a curse to this unfortunate country, inflicted upon us, doubtless for our sins, – that instead of being, as our vehement friend preaches 'God's message', his whole mission and teaching here were a genuine gospel of the Devil...[5]

However, Mitchel did admire Carlyle's prose, his opposition to utilitarianism, his support of structured hierarchal society, his criticism of O'Connell and his praise for the role of the hero. In the *Nation* on 7 February 1846, he even declared himself to be a Tory – and showed himself to be instinctively conservative.

> Often we think that if we were English, instead of Irish, we should be determined conservatives, jealous of change in the time-honoured institutions of our ancestors; intolerant of democratic freedom of speech, that rudely questions and takes to task the high traditions and stately usage of the ancient monarchy of England.[6]

For Mitchel, this tolerant reference to England was a rare moment of political empathy. Despite his sympathy for the Irish peasant, it places John Mitchel on the right of the political spectrum and indicates the future direction of his skewed decision-making.

Carlyle was only one of many visitors to John and Jenny's home. In *The Last Conquest of Ireland (Perhaps)* Mitchel fondly recalled the social life of this time, as the Young Irelanders visited each other's houses: 'Nights and suppers of the Gods, when the reckless gaiety of Irish temperament held fullest sway …Those nights, winged with genial wit and cordial friendship.'[7] Gavan Duffy, more prosaically but just as fondly, remembered Saturday nights; nights of 'tea and serious debate until 10pm; followed by 'a light supper, pleasant talk, fun and song until midnight…A cordial friendship warmed and harmonized these pleasant evenings.'[8] But such friendship did not stop political fractures; first as Young Ireland distanced itself from O'Connell's Repeal Association and then within Young

Ireland itself.In July 1846 Young Ireland, with Mitchel to the fore, was splitting from O'Connell's Repeal Movement over the 'Peace Resolutions'.

The earnest young men from the *Nation* reserved the right to use force to achieve their ends. For most in Young Ireland it was, initially, a theoretical position. If Ireland was a nation it had the right to bear arms. A nation could not rely solely on moral force, as advocated by O'Connell. In his famous *Sword* speech on 28 July 1846, Thomas Francis Meagher, whilst not seeking an armed rebellion, declared that he could not pledge himself 'to the unqualified repudiation of physical force in all countries, at all times, and in every circumstance'.[9] Meagher, 23 at the time of this speech, was born in Waterford where his father was a Catholic merchant and mayor. He moved to Dublin to study law, where he gained a reputation as an elegant and eloquent orator. He was perceived as a romantic figure, first in Young Ireland and years later as a Union commander during the American Civil War. He was also to become a significant character in the lives of John and Jenny Mitchel.

In 1867, in the *Irish Citizen*, in *Reminiscences of Mitchel*, John Mitchel recalled his first meeting with Thomas Francis Meagher, at an '82 Club banquet. Mitchel thought Meagher a 'rather foppish young gentleman, with an accent decidedly English'. Both men were aware that the room was full of attractive women, 'a breathing banquet of beauty' and their 'impressions of one another' were not favourable. However, Meagher called on Mitchel the next day and as they walked from the *Nation* office in D'Olier Street to meet Jenny at 1 Upper Leeson Street, they talked and John Mitchel was impressed by Thomas Francis Meagher.

> What talk! What eloquence of talk was his! How fresh and clear and strong! What wealth of imagination and princely

generosity of feeling! To me it was the revelation of a new and great nature, and I revelled in it, plunged into it, as into a crystal lake…he was always Irish to the very core.[10]

The Young Ireland fracture with O'Connell widened. In July 1846, O'Connell, anxious that the Repeal Association rejected violence both in theory and practice, introduced a resolution in Conciliation Hall to that effect. Following a bitter debate, and before the vote was taken, the young men from the *Nation* walked out. In a letter to John Martin, in December 1846, Mitchel hoped that they were 'done with Dan for ever…I hope we are going to be a little more outspoken and less politic at last.' In the same letter he wrote of his growing awareness of the Famine. He referred to 'terrible events in Skiberreen' and he chided his friend for trying to do too much for his labourers: 'I will not torment you further on the matter. Only remember that by trying to do more than there are means to do, a man may suddenly deprive himself of the power to do anything at all.'[11] Mitchel's laudable concern for his friend hints at the finite nature of his sympathy for the peasants. It was also prophetic as Honest John Martin's generosity did lead him into financial difficulties.

Relations with O'Connell were formally and finally undone with the founding of the Irish Confederation, in the Rotunda at the northern end of Sackville Street, now O'Connell Street, on 13 January 1847. The Confederation was to have a more practical and serious intent than the '82 Clubs.[12] They would drill, seek arms, march and eventually attempt a rebellion. As the Famine unfolded Mitchel's thoughts on physical force moved from the theoretical to the practical. His language and views became more colourful, more extreme. He referred to the 'harpy claw' in the 'vitals' of children; of the Irish beholding 'their own wretched food melting in rottenness … and they see heavy laden ships, freighted with the yellow corn their own hands have sown and reaped, spreading all sail for England.[13] His anger grew. In *The Last Conquest of Ireland (Perhaps)* he reflected on an electioneering visit to Galway, in 1847, with other Young Irelanders:

> I could see, in front of the cottages, little children leaning against a fence when the sun shone out for they could not stand, their limbs fleshless, their bodies half-naked, their faces bloated yet wrinkled, and of a pale, greenish hue…I saw Trevelyan's claw in the vitals of those children: his red tape would draw them to death: in his Government laboratory he had prepared for them the typhus poison. [14]

Charles Trevelyan was the Chief Secretary to the Treasury, and in charge of famine relief schemes. Whether, for Trevelyan, who bears much of the popular blame for the Famine, *being in charge of* was the same *as being responsible for* remains the topic of academic debate, but regardless Mitchel was contemptuous of British relief efforts. These included public works where people already weak from hunger were employed to break stones, to build roads and piers to get money to buy imported Indian corn. Public works only delayed the end. Mitchel wrote:

> We know the whole story... the father was on a public work... and so instead of dying in December they died in March...the poor wife wasting and weeping over her stricken children – the heavy-leaden, weary man with black night thickening around him – thickening within him ... but his darling wife is dear to him no longer: alas and alas! There is a dull stupid malice in their looks: they forget that they had five children, all dead weeks

ago and flung coffinless into shallow graves: nay, in the
frenzy of their despair they would rend one another for
the last morsel in that house of doom and at last in misty
dreams of drivelling idiocy, they die utter strangers. [15]

For Mitchel such scenes were the inevitable result of British policy, of
the various Famine Relief Acts. The failure of the potato was exploited
with the intention of 'shaking small lease-holders from the soil'.[16] As
the impact of the Famine moved to the top of the social scale, as rents
were unpaid, as many landlords faced unsustainable debt, the 1849
Encumbered Estates Act, Mitchel suggested, was passed because 'the
London Jews, money brokers and insurance offices required a speedier
and cheaper method of bringing property under the hammer'.[17] The
potato had failed across Europe but only Ireland, and the Scottish
Highlands, had an extraordinary famine. It was an 'artificial famine'.[18]
When it was over 'England was left, for a time, more securely in
possession than ever of the property, lives and industry of the Irish
Nation'.[19] Hence, for Mitchel, British policy during the Great Famine
was part of *The last Conquest of Ireland (Perhaps)*. The above reference
to 'London Jews' suggests Mitchel was anti-Semitic.

To Mitchel's disgust, as the winter of 1847-48 brought the
misery described above, Dublin 'had never before been so gay and
luxurious; splendid equipages had never before so crowded the
streets and the theatres and concert-halls had never been filled with
such brilliant throngs'.[20] However, although concerned, John Mitchel
and Young Ireland also continued to meet, to eat, to drink and to
sing. Many of them, like D'Arcy McGee, were as angrily eloquent
in their condemnation of British policy as Mitchel. It was McGee
who referred to 'sailing coffins'.[21] McGee, born in Carlingford on
13 April 1825 emigrated to Boston aged 17 and at 19 was editor of

the *Boston Pilot* newspaper. He returned to Ireland at the invitation of the nationalist *Freeman's Journal* but then became involved with *The Nation*. D'Arcy McGee, whose life was one of continuous political transformation, was to end his career as a founding father of Canada. It was to cost him his life.

Although angered by the Famine, the Young Irelanders, as a group, were of Dublin; they were of their class. Famine was something that was socially beneath and geographically beyond them. It was the cottiers, labourers and small tenant farmers in distant counties who were suffering most.

Despite this, it was John Mitchel, more than any other writer or politician, who shaped the nationalist perception of the Great Famine; Britain was to blame. It was, to use Tim Pat Coogan's book title, a 'Famine Plot'. However the causes and impact of the Great Famine were more complex than Mitchel's singular assessment. As Mitchel himself pointed out after the Great Famine 'many barristers, once loud in their patriotic devotion at Conciliation Hall, were appointed to Commissionerships…'.[22] (Such was to be the case with fellow Newry man and walking partner, John O'Hagan.) During the Great Famine not only was Young Ireland's concern more vocal in the condemnation of government policy than active in helping the distant destitute, but also many Catholics prospered. They operated as large tenant farmers, as merchants, as ship owners and agents.

Such was the case in Newry, Mitchel's mainly Catholic hometown. As multitudes of paupers swarmed into the town, the townsfolk complained of them begging on the streets.[23] Many wanted the penny charge at the soup kitchen, which was feeding nearly 1,200, dropped, not out of concern for the paupers, but to reduce begging on Hill Street. The ship-owning Carvill Brothers, a Catholic company on Merchant's Quay that owned saw mills, and an unusual shipyard that launched ocean going vessels sideways into the Newry Canal, did well. They imported timber from Canada and used the same ships to send emigrants, through Warrenpoint, across the Atlantic. As the Famine progressed the *Newry Commercial Telegraph* commented on its impact moving up the social scale.

> Emigration is taking place at an alarming rate. It is the industrious, thrifty class that is being drained. Day after day there are to be seen passing through the leading thoroughfare, on their way to Warrenpoint, carts upon which are seated ...young and hale looking men and women.[24]

Shipping agents, shopkeepers and guesthouse owners prospered from providing services for those leaving Ireland. That some in John and Jenny's hometown were inconvenienced or making money did not lessen the impact of the good work done by voluntary relief committees like that of Mrs Margaret Russell, who was the mother of Lord Russell of Killowen, and Queen Street neighbour of Jenny Verner. Mrs Russell's Newry Ladies Benevolent Society collected £157 and spent £97.7s in 'giving gratuitous relief in food, clothing and straw'.[25] It was therefore a social famine, with differential impact. The people of Ireland, Young Irelanders included, either responded and survived or not according to their class. Throughout Ireland the cruel potato blight was made worse by the country's uniquely flawed economic system. No other European country had such a widespread proportion of cottiers and labourers making up such a distinct and vulnerable underclass in society.

It was a geographic famine with different parts of the country, even different townlands, suffering to a greater or lesser degree. Between 1841 and 1851, along the Down-Armagh border, some townlands like Altnaveigh, Ryan and Savalbeg lost over 30 per cent of their population whilst others like Mullahglass, and Derrymore, also rural, gained 30 per cent.[26] Townlands with a quarry, a mill or a demand for carting services tended to do better. Townlands on marginal land suffered more. It was a political famine. In apologising for Britain's response to the Great Famine the British Prime Minister, Tony Blair, in 1997, said: 'Those who governed in London at the time failed their people through standing by while a crop failure turned into a massive human tragedy.'[27] As illustrated above, 150 years earlier Mitchel had though that, rather than simply 'standing by', the British Government had in fact taken advantage of the tragedy, and developed specific policies to clear the land.

Thus, the issues surrounding a study of the Great Famine, especially culpability, are complex. Continuing studies are needed to show how the Great Famine impacted on different classes, on towns and townlands; but perhaps Brendan O'Cathair got closest to an understanding when he suggested Mitchel's 'inflamed mind mistook the combination of laissez-faire economic dogma, parsimony, inefficiency and insensitivity for genocide.'[28] By February 1848 in advocating 'a deliberate study of the theory and practice of guerilla war'[29] and holding that 'armed opinion is a thousand times stronger than unarmed',[30] Mitchel's writing alarmed the majority of his Confederation colleagues. As he became even more militant, Charles Gavan Duffy found it necessary to 'censor' some of Mitchel's articles in the Nation. In doing so he ignited a mutual hatred that would last their lifetimes. The moderate Smith O'Brien was also horrified by Mitchel's increasingly extreme views although, unlike Gavan Duffy, he retained an admiration for Mitchel the man. Smith O'Brien wrote:

> Having being compelled on many occasions to express
> my dissent for many of the doctrines of Mr. Mitchel, it is
> right that I should say that all my personal prepossessions
> were strongly in his favour; that I believed him to be an
> enthusiastic lover of Ireland, a warm friend, an excellent
> husband, father and brother – amiable in all the relations
> of life.[31]

In February 1848, Smith O'Brien, disturbed by Mitchel's readiness to call for violent action, called a meeting of the Confederation to censure him. Mitchel was defeated by a vote of the Council of the Confederate Clubs by 317 to 188. He resigned from the Confederation Council and established his own more radical newspaper the *United Irishman*.[32] Mitchel had already stopped writing for the *Nation* because he claimed its editor had become 'constitutional and safe… with a view to some constitutional and parliamentary proceedings'. For Mitchel, this was too much like the policy of O'Connell's Repeal Association. Under Duffy's editorship, he thought the *Nation* had fallen 'into the merest old-womanly drivelling and snivelling, and the people are without a friend at the press'.[33] Hence, there was the need for Mitchel's *United Irishman*. On 12 December 1847 he had written to his mother, who wanted him to come back to Newry and resume his legal career, telling her that he was thinking 'of starting a new and most furious newspaper'. It was an accurate assessment of his intent.[34]

In London, the satirical magazine *Punch* enjoyed the irony of another split within the supporters of repeal and asked, 'How many disunited parties are required to make up a United Irishman? The Repealers have certainly repealed one union – their union with each other.'[35] An ailing Daniel O'Connell had died in Genoa, on his way to Rome, on 15 May 1847 and his son and successor, the much less popular John, was also enjoying the split within Young Ireland. To loud laughter in the now ironically named Conciliation Hall, he poured scorn upon Duffy and gave grudging respect to Mitchel and his young disciple, Thomas Devin Reilly:

> There is Mr. Duffy, the great warrior, now turned a decided moral force and 'patient courage man'. He has repudiated Mr. Mitchel and Mr. Reilly, because Mr. Mitchel and Mr. Reilly are honest, and do not hesitate to speak out the violent sentiments which once animated that party – they, at least, have no disguise about them.[36]

Mitchel's split with Gavan Duffy was bitter. Not so the split with Smith O'Brien and Thomas Meagher. As illustrated above, there was personal goodwill between John Mitchel and Smith O'Brien, between the middle-class son of the manse and the Anglo-Irish aristocrat. Meagher's emotions were in sympathy with John Mitchel's urgency and ardour and in the Confederation meeting which expelled Mitchel he declared, 'My strongest feelings are in favour of that policy advised by Mr. Mitchel. I wish to God I could defend that policy.' However, Meagher's reason was, reluctantly, with Gavan Duffy and he continued, 'I support his constitutional strategy not from choice but from necessity.' Meagher reasoned that the peasantry would not rise in rebellion. He put a hard rhetorical question to Mitchel:

> Who then are for it? The peasant and the mechanic classes we are told. These classes you will tell us have lost all faith in the legal agencies, and through such agencies despair of the slightest exemption from their

suffering. Stung to madness – day from day gazing upon the wreck and devastation that surrounds them, until the brain whirls like a ball of fire – they see but one red pathway, lined with gibbets and hedged with bayonets, leading to deliverance. But will that pathway lead them to deliverance? Have these classes which alone you now reply, the power to sweep like a torrent through that pathway dashing against the tremendous obstacles that confront them? You know they have not.[37]

Strong arguments like this over policy did not dent the growing friendship between Mitchel and Meagher. Yet, in the same debate Duffy, unlike Smith O'Brien and Meagher, had to defend himself against personal attacks from Mitchel. S.R.Knowlton has suggested that a major element in the feud between John Mitchel and Gavan Duffy was Mitchel's perception of himself as the spokesperson of the rural people. It was a claim much disparaged by Duffy. In 1854, writing to Mitchel and reflecting upon Mitchel's 1848 call to the peasantry to rebel, he wrote, 'When you answered for this insurrectionary spirit of the South, you, who had never actually crossed the Shannon or seen a Munster peasant on his own soil...'[38] In language that was both colourful and insulting, Mitchel, the country solicitor from County Down, derided Duffy as a 'drawing room liberal'.[39] He later wrote, 'Duffy could never sustain life without puffery; the breath of his nostrils was puff...You cannot get out of any man what is not in him, but yet this miserable grovelling of Duffy's is a bitter disappointment to me'.[40]

The bitterness of the debates between Mitchel and Duffy also highlighted a difference in character between John Mitchel and his father. The Revd Mitchel, given that he always made a clear distinction between the argument and the man, would not have written about an opponent in such an insulting manner.

John Martin and the young Thomas Devin Reilly moved with Mitchel to set up the *United Irishman*. John Martin was loyal to his best friend and, politically, the twenty-four-year-old Thomas Devin Reilly 'was of the calibre of Mitchel himself'.[41] Reilly, born on 30 March 1824, was originally from Monaghan and like many of Young Ireland it was while at Trinity that he became involved with the *Nation* where he came to admire Mitchel's character and radical ideas. Perhaps, apeing the 'Ten Resolutions' which Smith O'Brien hoped would commit the Confederation to constitutional methods and which led to Mitchel's expulsion, there were ten declared principles behind the setting up of the *United Irishman*. The tenth was Mitchel's lifelong governing principle: 'That no good thing can come from the English Parliament, or the English Government.' The third, stating that the life as a peasant was as sacred as the life of a nobleman was the basis of an open letter to Lord Claredon, the Viceroy. In the first edition of the *United Irishman* Mitchel declared:

> Just take our third axiom, *that the life of a peasant is as sacred as the life of a nobleman* – Why it seems a truism, and yet it is denied and set at nought by your 'laws', as you call them…if there is to be a *surplus*, who are the surplus?

At first glance this suggests Mitchel to be a Leveller. He challenged the aristocrat Clarendon 'to imagine how these questions are likely to find solution amongst an excitable Peasantry'.[42] However, in Michel's vision of a fair society the peasant is entitled to his sacred life as a peasant, the lord to his sacred life as a lord. That the peasant might or should aspire to better was not a consideration. For Mitchel the granting of Tenant Right would be sufficient to ameliorate the sacred life of the peasant. Although he was, for a time, attracted by James Fintan Lalor's ideas on peasant ownership of the land, Mitchel's biographer James Quinn noted that Mitchel 'still regarded the landed gentry as the natural leaders of the Irish people'.[43] In a letter to O'Brien, in 1847, Mitchel had advocated, paradoxically, that the Ascendancy might lead the revolution.[44] They simply needed to be convinced of the value of Tenant Right. However such an attempt, by Lalor, to interest landlords around Holycross, Tipperary in Tenant Right failed.[45] To Mitchel's disgust the landlords were not alone and Repeal Ireland generally shunned Tenant Right 'like poison'.[46] Mitchel despaired of landlords and expressed his shame, to Lalor, at having thought they might be won over 'to nationality and the rest of it'. He now thought the idea of 'conciliating classes' was 'humbug'.[47] In May 1848, in a letter 'to the Protestant Farmers, Labourers and Artisans of the North of Ireland', Mitchel rejected the idea of a class transcending unity of purpose and dismissed the landlords as possible rebels, but significantly, not because of their class but because 'they are "Britons"; their education, their feelings and what is more important to them, their interests are all British'.[48] Given that even in Ulster at this time most Presbyterians still regarded themselves as being Irish, for Mitchel, if the landlords were British they were the enemy. Thus the letter to Clarendon, elevating the value of the peasant to that of the lord, is more a challenge to British maladministration rather than to a social hierarchy, within which Mitchel would only want the peasant paternally and fairly treated. In later years Mitchel would demand humane treatment for the black man, but only within the institution of slavery. Now with complete editorial control of the *United Irishman* Mitchel goaded the British and called for a republic, to be achieved by a variety of means including the threat of physical force. One regular feature in the *United Irishman* was 'Our War Department'. Among other tactics it offered advice on how pike-men might 'receive' and defeat a cavalry charge: 'Cavalry always charge. Their great strength is in the impetus of the gallop. To destroy them it is only necessary to drill pike-men to go through the forms of *reception* with grace and effect.'[49] In the first edition Mitchel's friend Father Kenyon addressed the paper's eighth principle: 'That every freeman, and every man who desires to become free, ought to have arms, and to practice the use of them.' Born in 1812, Father Kenyon was a curate in Templederry, County Tipperary, who supported physical force and abhorred the moral force arguments. He defined the policy of the *United Irishman* when he wrote:

> I wish in the first place that all Irishmen were armed and able to carry arms... In opposition to all Quakers and quakerly-disposed persons, I firmly believe in the lawfulness of war...I account it amongst the duties of all freemen and of all men aspiring to be free to be prepared more or less according to the varying circumstances of their condition to wage war in defense of their hearths and altar.[50]

In a letter to John Martin, such sentiments caused Mitchel to describe this 'calm, good natured and jovial fellow' as '...the very wisest man I ever met.'[51] Father Kenyon, like John Martin, was to remain a lifelong friend of both John and Jenny.

Martin, writing in the *United Irishman*, whilst calling for 'a political and social revolution in Ireland' and supporting 'the right of the people of Ireland to rise up against this "Government" and drive it out of our country at bayonet's point', suggested a preferable and more peaceful way. He was much less aggressive than Mitchel and wrote that he was opposed to both French intervention and insurrection.

For Martin 'French Intervention would only be a lesser evil than English rule.' He thought the 'doctrine of lying in wait for an "opportunity"' in England's adversity was 'mean and immoral'. Insurrection was really just another name for civil war with Irishman killing Irishman. John Martin thought it unnecessary. An elected national assembly could ask the Queen to summon an Irish parliament. 'If this formal demand of the Irish nation be refused, the elected assembly – its authority sanctioned by the national will, and supported by the national guard – must assume and exercise the functions of legislation and government.'[52] This was a more cautious approach, more reminiscent of the limited success of the 1782 Irish parliament with its implied threat from the Volunteers, than that suggested by Martin's editor, John Mitchel.

The fervour, and widespread nature, of the 1848 spring revolutions in France and across Europe neutered caution, like that of John Martin and reignited the rebellious passion of Young Ireland. It swept Mitchel and his fellow writers in the *United Irishman* triumphantly back into the Confederation. In the Rotunda, his originally reluctant Young Ireland friends were ready for revolution. Mitchel reflected, 'Nobody would now be listened to there, who proposed any other mode of redress for Irish grievances than the sword.'[53] Dillon noted: 'The most cool-headed and sagacious of the Young Ireland leaders were hurried along with the general tide into a policy of physical force, the hopelessness of which they would in ordinary times have been the first to point out.'[54] Meagher, with his heart now ruling his head, declared, 'We must have it – bold strokes and nothing else.'[55] Even the cautious Gavan Duffy suggested,

'Ireland will be free before the coming summer fades into winter.'[56] Even Smith O'Brien began to sound warlike. On 15 March, at a meeting of the Confederation, Smith O'Brien followed Mitchel in advocating the study of guerilla war. Ironically, it had been Mitchel's call for a study of guerilla war[57] that had led Smith O'Brien to call for Mitchel's expulsion from the Confederation.[58]

With Smith O'Brien calling for a National Guard the Confederate Clubs marched and tried to arm themselves. They hoped for war in Europe, and preparations were made for a possible alliance with Chartists in England.

The Chartists, through public meetings, were seeking universal male suffrage and working-class representation in parliament. On 10 April 1848 they presented a petition, which gathered six million signatures, to the British parliament. In June 1848, when the Chartist leader, Manders May, was charged in Bow Street, London, part of the evidence presented against him was that he had called for the Irish Confederates and English Chartists to unite. According to the police evidence, May declared, 'It is the duty of Englishmen to join the Irish patriots in resisting the Government and obtaining the Repeal of the Union.'[59] Whilst Young Ireland sympathized with the Chartists, John O'Connell and the Catholic mainstream of the Repeal Association did not welcome support from a working-class, revolutionary group. With reference to a visit of Chartists to Young Ireland at the Rotunda, John O'Connell asked:

And what did they do? They got two or three vagabonds from Manchester to come over here, and Mr. Leech, the Manchester Chartist, and great gun of the evening (to whom by the way they gave a dinner on the past evening), preached 'Down with everything, not even excepting the Queen'. Nothing will satisfy that gentleman [laughter and cheers].[60]

Unsettled by the unrest caused by the European revolutions and fearful 'that Ireland was becoming steadily more combustible',[61] the Dublin government moved to prosecute John Mitchel, Smith O'Brien and Thomas Meagher. On 22 March, 'in a show of solidarity and strength' and with a crowd of followers the three men marched to the police headquarters, and returned on bail. However, despite moving towards Mitchel's position, O'Brien was uneasy. He thought the joint prosecution was 'a deliberate ploy to taint him and the Confederation with militant *United Irishman* views'.[62]

In early April O'Brien, Meagher and Richard O'Gorman went to Paris seeking support.[63] Upon their return, at a reception in the Music Hall, Lower Abbey Street, in honour of the Deputation to France, Meagher presented the Irish tricolour to the assembly. He hoped it would signify 'a lasting truce between the "Orange" and the "Green"'. He trusted 'that beneath its folds the hands of the Irish Protestant and the Irish Catholic may be clasped, in generous and heroic brotherhood'. John Mitchel, given his desire to convince his northern co-religionists of the value of Repeal, recognized the ethnic symbolism of the flag and proclaimed: 'I hope to see that flag one day waving, as our national banner, over a forest of Irish pikes...' Mitchel then quoted Thomas Davis's poem *Nationality*:

A Nation's Flag! A Nation's Flag!
...
Look you, guard it well!
No King or Saint hath tomb so proud
As he whose flag becomes his shroud. [64]

Although Mitchel's wish that the tricolour should become the flag of Ireland was not fulfilled until the early twentieth century it was a symbol of his desire for an Irish Republic, free from sectarian strife. It was also a symbol of the impact he was to have on both Pearse and de Valera as they sought to establish that republic. However, it was another flag, a foreign flag, that was to proudly shroud two of his children. This was a flag that divided people according to race. Both flags are wrapped around the paradox of the champion of the Irish peasant wholeheartedly supporting the institution of slavery.

In late April, the *Newry Examiner* reported John Mitchel chairing a meeting in Dublin 'urging the necessity of uniting with the workmen of England'. The same edition reprinted the *Nation's*, and Smith O'Brien's call for an armed National Guard 'for the purpose of preserving social order and protecting this island against all foes – domestic and foreign'.[65] Foreign meant the British government. Events were moving towards a clash with that government. In May, in a letter to the Repealers of Newry, John Martin condemned what he saw as 'a monopoly of political power in the hands of capitalists and landlords' – power that inflicted 'wrong upon the defenceless working classes'. Martin called for universal suffrage and the separation of church and state. 'The Church question I would settle by disconnecting all churches from the state. The compulsory support of one or two sects at the expense of all sects in common is robbery, and utterly at variance with the spirit and teachings of the Christian religion.'[66]

This was revolutionary stuff; such was the fervour generated by the 1848 spring revolutions on the continent. An excited Smith O'Brien reignited another old idea. In 1843 O'Connell had proposed a Council of Three Hundred, which he hoped would morph into an Irish parliament. O'Connell had imagined a conservative body (one which a younger, milder Mitchel was invited to join) that would mainly consist of landlords and wealthy merchants who would 'disarm the fears of the most timid, by rending impossible any violent revolutionary movement'.[67] In the event O'Connell abandoned his idea but now in the heat of the European revolutions O'Brien called for a revival of the Council of Three Hundred. The Prime Minister, Lord John Russell, feared such a council might 'wrest' power from Dublin Castle leaving the Lord Lieutenant 'powerless'. The *Newry Examiner* expressed the hope that O'Brien's 1848 proposed Council of Three Hundred would be a platform for unity and represent all shades of opinion, including the Protestant Repeal Association.[68] However it noted the silence on the topic from John O'Connell's Conciliation Hall and rejoiced in the election of radicals like John Martin for Newry and John Mitchel for Banbridge.[69] Like O'Connell's before it, O'Brien's more radical Council of Three Hundred never met.

Despite the above call for unity of purpose between the Irish peasant and the English proletariat, unlike his friend John Martin, John Mitchel's focus was more on rebellion against the British, rather than on an idealistic revolution. He may have called for a republic but on the 10 April 1848 he wrote in a letter (correspondent unknown) from 8, Ontario Terrace, Dublin (John and Jenny's second home in Dublin): 'You have correctly interpreted my views about Republicanism… In fact I am no bigot as to forms of government. And am a Republican now only because this democratic spirit is the most formidable enemy to British dominion in Ireland.'[70]

Later in the year, on board his prison ship in November 1848, following his trial, the exiled Mitchel's doppelganger, with whom he was having imaginary conversations about his politics, motivation and condition, was to suggest that his 'anxiety for the success of the French Republic' was 'born of not love of mankind, or even French mankind, but a pure hatred of England, and a diseased longing for blood and carnage'.[71] There is probably truth in this introspective exaggeration.

Six years later, in 1854, Mitchel made a similar reply to Gavan Duffy when Duffy reminded Mitchel that in the *Nation* he, Mitchel, had rejected Chartism. Mitchel enthusiastically accepted that he had written against Chartism, 'refusing to have anything to do with the "six points"' [male suffrage, protection for the voter when casting his vote, abolition of property qualification for MPs, payment of members, equality of electoral districts, and annual elections] and declaring some of the said points to be 'an abomination'. He continued. 'What of this? I never denied it…I courted their aid to destroy the British Empire, as I would now court the aid of the Czar to do the same'.[72]

Mitchel courted the Chartists, the Russians and anybody else for much the same reason he once courted the landlord. His primary aim was the removal of England from Ireland. John Mitchel, the Irish rebel, was associated with revolutionary ideas and causes not out of philosophical conviction but rather as a means of gaining support for his rebellion against England.

In his early-twentieth century introduction to the Gill edition of *Jail Journal* Arthur Griffith agreed with Mitchel. He wrote that Irish Nationalism 'is based on no theory of, and dependable in no wise for its existence or justification on the "Rights of Man", it is independent of theories of government and doctrines of philanthropy and Universalism'.[73] For both Mitchel and Griffith, Irish Rebellion was not French Revolution. John Mitchel, the man from liberal Presbyterian stock; the rebel from the tradition that brought the Scottish Enlightenment to Ulster, rejected Thomas Paine's *Rights of Man*. He fancied himself a Tory. Yet, neither did he follow his post-1798 fellow Presbyterians in embracing the economic opportunities offered by the emergent coalfields and Industrial Revolution. They were British coalfields and that would not do. Although, at a November 1847 Confederation meeting in Belfast, he unsuccessfully sought their support for his fight against Britain, John Mitchel removed himself from both minority liberal and majority conservative Ulster Presbyterianism. His politics sought a singular outcome, the withdrawal of England from Ireland.

Smith O'Brien and the Irish Delegation had returned from their 3 April meeting in Paris, with Alphonse de Larmatine, Minister for Foreign Affairs, with the Irish tricolour but only lukewarm expressions of support. For John Mitchel, and the young Thomas Devin Reilly, the flood tide of enthusiasm for rebellion, created by the revolutions in Europe, was ebbing[74] and in letters dated 3 May they resigned from the Confederation. In their letters of resignation both men made it clear that Smith O'Brien had already indicated it was they or he who had to go. However, in resigning Mitchel pledged his continuing support, especially for two key policies: 'It is needless to say that all the active measures proposed by the Council, of which I approve, shall have my warmest support; more especially the calling together of a National Convention and the enrolment of a National Guard.'[75]

Mitchel's resignation followed on from the 29 April 'Battle of Limerick' when, after an Old Ireland attack on their November Belfast meeting, and continuing street fights between Young and Old Ireland in other towns, Mitchel ignored Smith O'Brien's request not to speak on the same platform, not to participate in 'the proposed tour to the south'.[76] The Limerick meeting of about 300 confederation supporters was held in a disused Thomas Street factory. Mitchel, Meagher and Smith O'Brien were on the stage when, as recorded by O'Brien:

> Scarcely had the proceedings of the evening commenced when the groaning of the O'Connellite mob assembled outside the building was followed by the throwing of stones. Before long an attempt was made to set fire to the house by burning an effigy of Mitchel close to the window and a regular battery was established against the door.[77]

The words on the effigy, 'Mitchel, calumniator of O'Connell', made it clear who the target of the mob's anger was; but when Smith O'Brien went out to try and reduce the tension with an appeal for Repeal unity, it was he who was attacked and badly injured.[78]

By this stage the government, fearing the revolution called for by Mitchel, moved against him by passing the Treason Felony Act. The British had earlier failed to convict Smith O'Brien and Meagher; the new act would allow the political prisoner to be treated as a felon, a guilty verdict could mean transportation, not execution, and convictions would be easier to obtain.

The dismissal of treason, of rebellion, as mere felony, with its intended, attendant diminution of political and heroic status was to resonate through Irish history. It was the issue that led to the 1981 hunger strike, to the electoral rise of Provisional Sinn Féin and its eclipse of the constitutional Social Democrat and Labour Party (SDLP). Perhaps Mitchel's shade smiled? Certainly as he reflected on the 1981 hunger strike, Paul Muldoon, in his poem *Yggdrasil*, obliquely resurrected Mitchel's image and his 1854 overtures to the Russian Czar.

> It may not be today
> Or tomorrow but sooner or later

the Russians will water

their horses on the shores of Lough Erne.

Mitchel was arrested on Saturday 13 May 1848, at 8, Ontario Terrace. Inspector Guy allowed John Mitchel to finish the meal he was sharing with Jenny, his brother William, Devin Reilly and the family. He was then quietly and quickly driven away.[79] Inspector Guy's patience reflected a respect for Mitchel's status that was to be consistently applied during his time in captivity by the British. Meanwhile, in Newry, the *Commercial Telegraph* gloated. 'Mr. John Mitchel is now experiencing, in the companionship of burglars and pickpockets, a foretaste of that life of misery which is the felon's doom.'[80]

With Mitchel in Newgate Prison, Dublin awaiting trial, the city smouldered with resentment. Troops nervously patrolled the streets. There were large, silent marches. 'On these marches Mitchel's brother, William, headed the St. Patrick's Confederate Club in his brother's place' and the young Thomas Devin Reilly was Jenny's escort.[81] In his prison cell John Mitchel heard 'the measured tramp of ten thousand marching men'.[82]

There were reports of members of Mitchel's jury being threatened. The *Newry Examiner* reported that Mr Whitty, the jury foreman, had received the following warning: 'By the thundering God, you bloody Saxon rascal, your life, and your life only, shall pay the sacrifice of your Orange bigotry! Prepare your coffin.'[83] In contrast the *Dublin Journal* appealed to the conscience of the jury:

God's truth has been spoken and written by John Mitchel. He has proclaimed to the world the labourer's right to live in the land of his birth by the sweat of his brow; the farmer's right to the fruits of his labour, his capital and his skill. This is God's truth! Will you jurors pronounce by your verdict God's truth to be a seditious Libel -- a Felony? If you do, which God forbid you don't, the blood of that innocent man of truth, John Mitchel, be on you and yours for all eternity.[84]

O'Connor suggested Jenny gave white ribbon cockades to those who promised to unsheathe the sword.[85] The London *Times* reported the unrest in Dublin: 'Since the arrest and imprisonment of John Mitchel there have been nightly musters of the Confederate Clubs.' They marched to Newgate, in silence and with a discipline that would compare favourably to a regiment of Guards. At Newgate they 'gave three mighty cheers'.[86]

Six hundred members of the Dr Doyle Confederate Club marched to the steps of 8, Ontario Terrace, by the Grand Canal. The London *Times* recorded that an elegant and gracious Jenny received the marchers.[87] A deputation expressed its sympathy and support for her husband. They may have had their differences in the past but they would stop any deportation of their 'heroic brother, your husband', John Mitchel:

> Madam…However some of us Irish citizens may have disagreed on abstract questions, this tyrannical attempt by foreign usurpers of our country, binds us all together, henceforth, to rise or fall with him. We have now but one absorbing duty to perform – namely to prepare night and day for the purpose, should he be convicted, of restoring him in triumph to liberty and to you.[88]

Jenny replied: 'I have not hitherto allowed any fears I might feel for my children's safety, or my own, to interfere with that line of policy which my husband thought it his duty to pursue; and I do not intend to do so now.' She went on to say it would be the 'most fatal madness' to allow any confederate, including her husband, to be exiled.[89]

Repeal Ireland, in and beyond Dublin, appeared to share Jenny's anger at Mitchel's arrest. Flowery tributes and messages of support were sent from around the country, including one dated 18 May 1848 from his hometown, Newry:

> As your fellow townsmen…We hail you, sir, as the boldest and bravest champion of Irish independence. We admire in you the stern and unyielding proclaimer of simple, yet to some unpalatable political truths, the open and advised utterances of which, though now sought to be made felonious, is yet the imperative duty of every honest Irishman. With you sir we lose our country.[90]

Given this rush of feeling there was a great increase in the number of Confederate Clubs – from 30 in May to 150 all over the country in July – with 50,000 members.[91] In the event Jenny was disappointed and years later expressed her frustration to James Stephens, who himself was to fail to unsheathe the Fenian sword.[92] She mistrusted those who 'preached the sword flashing but carried it sheathed'.[93] Dublin did not ignite. With the exception of John Martin[94] and a minority of others, like W.B. Yeats's young John O'Leary, not yet in his Fenian grave, Young Ireland was persuaded of the advisability of not attempting a rising or a rescue of John Mitchel, until after the harvest.[95] To this end a delegation from the Confederate Clubs visited Mitchel in Newgate Prison and asked him to confirm their decision. Having heard, and overestimated, the tramp of marching men, and believing that the Dublin Confederate Clubs did not agree with the leadership and were ready to rise in his support, Mitchel 'refused to sign a paper...deprecating all attempts at rescue'.[96]

At his trial, despite the best efforts of the eighty-two-year-old former *United Irishman* Robert Holmes, the brother-in-law of Robert Emmet, Mitchel was found guilty. For Mitchel, having Robert Holmes as his lawyer established a patriotic continuity with 1798 and 1803, even if, beyond rebellion against England, he shared few of the egalitarian ideals of the United Irish. With measured sympathy the *Newry Commercial Telegraph* announced the guilty verdict in its second edition on 27 May. It commented:

> Alas for misguided honesty, misdirected zeal, ill regulated, miscalculating and over trustful enthusiasm ... diabolical though the measures he proposed were in the sight of men of peace, he was as candid in the expression of his sentiments as he was sincere in holding them ... John Mitchel was a downright, unreflecting maniac.

However, the *Newry Telegraph* did allow that John Mitchel was a 'profoundly compassionate man'.[97]

John Mitchel was sentenced to fourteen years' transportation. In his speech from the dock he presented himself not as a criminal but as a Roman hero. 'The Roman who saw his hand burning to ashes before the tyrant, promised that three hundred should follow out his enterprise. Can I not promise for one, for two, for three, aye, for hundreds?'[98]

There were shouts of support in the courtroom with Reilly, Martin, Father Kenyon and Meagher answering, 'Promise for me.' In the event John Martin and Thomas Devin Reilly fulfilled that promise by founding the *Irish Felon*, as did Richard Dalton Williams and Kevin Izod O'Doherty. They published the *Tribune*. Both papers were, like the *United Irishman*, short lived. John Martin surrendered to the authorities. Devin Reilly escaped to America: Williams and O'Doherty were arrested; Williams at the home of Dr Antisel[99] who, like Thomas Francis Meagher, was to achieve high rank in the Union Army and who, after the Civil War, would be a good friend to Jenny, especially as she tried to get John released from a Union prison where he was being ill-treated. Later, in November 1848, Williams was found 'Not guilty of intent to depose the Queen.'[100] O'Doherty was not so lucky. Years later, in 1885, the young medical student from 1848, Kevin Izod O'Doherty, who was married to the poet 'Eva', Mary Eva Kelly from Galway, and the *Nation* recalled his day in court. Instead of presenting himself:

> ...before the Court of my Examiners at my College I was called upon to appear before a much more terrible tribunal, and one more difficult to pass through unscathed when I was required to answer the charge of having levied war against her Majesty...I had been one of those...who shouted in accord with Mitchel's appeal that for everyone like him who was sent into exile a dozen would be found to take his Place.[101]

Given that Mitchel viewed himself as a heroic Roman it is not surprising that, in *Jail Journal*, which he began on 27 May 1848, the British were labelled Carthaginians. For Mitchel, educated in Dr

Henderson's Classical School, human thought had advanced little from classical times. Nineteenth-century technological innovation he acknowledged as unwelcome change, not progress.

At first the Carthaginians gave him prison clothes but then allowed him to retain his own. Over the next five years it was one of many concessions to his political and gentlemanly status. However, he was still in chains, in his cell, when he said goodbye to Jenny and his sons, John and James. He was then escorted 'by a large force of cavalry' through Sackville Street, now O'Connell Street. At Carlisle-bridge, now O'Connell Bridge, there was 'considerable groaning as the carriage passed, but with this exception there was no other indication of feeling.'[102] However, in its edition the following day, the *Times* reported that at Seville Place on the North Strand the police were attacked by a mob, 'the chief leaders of which were women'. It noted, 'one amazon was conspicuous by her daring. She hurled stones and brickbats, with unerring aim at the heads of the constabulary, cursing lustily the cowardice of the men of Dublin in leaving the fighting to the women.'[103] Although not as lustily expressed, it was a sentiment Jenny agreed with. From the North Wall a waiting steamer, the *Shearwater*, took John Mitchel to Spike Island, Cork. The suddenness of his departure took much of Dublin by surprise but the Nationalist *Newry Examiner*, perhaps fancifully, recorded thousands 'flying down the quays anxious to get one parting glance at the patriot' and Mitchel waving to a numerous crowd at Lighthouse Point where 'a wail (it could not be called a cheer) arose from the multitude.'[104]

John Mitchel's brother, William Haslett Mitchel, wrote to the newspapers protesting that although he had official permission to visit John after his conviction he was told, at 3pm, to call back in the morning. At 4pm he heard that his brother John 'was since carried off in the prison van to Howth on his way to Norfolk Island'.[105] He was misinformed.

Also at about 4pm a body of police took over the office of the *United Irishman* and carried off the type on a dray. Subsequently, however, it transpired that Mr Charles Gavan Duffy had, on the previous day, purchased all the materials, and having intimated this circumstance to the authorities, orders were issued to restore the property.[106] This meant the premises and machinery were available to John Martin when he set up the *Felon*. Despite the past and growing enmity between Mitchel and Duffy, in May 1848, the two able, young journalists were still on the same side. Two months later on 8 July 1848 Duffy and the *Nation* would suffer the same fate as Mitchel and the *United Irishman*. To Mitchel's disgust three juries would fail to convict Duffy on a charge of felony.[107]

CHAPTER THREE

I Hope To Do My Children
Some Good Before I Die

After John's arrest Jenny went to stay with Thomas O'Hagan, in whose house she and John had 'spent many pleasant evenings'.[1] Ironically the rising barrister, later Lord Chancellor of Ireland from 1868 to 1874, had refused to be a prosecuting lawyer at Mitchel's trial. Jenny stayed a number of weeks with Mr and Mrs O'Hagan, where she received many well-wishers. With the loss of John's salary and the seizure of his property, under the conditions of the Treason Felony Act, the Mitchels were destitute. A National Fund was organized and contributed to by many businessmen across the island including Francis Carville, the Newry shipbuilder and owner who chaired his local fund.[2] Sympathy for John Mitchel and his family extended across Ireland and through O'Connell's Old Ireland. The following letter, from Castletown Devlin, County Westmeath, suggests that, whilst indignant at the perceived injustice done to John Mitchel, many remained out of sympathy with his extreme views and still favoured the deceased Daniel O'Connell.

The generous and spirited principle of this parish although not fully agreeing with the wild political doctrine propounded by the impudent John Mitchel, yet could not but boldly express their indication at the injustice done to him … alas poor Ireland, every day more and more feels the loss of her ever faithful and honest friend, the illustrious O'Connell.[3]

Daniel O'Connell's son, John, who had predicted, and feared, that if Mitchel was imprisoned he would become a martyr, contributed £5.[4] Jenny would not have been impressed. She listed John O'Connell as one who had failed to support her husband.[5] Nationally £2000 was raised. The London *Times* sneered at the amount. Jenny and the family moved between Newry, Carlingford and Belfast – the summer of 1848 was spent in Carlingford, for the sea bathing. Jenny must have been cheered by the 3 June 1848 declaration by the *Newry Examiner* that Ireland's first duty was to the family of the victim. 'John Mitchel has left to our protection that wife whose highest praise is that she was the worthy partner of his loftiest ambitions … that incomparable wife and mother … and now Mary Mitchel and her children, his children are the adopted family of Ireland.'[6] Perhaps she was less pleased that they got her name wrong, as they had the number of their children in a previous edition – six 'orphans' mentioned instead of five.

However, not all Confederate Club members, nationally or locally, shared in the admiration for John Mitchel. David Ross of Bladensburg, a landlord from Rostrevor, County Down and Chairman of Newry's Foster Confederate Club, before it became the Mitchel Club, resigned from the club. He disassociated himself from a resolution supporting Mitchel.

It was Ross who had chosen the name Foster for the Newry club, in memory of the last Speaker of the Irish House of Commons. Although a 'patriot', in 1793 Speaker Foster voted against Catholic emancipation, and probably opposed union for the same reason, fearing Westminster would be more likely to grant Catholic emancipation.[7] At the inaugural meeting of the Foster Club, on 11 February 1848, in the week after he had voted to support Smith O'Brien in expelling Mitchel, Ross had declared, 'much as I admire Britain I am not ready to give up the Irish character.'[8] Now, in May, he wrote, 'Cherishing as I do, my allegiance to our most Gracious Sovereign, I can feel no sympathy for a gentleman who openly avows his disloyalty.'[9] For Ross, and many followers of O'Connell, repeal under the Crown was a consistent position that harked back to the Constitution, the Irish parliament and the volunteers of 1782.

However, the *Examiner* was bitter in its defence of John Mitchel. It wondered why Ross, a man from a family of soldiers, should object to war. 'Look to your pedigree – look forth from your windows upon a monument of war – savage and disgraceful war – and blush.'[10] The monument mentioned is a 99-foot obelisk, in Rostrevor, to Major General Robert Ross; the man who, in the war of 1812–14 burned the White House on 24 August 1814. However, despite the vitriol of the *Examiner*, that the Major General's son was involved in Irish politics on the side agitating for the repeal of the Act of Union is an indication of the breadth of support for Repeal. The landlords, the ascendancy, had lost much of their power and status with union and some, like David Ross, sought its repeal under the Crown.

Mitchel was now recording his experiences and reflections in his polemic, *Jail Journal*. He was aware of his family's suffering and the price they were paying for his ideals. He wrote, 'At Charlemont Bridge, in Dublin, this evening there is a desolate house … five little children very dear to me none of them old enough to understand the cruel blow that has fallen on them this day, and above all – above all – my wife.'[11]

At Spike Island, Cork Harbour, despite being told he was not to be treated like a common convict, Mitchel was again put in and out of convict clothes. John Mitchel was amused at the confusion. In *Jail Journal* he teased the Lord Lieutenant. 'Come, my Lord Clarendon, either I am a felon or not a felon.'[12] He wrote a 'cheerful letter' to Jenny and wondered how his family was faring. He worried that his old brown summer coat may not be warm enough but the prison authorities provided him with 'a few changes of linen and other small indispensables'. An indication of John Mitchel's national fame, or notoriety, was that the prison surgeon, a young man from Monaghan, asked him to sign autographs for some of his lady friends. Mitchel wished 'the sweet girls much joy'[13] with his signatures.

On 1 June 1848 John Mitchel left Spike Island, and Ireland. On board the *Scourge,* as it sailed for Bermuda, John Mitchel was treated as a gentleman. The ship's officers provided books, newspapers and discussed politics with him. He even found the last copy of his own newspaper, *United Irishman,* in his cabin. Reading it, a copy to which he had been unable to contribute, he realized his two closest associates would be arrested. 'Good Martin! Brave Reilly! But you will be swallowed, my fine fellows. Government has adopted a vigorous policy.'[14] The 'vigorous policy' meant constables entered Martin's *Felon* newspaper offices on Friday 7 July, forced open the editor's desk and seized all accounts, correspondence and manuscripts. John Martin, however, was not present.[15]

Mitchel dined with Captain Wingrove. He drank the commander's good wine, whilst explaining to the officer what a packed jury was.[16] When news of such lenient treatment reached London, Sir William Verner, Jenny's uncle, was angry. He asked in parliament if it was true that when John Mitchel was put on board the *Shearwater,* to be conveyed to Spike Island, he was 'entertained by the officers in a way that was unbecoming a convicted felon?'[17]

Despite continuing hostile questions at Westminster from Sir William Verner and others about Mitchel's lenient treatment, the British, the *Carthaginians* (he being a noble Roman), continued to treat John Mitchel as a gentleman. The answers to these parliamentary questions tended to be vague and referred to Mitchel's health or 'Mr. Mitchel's former position.'[18] However, a letter from T. Redington, from Dublin Castle, to Captain Wingrove, the officer commanding HMS *Scourge,* dated 30 May 1848 had already made it clear John Mitchel was not to be treated as a common criminal.

> John Mitchel, whom you have been instructed to convey as a prisoner to Bermuda, should, during the voyage, receive as much indulgence as is compatible with his safe custody. He should not be ironed, nor is it necessary that he should wear convict dress … he is, therefore, during his passage, not to be treated as a common criminal, or treated with unnecessary severity.[19]

In this case gentlemanly treason was taking precedence over low felony. Given Mitchel's love of hierarchy, his almost Braminian view of society and his view of himself as a political martyr, he was not displeased.

At the same time as he was asking questions in Westminster Sir William's niece, was anxiously waiting for news of her husband. She wrote to John Martin, 'It is very strange I have not heard from John yet. Everyday seems a year and yet I try to keep myself busy with the children.'[20] In Bermuda, where he arrived on 20 June 1848, John Mitchel was housed on the convict hulk *Dromedary,* but despite the two-inch cockroaches, his conditions were far superior to those of the ordinary convicts, one of whom was assigned as his servant.[21] Mitchel despised his fellow convicts' 'brutal obscenity and stupid blasphemy', but even when hearing them being flogged caused him to gnaw his tongue, he still did not 'think it wrong to flog convict felons when needful for preservation of discipline'.[22] If he died in Bermuda John Mitchel did not want to be buried in their 'unblessed company'.[23]

On 4 July the mail steamer took a letter to Jenny, in Newry, telling of his long journey. In Newry, the Confederate Club, having changed its name from Foster to Mitchel, waxed lyrical about the new Irish tricolour, Mitchel's 'national banner'[24] and their hopes of rescuing their exiled leader. The Mitchel Confederate Club was fanciful about the 'felon flag'.

> Oh how we long for the day when … we shall see a ship
> of war – with an Irish tricolour at her peak sail for the
> still vexed Bermoothas to set our captive chieftain free.
> But we must free our country first, and then liberate our
> hero, of whom our town is so justly proud. [25]

One hundred years later in November 1948 an Irish navy ship, the LE *Macha*, flying the tricolour, did sail from Ireland to bring home an Irish hero. In this case it was the remains of W.B. Yeats, who in two of his poems, 'cast a cold eye' on Mitchel's prayer for war (*Bulben*) and consigned his romantic Ireland to O'Leary's grave (September 1913).

Given her disappointment when Dublin failed to rise, Jenny would not have been impressed by the tricolour fantasy, especially since, following Newry's placement under martial law, the Newry Commercial Telegraph was able to sneer that 'mock heroics are out of season'. It recorded the John Mitchel Club of Newry voluntarily dissolving 'in perspiration'.[26] The town, like many others, was searched for arms. The Out-Pensioners (retired soldiers) were ordered on duty, to bolster the Newry Garrison, and pikes, nine feet long, were found in the business premises of George Guy and a Mr Byrne on Merchant's Quay.[27] As part of this clampdown, in the Newry area, and seeking to arrest John Martin, police searched his house in Loughorne. He was not there but following the raids there, and in Dublin, John Martin's uncle, the diarist James Harshaw, (a farmer of 80 acres, mentioned in a previous chapter as having given evidence to the Devon Commission), recorded Martin putting his affairs in order and surrendering to the authorities in Newgate, Dublin.[28] He too was charged under the Treason Felony Act, for articles published on 24 June 1848 and 1 July 1848 in the *Felon*.[29] On Saturday 8 July, despite a large crowd 'gathered round the office in Trinity Street', police Detective Sergeant Gargan seized all copies of the *Felon* from here and from the press-room on Ormond Quay.[30] The *Felon* was no more. On 17 July, Jenny wrote to its ex-editor, John Martin, in Newgate jail. She was angry and bitter, perhaps humorously so:

> The leaders have a great deal to answer for. Now I do think if there is another conviction, no matter in whose case, the moment the judge passes sentence he should be shot, next the Attorney General then the Sherriff and lastly the whole jury. That is what ought to have been done in John's case and if the men are not wholly slaves they will do it. [31]

Her anger was directed especially at D'Arcy McGee and Gavan Duffy, but she retained warm feelings for Smith O'Brien and Thomas Francis Meagher. McGee was to become a founding father of Canada and Duffy, who had clashed with Mitchel in the *Nation,* was to be knighted for public service in Victoria, that included the post of prime minister. Mitchel's nephew, William Hill Irvine, born in Dromalane, in 1858, was also to be prime minister of Victoria.[32] On 4 August John Mitchel received a large trunk from Jenny with clothes and books. Included were 'exquisite coloured daguerreotypes' of Jenny, his mother and two closest friends, John Martin and Fr Kenyon. On 20 August he received letters from home and the news, 'Wife and bairns at Carlingford for the Summer.' The news also mentioned the arrest of many Young Irelanders, including Meagher and Duffy. Mitchel especially rejoiced at the imprisonment of John Martin, Kevin O'Doherty and R.D. Williams for their 'felonius' writing in the *Felon* and *Tribune*. With high profile arrests like these he was pleased events appeared to be moving as they had done before the 1798 Rebellion. He wrote, 'and in short, everything goes in the genuine '98 style I like all this very well.'[33] However, he suffered from attacks of asthma – 'Asthma! Asthma! The enemy is upon me.'[34] In Bermuda Mitchel was often sick, depressed and, at times, very uncomfortable. He nearly died on the hulk and considered suicide. 'Suicide I have duly considered and perpended, and deliberately decided against.'[35] John Mitchel gave six reasons for rejecting suicide, including (ironically, given future events) reason five; 'Because I have so much to live for – many duties but half discharged or wholly neglected – young children brought into the world, and allowed to grow up hitherto, like an unweeded garden … I hope to do my children some good before I die.'[36] In the years that followed John Mitchel's children would suffer exile, war and death because of their father's politics and decisions.

In a letter dated 5 March 1849, to his sister Matilda, at Laurel Hill, Dublin Road, Newry, he wrote of his despair, 'of the sickness and pain, and sleepless nights'. However, he defiantly declared, 'But all these things are as nothing to a man unless they conquer him and they shall not conquer me ...' In the same letter, given future attitudes and events, he prophetically lambasted the United States for its 'ardent and devout worship of the great dollar', its similarity to Britain, and suggested that if he ever settled there it will be in the wilderness, 'westward of lake Superior.' In later years Mitchel was to try and turn his back on progress and live in a wilderness in Tennessee.[37] Although his sister Matilda, married to Doctor Dickson, opposed Mitchel's politics – and there was a period of coolness – they remained affectionate and close. He confessed to Matilda a liking for 'the most stercoraceous of the "fashionable novels"' and a great appetite for 'the blessed Sir Walter Scott' whom he strongly recommended for Matilda's children[38] despite Scott dedicating his stories 'To the King's most Gracious Majesty.' However, as Mrs Anderson was to comment, years later in the American Confederacy, Mitchel would probably not have been so generous if Scott had been an English writer.

Asthma continued to afflict and depress John Mitchel but a London newspaper, thrown secretly into his cell, maintained his interest in Irish affairs; he read of the attempted rising at Ballinagry; of the arrest of the leaders and the death sentences being commuted to transportation. He dismissed their efforts as 'a poor extemporised abortion of a rising in Tipperary, headed by Smith O'Brien.'[39] Following his sickness and depression and on being told he was being sent to Africa John Mitchel was pleased when, on 22 April 1849, he saw 'the cedar groves of Bermuda sinking below the hazy horizon.' He was further cheered by news from Newry and in reply he told Jenny of his improving mood and health. He recorded his optimism in *Jail Journal*:

All well at home. I have written a very long and cheerful letter to my wife; for indeed matters begin to look somewhat brighter for us. I begin to see daylight: my health has been improving rapidly; will probably continue to improve at sea: and why may it not be completely re-established in the climate of Africa?[40]

On 12 July 1849, sailing first for Brazil and then South Africa, he was still in better spirits as he reflected on the sectarian activities of his fellow northerners. 'I trust the maniacs in the North of Ireland are not cutting each other's throats today.'[41] His desire for 'Irishmen of all bloods to stand together'[42] against England was a consistent theme throughout his life. In Brazil, on 20 July 1849, John Mitchel encountered his first 'merchantable' slaves. He saw them as fat, merry and not overworked, their condition not as abject as it would have been under Anglo-Saxon ownership. The actions of the British continued to be the yardstick of Mitchel's morality. Prophetically, given his future stance on the issue of slavery first in the USA and later in the Confederacy, he wondered: 'Is it better then, to be a slave of a merciful master and a just man, or to be a serf to an Irish land-appropriator? God knoweth.'[43] By the time he was living in the USA Mitchel knew. By then he, controversially, had no doubt the American slave was in a better position than the Irish serf.

Thoughts of home were always with him and on the 12 August 1849, while sailing from Brazil to Africa, he poignantly wrote:

It is deep in the night ... we are not far from the meridian of Newry, though six thousand miles to the south and I know that this white disc struggling here through Atlantic storm clouds is the very globe of silver that hangs tonight between the branches of the laurels of Dromalane. [44]

With his melancholy thoughts Mitchel was pleased to converse with the only woman on board, and to hear 'the liquid music that distils from a kindly Munster tongue'. Mitchel confessed that if Mrs Nolan, the wife of a sergeant, had not been fifty years old he would have fallen in love with her. Even though he was comfortably far removed from the other prisoners, at night, their mournful singing of some Irish air carried him 'back to old days when I heard the same to the humming accompaniment of the spinning wheel'.[45] The voyage to South Africa took five months but for Mitchel it had been neither long nor wearisome and he was ready to stop his 'blue water dreaming, and gird up my loins to meet whatsoever new thing Africa may bring forth'.[46] He was disappointed. The citizens of the Cape Colony refused the convicts entry and there was a standoff with the British authorities. Mitchel agreed with the Dutch and British settlers. Colonies should not be turned into 'sinks or common sewers of felony'.[47] However, significantly, he expressed no sympathy for the black South Africans, the 'caffirs'.

For months, Mitchel had to wait on board the *Neptune,* in Simon's Bay. Supplied with papers, he learned that Duffy had restarted the *Nation.* Since Mitchel was angry that Duffy had avoided the fate of other Young Irelanders, by producing witnesses to 'prove his moral-force character', the news of a revived *Nation* did not please him; that the *Times* praised this revived Young Ireland organ disgusted him and he dismissed Duffy and his efforts as 'dishonest'.[48] On 20 January 1850 Mitchel noted he was suffering another attack of the 'damnable asthma'.[49] On the 19 February the *Neptune* left Cape Town, and after a long period of sickness at sea, Mitchel arrived in Hobart, Van Diemen's Land on 7 April 1850. The journey had taken so long his fellow Young Irelanders had had their rebellion, of sorts, in Tipperary and many were now themselves prisoners in Van Diemen's Land. Among those imprisoned were Thomas Francis Meagher, John Martin, Kevin Izod O'Doherty and Smith O'Brien. O'Brien, unlike the other Young Ireland prisoners, had refused the 'ticket-of-leave' status that would have allowed him a farm and freedom of movement on the island, provided he did not try to escape. Even with 'ticket-of-leave' status the Irish political prisoners were not allowed to associate – but they did.

Mitchel recorded that once in Van Diemen's Land, because they had not been allowed entry to Cape Town, the 'real convicts' from the *Neptune* were set free.[50] In reality, nineteenth-century Van Diemen's Land was not a prison in the conventional sense. Convicts were only chained in road gangs or sent to penal stations, like Port Arthur, for crimes, or breaches of discipline like answering back, committed on the island. Upon landing, they were used on public works, as farm hands, as mill workers, as servants or as clerks. Good behaviour was rewarded 'with small payments of tobacco, rum and cash, or perhaps even a precious pardon, which would restore their freedom to travel or earn a living'.[51] On the other hand, punishments for trivial breaches of discipline were severe and frequently involved solitary confinement and flogging on a triangle. In general, the skilled craftsman was better treated than the unskilled. The middle class and political gentleman, Mitchel, was offered 'ticket-of-leave' status. He accepted it, 'as the majority of my friends have done, especially as Dr Gibson informs me the close confinement of Maria Island [where Smith O'Brien was being held] would probably kill me at once'.[52] Because of his poor health, John Mitchel was granted another concession. He was allowed to live with John Martin in Bothwell, in the bleak Fordel cottage. John Martin had arrived in Van Diemen's Land in November 1849, having loyally set up the *Irish Felon* newspaper to support and to continue the work of his convicted friend. In the last of only three editions of the *Irish Felon*, in the face of the country being proclaimed, and as a witness to famine he advised, 'Stand to your arms! – resist to the death! – better a hundred thousand deaths than to leave Ireland another year disarmed, cowed and defenseless to the mercy of that fiendish despotism.'[53] He was prosecuted for this and other articles in which he asked the people of Ireland to 'read, mark, learn and inwardly digest.'[54] At this stage John Martin was almost as radical as John Mitchel. He would not remain so.

By 12 April 1850 John Mitchel was 'sitting on the green grass by the bank of a clear, brawling stream of fresh water'. Opposite sat 'John Martin, sometimes of Loughorne, smoking placidly, and gazing curiously on me with his mild eyes'.[55]

Those mild eyes saw a physically weakened Mitchel who, despite his travels, was 'as fierce as ten lions, and bullies me outrageously.'[56] Martin's jovial reference to bullying was contained in a letter to Meagher. In also writing to Meagher Mitchel countered, 'I intended my selection of this Bothwell district as a very great benefit and high compliment to Martin. And the infernal old fellow does not seem to view it in that light at all.'[57] Such was the easy humour between old friends. When Mitchel disembarked from the *Neptune*, Meagher too was shocked at the 'wretched' state of his health: 'I would not give him ten shillings for the purchase of his life, the first evening I met him here.' He and O'Doherty met Mitchel and Martin at their clandestine meeting place 'at the point where the three districts of Campbell Town, Bothwell and Oaklands unite'. Despite talk of old times and songs, 'a dark shadow seemed to be resting over the little party.' However, soon after that meeting Mitchel rallied. He recovered from asthma and 'became actually radiant with good health'. Within a few weeks he was as youthful looking as the young medical student O'Doherty.[58] Mitchel liked Bothwell. His descriptions are imaginative, onomatopoeic. It is not the usual description of a jail:

Mother earth breathing her vital fragrance for ever, for ever swinging the censer of her perfumes from a thousand flowers; for ever singing her eternal melodies in whispering tree-tops and murmuring tinkling, bubbling streams – certain it is I feel a kind of joy. In vain I try to torment myself into a state of chronic indignation: it will not do here.[59]

He immensely enjoyed John Martin's company and that of Meagher and the other exiled Young Irelanders. They continued to meet at Lake Sorel where their 'dungeon-districts' touched.[60] Mitchel, who had looked 'wretchedly thin and weak and exhausted' and could 'hardly walk a few yards without panting for breath'[61] was nursed by John Martin and had grown stronger to the extent that he was now able to fight with his friend as to who would sleep on the bed and who on the sofa. Martin recorded the incident in his diary:

Then we had a long row about the important question of who should sleep on the said sofa tonight – there being but one bed, viz my mattress, till the new bed tick be filled with straw or wool or something. He was obstinate & cross, and would occupy it himself in spite of me. I proposed to abide by the solemn decision of toss-up … He attempted repeatedly to force me out of the room.[62]

The sofa was broken in the struggle. Mitchel sulked and poor Martin eventually found himself out in the cold and on an old mattress. Such was the nature of their relationship and characters, with Mitchel being aggressive whilst Martin sought accommodation and compromise.

In Van Diemen's Land the Irish political prisoners were well received by the settlers. They were perceived as distinct from the

71

convict class. John Mitchel was especially popular. He made friends easily, including the widowed Mrs Jane Williams and her father, Mr Reid. Mrs William's late husband had been a British officer. Her house, Ratho, was a favourite place where 'the books, music, flowers – and the gentle converse of high bred women, could not fail to soothe and soften an exasperated soul in any but its darkest hour.'[63]

Although, no supporter of women's emancipation Mitchel respected the opinion and views of Mrs Williams, with whom he was to correspond for years. Private letters, especially to respected female friends, were to provide insights into Mitchel's personal and public views on many controversial issues, throughout his life. Such was the case with Mary Thompson, the poetess Ethne of the *Nation*.[64] She lived in Ravensdale, between Newry and Dundalk and personal letters to there, from both John and Jenny, were to reveal much about their family and their politics – especially with regard to slavery. As Mitchel settled into life in Van Diemen's Land he realised there could be a degree of material and social comfort and he thought Jenny and his family might be able to join him. Despite the above sofa wars, he sought John Martin's advice, 'as to whether I should at length allow my wife and family to come out to Van Diemen's Land'. On 22 July 1850 he wrote in his journal 'I do so pine for something resembling a home – something that I could occasionally almost fancy a real home … I have written this day to Newry, inviting all my household to the antipodes. Pray God, I have done right.'[65] John Mitchel was not only inviting his family to Australia but also into a future that would eventually see them become involved in a civil war on the other side of the Atlantic, on the wrong side of history.

CHAPTER FOUR

'John Will Not Have Me Use The Word "Home" In This Country'

Jenny had been waiting for, and welcomed, the letter from John inviting her to Van Diemen's Land. With her five children, two servants, several trunks and boxes she sailed from Warrenpoint to Liverpool.[1] On 23 January 1851, the family then set sail on the *Condor* to Melbourne. They were seen off by John Mitchel's brother-in-law Hill Irvine, married to Margaret, and by Fr Kenyon who, following his support of physical force rebellion, had been persuaded into retirement from public life by his bishop, Dr Kennedy.[2] The *Evening Post* of 14 June 1848 carried a letter, inserted by the bishop but written by Father Kenyon, denying 'sentences from which a meaning, at variance with my own sentiments and sound morality, may be deduced'.[3] These vague words, offered in atonement, were sufficient to allow Fr Kenyon to retain his parish. The priest's sympathetic biographer Fogarty wrote, 'From this time forth, the hearty, buoyant, responsive part of his nature – the part Mitchel loved was buried …'[4] However, Fr Kenyon remained a Mitchel family friend. As befitted their class Jenny and the family had cabins and dined at table, but for Jenny especially there was still the discomfort of a six-month odyssey and a long period of seasickness.

On 23 May John Mitchel received a letter from Jenny. His whole household, including a servant, had arrived in Adelaide, South Australia from Liverpool. They had taken passage for Melbourne, not realizing the *Condor* was going to call at Adelaide: 'A business which will hold them a full month.'[5] Jenny was impatient and sent word to her husband with a ship's captain that she would take passage on a brigantine, sailing to Launceston.[6] Mitchel immediately took the night mail coach to Launceston. Terence Bellew McManus who, following the rebellion, was sentenced to be 'hanged, drawn and quartered at Clonmel in October 1848'[7] but was transported instead, had escaped from Launceston for California some weeks previously. Mitchel, who arrived there before his official permission, was therefore suspect. The Magistrate perceived Mitchel to be haughty and disrespectful and ordered him to jail. When Mitchel's papers did arrive he was released and spent nine days waiting with an old friend, Mr Pooler, a merchant from Armagh. He then discovered, in a letter from Kevin Izod O'Doherty, that the brig *Union* had arrived in Hobart 'carrying my expected consignment.'[8] Mitchel arranged to meet his family inland at Greenponds and set off by coach. The journey from Adelaide to Hobart, as described by Jenny, was stormy, dangerous and frightening. She wrote to Mary Thompson:

> I despaired of ever seeing V. D. Land … The Captain of the *Union* said he had never been at sea in worse weather. We were driving about for several days without a shred of canvas, just the bare masts and the wind howling through them. Such seas it were impossible to describe … [9]

Alas, John Mitchel was not waiting for them. The family faced another two-day trip, overland to an inn at Greenponds.

Jenny and John were reunited on 20 June 1851, eleven months after he had sent word, and three years since they had been parted in Newgate prison. Mitchel wrote with powerful understatement: 'Greenponds – Today I met my wife and family once more. These things cannot be described.'[10] One assumes that that night they did not read Disraeli's *Young Duke*. (As they had done when Jenny's 'father' caught them in Chester.) John had a present for Jenny; a chestnut mare, Fleur-de-Lis, which he rode the following day while the family, in a spring cart, travelled through the rain and snow to Mrs Beech's hotel in Bothwell. Mrs Beech was known for her kangaroo steaks. Here they were reunited with John Martin and 'spent such an evening as seldom falls to the lot of captives'.[11]

Mitchel was not well when he met his family. In the previous week, 'the old demon asthma had returned and clung to him with all its former force and cruelty'. His friends were disappointed that Jenny did not find him 'in buoyant health and sparkling form'.[12] Over the next few weeks he had a very slow, unsteady and painful recovery. The family then settled into another period of domestic tranquility with 'pure air, glorious forests, lovely rivers, a thinly populated pastoral country and kind friends'.[13] In August they occupied Nant Cottage, 'with a 200 acres farm and a good enough little house with a large garden and various conveniences, and altogether it is a very nice little place. Mitchel is very delicate but all the rest are well'.[14] With his family around him John Mitchel's health improved and he enjoyed farming. Others looked forward to meeting the beautiful Mrs Mitchel. Mrs Connell, from a non-convict Irish settler family, wrote to John Martin to:

> Remind Mr Mitchel of his promise the night he came
> here that he would bring Mrs M., if ever she came to

V.D.L. No tyrant can confine her to a district ... I hope she is a real croppy; you know we have plenty of room for all the little rebels.[15]

Of this time Mitchel wrote:

> Mrs Mitchel and the children enjoy themselves exceedingly for our cottage is in a beautiful spot, three miles from Bothwell township, with the River Clyde running in front of it and fine hills all around covered in wood. My wife has grown a great equestrian ... Martin lives four miles hence.

Four hours a day were devoted to lessons, followed by riding or roaming the woods with the dogs.[16] O'Connor, Jenny's biographer, described it more romantically as a time 'for stitching them together as a unit of fidelity that would never unravel'.[17]

In the Australian spring of 1851, with the children safely in the care of John Martin, Jenny and John set out on their horses, Fleur-de-lis and Tricolour, on an odyssey to visit Smith O'Brien, who had accepted ticket-of-leave and 'comparative liberty'.[18] He was now the tutor to the children of a local doctor at Avoca. As Mitchel travelled he felt he was in 'a small misshapen, transported, bastard England'[19] and the sight of lounging constables made him feel 'the whole wide and glorious forest is, after all, but an umbrageous and highly perfumed dungeon'.[20] However, Mitchel's descriptions of the countryside and the journey tell of his love of the landscape and the pleasure of his wife's company.

They stayed in a small inn, travelled in valleys and over mountains, 'belted with magnificent timber'[21] that reminded

Mitchel of counties Donegal and Down. For the final stage of the journey, to Avoca, they transferred to a public conveyance. Their horses were taken to the Sugar-Loaf by Mr Connell, whose wife was eagerly awaiting Jenny's visit.

The visit to Smith O'Brien was bitter sweet. Whilst rejoicing in his company Mitchel regretted that Smith O'Brien, following both a failed rebellion in Ireland and an abortive attempt to escape from Van Diemen's Land, had accepted defeat. Smith O'Brien described his failed bid for freedom and his betrayal by Captain Ellis of the schooner he was attempting to escape in. 'Ellis had gone to Government House, and there had sold him for certain moneys.' During the escape attempt, as Smith O'Brien struggled in the water, he claimed the three 'rascals' in the schooner's rowing boat refused to help him and thereby alerted the constable. He also told Mitchel about the behaviour of the priests in Balingarry and how they had dissuaded people from joining the rebellion. Mitchel had other words for their 'priestliness'; words like cowardice and treachery;[22] words that would later land him in a written fight with Archbishop Hughes in the United States.

As they walked and talked Smith O'Brien gallantly protected Jenny from a large black snake she was about to step on.[23] Both she and John were enjoying the company of a man they loved and respected. When the time came to part, on 16 October, they all walked two miles together and then John and Jenny 'watched him long, as he walked up the valley side on his lonely way; and I think I have seen few sadder and prouder sights.' Jenny was moved to tears.[24] On the return journey they picked up their horses at the Connells of the Sugar-Loaf. The Connells were a frontier family, a settler family from County Cork who had clashed with 'black Tasmanians'. On one occasion, when Mr Connell was away, Mrs Connell and the children disarmed and overpowered four white bushrangers who had tried to rob them. In *Jail Journal*, Mitchel retold Mrs Connell's stories without any trace of empathy for the black Tasmanians who, 'have all disappeared before convict civilization'.[25]

On 18 October John and Jenny left the Sugar-Loaf and, initially guided by young Connell, made their way up 'rude tracks' through the mountains. As 'they led their horses up a steep ridge they met a man with a gun, greyhound (that had belonged to the escaped Terence Bellew McManus) and wearing 'a cabbage-tree hat'. It was Thomas Francis Meagher who had walked out four miles, over the steep ridges, to meet his friends. Their visit with Meagher and his 'lady of the sylvan hermitage'[26] was light-hearted and active.

Meagher had found exile lonely, had craved female company and the previous February married the unaccomplished Katherine Bennett. Katherine was the daughter of a convict highwayman. Their union invited snobbish criticism from Meagher's Young Ireland colleagues, including the Mitchels and John Martin. All were of their class, including Jenny and 'Honest' John Martin, who lived up to his name in expressing an opinion:

> The Bride looked well and so did the groom. She seems
> a very quiet, gentle and inoffensive girl. It is a pity (so far
> as I have learned) she neither sings, or plays nor draws,
> nor paints, nor has any decided turn for literature, or
> any great enjoyment or interest in it, or any feeling of
> patriotism or any enthusiasm of character, or any marked
> talent, or accomplishment or decided character ... [27]

Meagher strongly dismissed such objections as 'the opinion of the frivolous, the fashionable, the sordid, the worshippers of the dollar, and of the flimsy phantom known as Birth'.[28]

While staying with Meagher the Mitchels sailed in a small boat 'hauled up here through Bothwell, a distance of seventy-five miles by six bullocks'.[29] The *Speranza* was the small boat Meagher named after the pen name in the *Nation* of the beautiful Young Ireland poetess Jane Francesca Elgee. She was the future mother of Oscar Wilde.

The Mitchels had 'a delightful sail to various points on the lake … and as we float here at our ease, we are willing to believe that no lake on earth is more beauteous than Sorel'.[30] On first meeting Meagher, in Dublin, Mitchel had described conversation with him like diving into a crystal lake. Now, with Meagher, he and Jenny enjoyed sauntering and conversing on the lakeshore, 'where gleams and ripples purer, glassier water mirroring a brighter sky'.[31] They discussed Irish and Australian politics. Meagher was interested in the efforts of the colonists to become a normal non-convict colony. Mitchel had that interest too, but mainly as a means of embarrassing the British. 'Our interest in the matter is much heightened (at least mine is) by the inevitable satisfaction of which I needs must feel at every difficulty, every humiliation, of the Carthaginian Government'.[32] John Mitchel was consistent. His fight had many theatres but one clear focus. The ride home to Nant Cottage, the children and John Martin was idyllic. The air they breathed crossing the high lake country was 'wafted to us from the wine-dark Indian Ocean, or the perfumed coral-isles of the sun-bright Pacific'.[33] Mitchel carried 'a young kangaroo in a bag (a present to the children from the good family at the Sugar-Loaf), and with this nursling resting on my arm it is as much as I can do to manage my horse'. The children were walking in the fields, with the dogs and John Martin, when they saw their parents ford the river; they ran to meet them 'with a welcoming outcry: and there is joy at Nant over the little kangaroo'.[34] Thus, Jenny and John spent time together travelling to visit friends, riding and sailing on Lake Sorel. Jenny refused to swim because of a fear of snakes. Given her life story it may have been her only fear. In letters to Mary Thompson of Ravensdale, she described her life and expressed both her contentment and irritations. 'I continue to like this country very much, and if we could get rid of the convict servants and the snakes and had you and one or two other of our friends here I would be contented to remain here all my life'.[35] The children bathed almost every day in the river Clyde that flowed in front of their house. The house was situated on a small hill, surrounded by one hundred acres of pasture.

The Mitchels lived as farmers on their two hundred and eleven acres. Jenny wrote, 'We use our own mutton, bake our bread and make our own candles. Certainly it is a new sort of life to me and on the whole a very pleasant one.' Jenny herself was actively involved. 'I have got 4 fine cows, 2 just calved and the others near it (I say I have, for the cows are mine own) and so I carry on great dairy operations'.[36] Although there were mice, and therefore 'two fine cats', the rats introduced by ships to Van Diemen's Land had not yet migrated from Hobart and Launceston. As well as farming John was the teacher for his sons. Henrietta, once 'an idle careless little puss' was 'promoted to her papa's charge' and became a keen reader, although, unlike Minnie, she was not so good with the needle; a useful skill since clothes wore out quickly and there were no tailors or dressmakers close by. Jenny commented that although she became ill in the hot season, the children were 'in almost perfect health'. The climate had been very good for Minnie and Willie, who had both been considered to be delicate. Willie was now 'a great stout fellow' whose interest was in horses and dogs.[37] Jenny, a daughter of an Ascendency family, the young lady from the drawing room in

Queen Street, Newry and from Miss Bryden's school, the political hostess from 8, Ontario Terrace, readily accepted, and enjoyed, the life of a farmer's wife.

John Mitchel and his sons went on kangaroo hunts. On such a hunt, in admiration but with little sympathy, Mitchel described finding a female kangaroo killed by their dog, Dart.

> We found the first kangaroo lying at the root of a gum tree. It was a very large female … we found in her pocket one of the young ones, that she has not time to throw away. The females, always as they rise from their lair, at the sight of the enemy, put their hands in their pockets and throw their young ones into some place of safety … This one had fought desperately for her life and her little *joey,* as the young are called … Round her lay a plenteous pool of blood; her head was almost torn off.

The dog's 'vengeful muzzle' was drinking up the kangaroo mother's life. Mitchel thought the day's sport even better because 'the kangaroo is becoming scarce all over the inhabited parts of the island'.[38] As with his recognition that black Tasmanians had all but disappeared from the island, this is simply a statement of fact. In a letter to Miss Thompson he was to suggest epidemics were useful in getting rid of the physically weak who would otherwise linger and, more tellingly, in the light of his condemnation of Famine policies of the Carthaginians, 'even propagate, perhaps, their unhappy species'.[39] However, when the blood of his own sons soaked into the soil of a Confederate lost cause, he was to accept it without complaint. He was consistent.

But for now life was good. Yet, no matter how strong the rustic seduction Mitchel fought it. Jenny complained, 'John will not have me use the word "home" in this country'.[40] Despite this, as evidenced above, Mitchel wrote with affection and admiration for the lake country.

John Martin, who moved in with the Mitchels, also objected to the idea that they were free in Van Diemen's Land. 'We are a good deal annoyed at seeing a paragraph in the Colonial papers, copied out of some grossly stupid Irish paper, to the effect that Mitchel has become an extensive and prosperous farmer' who was enjoying life with his family and the 'amiable John Martin'.[41] Despite their protestations, Mitchel's treatment, and Martin's, by the Carthaginians, hardly merited the title *Jail Journal*. In September 1852 Jenny gave birth to another child, a little girl, Isabel, or Rixy as she was affectionately known within the family. 'The dearest, sweetest, loveliest child that ever a mother's heart could desire'.[42] John Martin referred to her as 'native girl'.[43] Within the Mitchel household such nicknames were signs of affection and in a letter to O'Doherty Martin revealed that he was the 'religious instructor', Mitchel was the 'head waiter' and Jenny was 'an admirable barmaid'.[44]

On New Years Day, 1853, after an absence of many months from his journal, Mitchel's pen declared, 'Of literature I am almost sick and prefer farming and making market of my wool'. The atmosphere of Van Diemen's was 'stupefying the brain'.[45] He noted, 'there is more languor, and less excitability among Tasmanians, native or imported, than I have ever witnessed before'.[46] It had a narcotic effect and if 'it has not removed, it has surely softened the sting, even of our *nostalgia*'. He and John Martin had 'quaffed in these gardens the cup of lazy enchantment'. The sound of the external world was 'deadened, softened, almost harmonized, like the roar of ocean waves heard in a dream, or murmuring through the spiral chambers of a sea-shell'. The papers, sometimes four months old, were 'lazily and sleepily' read.[47] John Mitchel was happily perplexed by the behaviour of 'two or three horrible cut throats' that worked for him. They had been transported from Ireland for 'seizing arms' which within the prisoner community was 'a respectable sort of offence'.[48] In bringing in his hay harvest they were model workers. As Maxwell-Stewart and Susan Hood have pointed out early colonial Australia was not a gaol. Prisoners who worked hard and without complaint were often rewarded, with material incentives or ultimately a pardon. On the other hand, those who incurred the wrath of their masters or government officials risked demotion to road and chain gangs.[49]

The ultimate sanction was banishment to a penal station like Port Arthur; overall about 16 per cent of prisoners ended up being detained.[50] Thus, Mitchel's convict workers were relatively well treated by the authorities and, despite liking wine, appeared to benefit from lenient treatment. Indeed, over his three years in Van Diemen's Land, and despite living in an isolated and therefore vulnerable place, Mitchel and his family had experienced very little crime.[51] Mitchel suggested the reason was a mixture of the prisoners being well treated and the severity of the punishments.

Yet, despite the evidence he observed – evidence that was strong enough to allow his family to feel secure and sleep in Van Diemen's Land 'as peacefully, as they ever did in Banbridge'[52] – Mitchel's instincts would not allow him to accept the progress of the convict class. Although, as he was to outline in his speech in Virginia University in 1854, he did accept that individuals might seek improvement. This tension between the observable evidence and his instincts made him uneasy. Most prisoners are free in their imaginations and physically detained. Physically John Mitchel enjoyed Van Diemen's Land, and the freedom and security of its economic system and landscape. However, in his imagination he was a prisoner. He was aware of the paradox. Perplexed by this, by the good behaviour of his convict servants, by the evidence before him, he wrote:

> … simple Arcadian shepherds – instead of rejoicing in their improved conditions and behaviour, I gaze upon them with horror, as unclean, and inhuman monsters, due long to the gallows-tree and oblivion; and then the sunlight of this most radiant land takes a livid hue to my eyes! The waving whispering woods put on a brown horror like the forests that wave and sigh through Dante's Tartarean vision. The soft west wind that blows here forever has a moan like the moan of damned souls. The stars look dim; and on the corner of the moon there hangs a vapourous drop profound. The Devil's in it.[53]

Mitchel's guilt at enjoying aspects of his captivity and the possibility that the convicts, as a class, might be making progress were unsettling to his classical view of the world. In *Jail Journal*, in his imagination, he retreated into that world. As he continued to write, the 'Arcadian Shepherds' bringing in his hay became 'Tartarian reapers of Erebus!' reaping a 'harvest of Hell; and preparing the ground in these Cimmerean regions of outer darkness to yield crops of abomination and horror…For is not the human species making "Progress?"[54] For Mitchel, progress that might allow the convict class to advance was a vision of hell. For Mitchel the 'vapourous drop profound' with the Devil in it was to hang and then fall catastrophically into his classical view of the world, his almost inert hierarchal view of

84

society when, years later, the Confederate Congress voted to allow slaves to become soldiers; for Mitchel this was something wrong and unnatural.

If the aging newspapers were casually read not so a forty-five page letter from Devin Reilly whose reference to Gavan Duffy as 'Mr Give-in-Duffy' pleased Mitchel, who thought Duffy should not have resisted a guilty verdict and deportation. Reilly had escaped to the USA, was editing the *Democratic Review* and was married to an Irish girl. In the letter he wrote of losing his son whom he had named after Mitchel, and soon after that tragedy he had to again rise from his writing to bury his little daughter.[55] His wife was sickly and only an interest in American politics kept him going. Commenting on the sad circumstances in the letter John Martin advised that Devin Reilly would be better off with them to have an opportunity to 'lay up thought, instead of wasting and squandering it ... Better be a shepherd at the lakes till better times.'[56] Mitchel strongly disagreed. 'I tell that you I envy Devin Reilly for being alive – alive as you and I will never, never be alive again.'[57]

News of Thomas Francis Meagher escaping to the United States further unsettled John Mitchel. Before fleeing, Meagher had written to a police magistrate withdrawing his parole[58] but ironically, given future controversy about his own leaving of Van Diemen's Land, John Mitchel was very critical of his friend's behaviour. An almost Arthurian sense of honour was central to Young Ireland's view of itself. Mitchel wrote harsh words on the topic to Miss Thompson:

> You have heard of course all about Mr Meagher's escape. We are not here content with the manner of it – assuredly if we could think the obligation of our parole could be so easily satisfied – there is not one among us

who would not have been north of the equator long ago. It is painful to say this, but his leaving V.D. Land so as to let even a question be raised about his good faith was a grievous wrong to us and to our cause.[59]

Unsettled by Devin O'Reilly's epistle, and with Meagher already gone, Mitchel was ready to escape.

1. The plaque on the pavement in Dawson Street, Dublin, commemorating the first meeting of the Grand Orange Order.

2. Jenny Verner: 'Jenny was a masterpiece in miniature'. (Courtesy Pat Brown)

3. Revd John Mitchel: He 'fairly observed the legitimate distinction between persons and opinions...' observed Revd Bagot. (Courtesy Non-Subscribing Presbyterian Church, Newry)

4. Mrs Mitchel, John's mother: 'There was a clearness, and energy and a decisiveness about her modes of thought and action which powerfully impressed and fascinated those who had the advantage of her friendship.' (Courtesy Pat Brown)

5. John Mitchel: the rebel with the cultivated looks of Byron. He loved walking, talking and smoking. (Courtesy Pat Brown)

6. Jenny's home, 52 Queen Street (now Dominic Street) Newry. Jenny eloped through the middle door. The end house below the chimney was the boyhood home of Lord Russell of Killowen, a nationalist who defended Parnell and became Chief Justice of England.

7. Drumcree Church, near Portadown, where John and Jenny were married in the tower. The rest of the building did not exist in 1836.

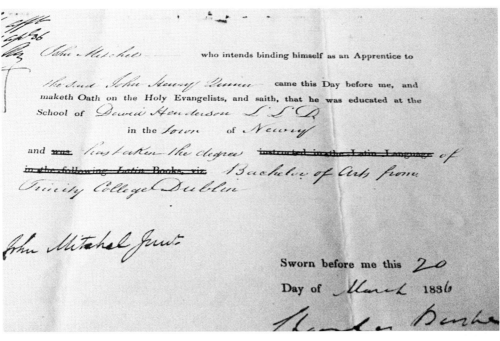

8. Apprentice Solicitor: John Mitchel's Certificate of Legal Apprenticeship dated 20 March 1836. (O'Connor Papers)

9. Thomas Davis invited Mitchel to join the council of the '82 Club. When Davis died on 16 September 1845 John Mitchel replaced him at the *Nation*, with a very different pen.

10. 1 Upper Leeson Street: the Mitchels' first home in Dublin, with the white doorway nearest the bridge over the Grand Canal. Here there were 'nights and suppers of the Gods, when the reckless gaiety of Irish temperament held fullest sway…'.

11. Thomas Francis Meagher in 1848: 'How fresh and clear and strong! What wealth of imagination and princely generosity of feeling! To me it was the revelation of a new and great nature, and, I reveled in it...'. John Mitchel on Meagher.

12. Rotunda, Sackville Street (now O'Connell Street, Dublin). Here the Confederation was to have a more practical and serious intent than the '82 Club.

13. Charles Gavan Duffy: It was Duffy who invited Mitchel to Dublin but he was more cautious than Mitchel and became a lifelong enemy.

14. The Tricolour: when Meagher introduced it in the Music Hall, Lower Abbey Street, Mitchel proclaimed: 'I hope to see that flag one day waving, as our national banner, over a forest of Irish pikes'.

15. William Smith O'Brien: Smith O'Brien, the Anglo-Irish landowner and Mitchel, the son of the manse, often disagreed but, unlike Gavan Duffy, O'Brien remained a favourite family friend.

16. Judges Dunne, Lefroy and Moore at Mitchel's trial: if there was to be another trial, Jenny suggested, '…the moment the Judge passes sentence he should be shot…'.

17. 8 Ontario Terrace was John and Jenny's second canal-side home in Dublin. From these steps an elegant Jenny urged the crowd not to allow John Mitchel to be transported.

DUBLIN TOURISM

JOHN MITCHEL
1815 - 1875

JOURNALIST, SOLICITOR
AND PATRIOT
FOUNDER OF THE
UNITED IRISHMAN

LIVED IN THIS HOUSE

18. Plaque on 8 Ontario Terrace.

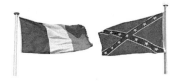

CHAPTER FIVE

Nicaragua – Agent Dropped From the Sky

On 13 January 1853 Mitchel wrote: 'A new personage has appeared amongst us – dropped from the sky or from New York.'[1] It was Nicaragua (P.J.) Smyth, an agent of the Irish New York Directory, sent to aid the escape of Young Ireland, including John Mitchel. In later years Smyth was to become a Home Rule MP, and even a minor establishment figure[2] but now he was a young, patriotic adventurer. An unpublished family manuscript suggested he was named Nicaragua because of his, 'previous journalistic support for railway projects.'[3] Mitchel realized his escape plans meant more turmoil for the family, but Jenny was supportive: 'Yet my wife does not shrink from all this risk and inconvenience. She sees all the terrible evils and disadvantages of rearing a family in such a country as this, and under such circumstances as ours; and instead of dissuading, urges me strongly on the enterprise.'[4] Jenny's support of Mitchel's plans was a constant throughout their troubled lives.

To escape, a fast horse was essential and Mitchel sought, and bought, a white 'half Arab' from Mr Davis the local police magistrate. Mitchel enjoyed the irony: '… and the idea pleased me, of buying my enemy's horse to ride off upon; which would have the double advantage of strengthening me and weakening the enemy.'[5] The first attempt to escape, which was to include 'John

Knox' (Mitchel's nickname for Martin), was 'blown to the moon'[6] by informers. Nicaragua was arrested, not as himself but as John Mitchel, when trying to warn the waiting ship, the *Waterlily*, of the plan's failure. He was eventually released, a sick man, but only after the real John Mitchel had presented himself. Mitchel was angry that the authorities thought he might escape without first resigning his ticket-of-leave. It took Nicaragua two months to recover.

In Nant Cottage on 6 June new escape plans were discussed, but this time John Knox opted out because, given the winter weather, he might 'be subjected to too much hardship' and because his looks would have been difficult to disguise.[7] In *Jail Journal* John Mitchel provided a detailed, and inevitably subjective, account of his escape.

On 12 June John Mitchel and Nicaragua Smyth set off, on horseback, for the police office in Bothwell. They met 'James (boy number two) coming at a gallop from Hobart.' James handed his father a note from the shipping agent, stating that the ship Mitchel was to escape in had gone. Mitchel decided to proceed anyway. He walked into the Bothwell police barrack and, armed with pistols, said to Mr Davis and his clerk: 'Mr. Davis here is a copy of a note which I have just dispatched to the Governor ... '. Mitchel handed over the following note resigning his 'ticket-of-leave':

Bothwell , 8th June 1853

To the Lieut. Gov., etc.-
     Sir, ----I hereby resign the 'ticket-of-leave,' and withdraw my *parole.*
I shall forthwith present myself before the police magistrate at Bothwell, at his office, show him a copy of this note, and offer myself to be taken into custody.

Your obedient servant,

John Mitchel

The magistrate and constables failed to react as Mitchel, whip in hand, pistols in breast pocket, bade them good morning, put on his hat and walked out. A constable was holding two horses, one in each hand. Mitchel and Nicaragua walked past him, jumped into their saddles and, to the cries of the officials and laughter of the crowd, galloped out of Bothwell. In a forest, they exchanged horses, exchanged coats, and separated; Nicaragua, on Fleur-de-Lis, to arrange a ship; Mitchel to avoid capture. He 'resolved not to be taken alive'.[8]

With a pre-arranged guide, the son of an English settler who knew every nook on the island, John Mitchel headed into the winter landscape for the district of Westbury, 'which is chiefly inhabited by Irish immigrants and where we should be within a days ride of Bass's straights'.[9] The journey along the shore of Lake Sorel and over the mountains towards Job Sim's shepherd's hut was difficult. At midnight, despite hearing Job's dogs below, the descent down the steep slope was judged too dangerous and they decided to stop for the night. Tired, thirsty and starving, they lit both a fire and their pipes. Exhausted, they tried to sleep on the rocky ground, by the fire, 'until awakened by the scorching of our knees, while our spinal marrow was frozen into a solid icicle'. They turned around but, 'in five minutes our knees and toes were frozen, our moustaches stiff with ice – our spinal marrow dissolving away in the heat. Then up again – another smoke, another talk.'[10] Next morning they arrived at Job's. Job, too, was an Englishman. He had also helped Meagher in his escape. In Job's, as Meagher had done, Mitchel made a 'complete transfiguration' of himself.[11]

Over the next month and ten days, in the depths of the winter, there were long horseback rides, trips along estuaries in small open boats and failed rendezvous with ships. There was help and accommodation from both Irish and English settlers.

For example, to the north west of Van Diemen's Land a young Irish couple called Burke hid John Mitchel in their isolated farmhouse for over a week.[12] Then following the failure of a brigantine, the *Don Juan*, to show on the shore of the Port Sorel inlet, an Englishman, farmer and part-time ferryman called Miller also helped Mitchel. Miller did not like Sir William Denison, the Lord Lieutenant of Van Diemen's Land. Mitchel suggested that Miller would 'go any length in my service; not perhaps, that he loves me more, but that he loves Sir William less'. Any length included an offer to intercept, rob and drown any constable carrying dispatches, and seeking Miller's help as a ferryman. While staying at Miller's farmhouse Mitchel was on the shore, within a mile of a sleepy village, which he observed through a telescope and 'which seems to be peopled by constables sauntering about with their belts and jingling handcuffs'.[13]

On 6 July, Mitchel left Miller and, with the two Burkes, rode to Launceston where he 'got rigged up instantly as a catholic priest – shaved from the eyes to the throat; dressed in a long black coat, with an upright collar, the narrow white band around the neck, and a broad black hat'.[14] The plan was for Mitchel to board a steamer bound for Melbourne but, due to increased surveillance, the Captain refused to take him and suggested he make his way fifty miles downstream before boarding. There followed a nocturnal journey in an open rowing boat, through a wet and stormy night. An exhausted Mitchel slept on the bottom of the boat but the steamer did not wait for him. They arrived to see it disappear. There followed another wet, windy and 'weary pull up the river again'. They were twice on the reefs.

As Mitchel's adventures continued, much of the time he was Father McNamarra, so well disguised that 'in truth, if my wife had met me in that walk, she could not have suspected me'.[15] As he was escaping John Mitchel wrote letters to Jenny and his mother. In a letter to his mother he feared he may never see his 'good and brave and affectionate' Jenny again. Ironically, given future events, he feared he might not be able to give her a peaceful home in America. Concerned it may be his last letter, Mitchel wrote of 'the scenes of his father's fireside' at Dromalane, and of his remorse at causing his parents 'grief and anxiety'.[16] Still disguised as a priest, this time the Revd Blake, Mitchel took the night mail from Launceston, 120 miles south, to Hobart. One passenger, Mac Dowell, had met Mitchel before but did not recognize him. However, he did comment that the Reverend had no luggage. At one point the coach was near Bothwell and Mitchel gazed 'wistfully up at the gloomy ridge of the Den Hill'. Beyond the hill lay his 'little *quasi*-home … with all its sleeping inmates lulled by the murmuring Clyde'.[17]

At four on a winter's morning, at Greenponds, where he had, at last, met Jenny and his children when they arrived from Ireland, the chief constable looked into the coach; Mitchel clutched the pistol under his soutane, but he was not recognised. When he arrived in Hobart even Nicaragua did not know him and thought Mitchel was a detective come to arrest him. Nicaragua was able to tell Mitchel that his escape was being celebrated in song, that the police magistrate, Mr Davis, lived in fear of John Martin attempting an escape and that it was said John Mitchel had bought the man and not the horse.[18] Mr Davis, in turn, had blamed and sacked an English constable for taking a bribe. Mitchel denied this but mused that the poor constable was open to a bribe, 'wanted a bribe, and deserved a bribe'.[19] However, when planning Mitchel's escape Nicaragua had, by the 'prudent employment of some money'[20] made sure there would not be extra guards. As their feud developed Gavan Duffy was to use Mr Davis's version of events to accuse Mitchel of surrendering to a policeman whom he had already bribed not to arrest him. It therefore followed that Mitchel's resignation of his ticket-of-leave was spurious and dishonourable.[21] The issue remained a matter of prejudice. However, as with much of the detail of Mitchel's escape and the content of this chapter, it was he who wrote the story. Numerous strangers aided Mitchel's clandestine journey through Van Diemen's Land. He wrote to the Burkes musing as to why they and so many people, strangers, had helped him:

> I cannot leave Van Diemen's Land without writing one line to bid farewell to you, and my friend John Burke. Though I never saw either of you until a month ago I cannot help regarding you as brother and sister ... The only thing that puzzled me was why you all took so deep an interest in my escape but I have not the vanity to think it was all on my own account. It was for the sake of our well beloved old country, in whose cause I am proud to suffer. And if I live you will yet hear of my doing, or more probably suffering more in the same cause.[22]

With Mitchel in Hobart, Nicaragua left for Bothwell and Nant Cottage to help the family make ready to leave for the USA by selling stock. Jenny received kind help from her neigbours. Fleur-de-Lis, a favourite, and one of the horses involved in the escape, went to a young lady. The cottage and furniture went to an Englishman.

The Mitchel family arrived in Hobart, with Nicaragua, and boarded the *Emma*, bound for Sydney. Further downstream in moonlight, after the authorities had cleared the ship, a Mr Wright boarded. John Mitchel's family, sitting in the moonlight on the poop deck, ignored him. Two years later Jenny wrote, 'So well was he disguised that neither Henrietta, Willie or Minnie recognized him.'[23] However, O'Connor described how young Willie did not understand and had to be restrained, by Nicaragua, from running to his father;[24] a double embarrassment as Mr Wright was both a felon and was dressed as a catholic priest. Years later, in his diary, Willie's friend, Captain John Dooley of the Confederate Army, recorded that Willie had asked one of the gentlemen, who was helping Mitchel to escape, if his father was on board. The gentleman took Willie to the cabin window and 'held him out over the dashing ocean's foam and told him if he wished to avoid a watery grave never to breathe his father's name whilst on that ship'.[25] If this account is true the gentleman was probably Nicaragua acting as guide and protector to the family.

On 23 July at Sydney, after getting rid of the chief search officer by taking him to his cabin, giving him brandy and telling him a jocose story, Captain Brown took Mr Wright ashore in his own boat. Mr Wright did not presume to bid farewell to Mrs Mitchel, to whom he had not been introduced. Captain Brown took Mr Wright to the home of the ship's owner Mr McNamarra, who had also sent the *Don Juan* to the north of Van Diemen's Land in the failed attempt to pick up Mitchel. Nicaragua found lodgings for Jenny and the family at Wooloomooloo.

The *Sydney Empire* warmly welcomed 'the gifted and beautiful wife of the Irish exile'. While not presuming 'to offer an opinion on his revolutionary project', it mused that her heart 'must have been tried to its innermost core in the conflict between affection, united with maternal solicitude, and … her duty to husband and her country'. Whilst, as we have seen in the *Newry Examiner* and *Louth Advertiser*, such hyperbole was not unusual in nineteenth-century papers, and the reference to Jenny 'participating in his halo of intense excitement'[26] was inevitably incomplete, it unconsciously anticipated not only many more severe trials but also her stoical and steadfast response. In McNamarra's carriage John Mitchel, who was now Mr Warren, went out to the South Head lighthouse, climbed the steps, admired the view but thought Donegal's Lough Swilly superior. Jenny visited John in McNamarra's, with letters of congratulations from Smith O'Brien and John Martin on his continuing escape. It was decided Mitchel would take the one berth available on the *Orkney Lass* to Tahiti. Jenny and the children would sail at a later date with Nicaragua.

Mitchel was on board the *Orkney Lass* ready to leave but some sailors jumped ship in search of gold. They were arrested and the police were called to investigate. Whilst the 'water police' were on board Mitchel walked 'coolly, conversing agreeably with other passengers'.[27] However, with the ship's departure delayed John Mitchel returned to McNamarra's. He visited his family at their lodgings. With further delays, and to the consternation of Mr McNamarra, John Mitchel even went for an evening to have oysters in a tavern. On 2 August, with Mitchel on board, the *Orkney Lass* set sail for Tahiti. It was searched but 'the man five feet ten in stature, with dark hair, was recognized by no enemy'. Four English actresses, preparing for a show in Tahiti, rehearsed and made the cabin 'uninhabitable by practicing in the evening'.[28] On 25 August John Mitchel arrived in Tahiti.

Although in a French territory, he remained as Mr Warren. He enjoyed visiting the town, being entertained on a French frigate, swimming with the *Orkney Lass*'s captain, and exploring the countryside. He thought the English actresses' concert a failure, mainly because the French governor and officers did not attend. An audience of Tahitian women, and the son of Queen Pomare, whom he visited, did not impress John Mitchel either.

On 13 September an American barque, the *Julie Ann,* arrived off shore. Mitchel using a telescope saw a rowing boat leave the *Julie Ann* and head for the shore. 'Anxiously I watched the boat; and while it was still a mile off I recognized one of my own boys sitting in the bow, and Nicaragua beside him. They have come for me.' On board the *Julie Ann* John Mitchel took of his hat in homage to the Stars and Stripes.

Foreshadowing future events, when he would tragically support the Confederacy, it was an unintentionally ironic gesture. For Mitchel this was the happy end of his captivity. 'I am surrounded by my family, all well; we are away before a fine breeze for San Francisco; my "Jail Journal" ends, and my "out-of Jail Journal" begins.'[29] The joy at being a family again did not relieve Jenny of her seasickness as the family sailed for California.[30]

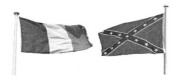

CHAPTER SIX

Through Nicaragua with *Nicaragua*

On 9 October 1853 John Mitchel and his family sailed into 'the long wished for Gate of Gold',[1] San Francisco. He was accorded a hero's welcome and was a guest of the city and its mayor. Jenny, recovering from the long sea journey, enjoyed daily journeys in a fine carriage with white horses.[2] Mitchel, without Jenny, was feted at the 'grandest of banquets, presided over by the Governor of the State'.[3] As Susannah Bruce has pointed out, in 1850s San Francisco this was not unusual. As escaped heroes of 1848, both Terence Bellew McManus in 1851, and Patrick O'Donohue in 1853 (from Carlow, who was deported in 1848 and produced the patriotic paper *Irish Exile* in Van Diemen's Land), had received similar welcomes.[4] Once in San Francisco McManus and others tracked down, seized and tried Captain Ellis, the schooner captain who had betrayed Smith O'Brien as he attempted to escape from Van Diemen's Land. However, the 'midnight court', under the tree where Ellis was 'destined to swing', let him go 'for want of sufficient and satisfactory evidence then producable'. Naturally, Mitchel contrasted this respect for available evidence with flawed British courts and packed juries in Ireland.[5]

Although an 1848 Irish hero, a status enhanced following his escape from Van Diemen's Land, McManus's business career in

America was to fail and he died in poverty. However, it was as a disinterred corpse that Terence Bellew McManus was to be of most value to Ireland's cause. In November 1861, the Fenians increased their strength and popularity by organising a massive funeral in New York, where even Bishop Hughes 'seemed to offer tacit approval of the Fenian Movement'.[6] The corpse of Terence Bellew McManus was then repatriated to Dublin where thousands viewed his body, before burial in Glasnevin.[6] As Michael Hanaghan, in *Globalization and Resistance*, has observed, 'The McManus funeral is often portrayed as a turning point marking a revival of nationalism in Ireland'.[7] It was a significant early move by the Irish Republican Brotherhood in preparation for, and to ferment support for, the 1867 rising.

San Francisco, in 1853, was a fast growing, young city with large Irish immigrant and second-generation populations of 4,200 and 1,400 respectively.[8] With a population of only 1,000 in 1848, it had not developed the same anti-immigrant tradition, or concentration of 'know-nothings', as the longer-established east coast cities.

'The pinnacle of American nativism was the Order of the Star Spangled Banner, also called the American Party but most well known as the Know-Nothings for their habit of denying all knowledge of the secret organization's traditions'.[9] The Know-Nothings sought to protect America's Protestant ethos. Immigrants, especially Irish catholic immigrants, would need to be 'fully Americanized before exercising the rights of Citizenship'.[10] Mitchel would use his pen, and on one occasion in Knoxville, his cane, against them. Despite Terence Bellew McManus entertaining the Mitchel family at his ranch near San Jose, John was impatient to be with Meagher and the large Irish community in New York. There he could, most effectively, write and speak for Ireland. Jenny was on the move again. After three weeks in California, on 1 November

1853 the Mitchels and Nicaragua were on board the *Cortes* sailing for Nicaragua. They passed Guatemala and the pirate ship *Caroline*, sailing towards the crescent-shaped bay of San Juan del Jour.[11] Again, Jenny suffered from mal de mer. The sea journey was followed by a most uncomfortable 15 mile mule-back ride to Virgin Bay on Lake Nicaragua. Isabel (Rixy) was carried in front of her father and two gentleman helped with the other younger children. The Mitchels crossed the lake on a paddle steamer, with 700 other passengers, to the outlet of the San Juan River, where rapids meant a night in 'a most comfortless hotel'. There followed a quarter mile walk, past the rapids to another steamer for the journey to San Juan on the Atlantic coast. Mitchel was amused when, as they sailed downriver, some of the passengers 'occasionally gently titillated' alligators, with revolver shots. The 'high walls of luxuriant tropical foliage' impressed him.[12]

At Greytown, on the Atlantic coast, the Mitchels awaited the arrival of the *Prometheus*, which would take them to New York. In two rooms at the Lyon Hotel Jenny endured extortionate prices and incessant mosquito attacks; but Mitchel did find a primitive restaurant with good claret. Angry that he was in a British Protectorate Mitchel, ethnically superior and consistently anti-British, wrote of 'the Mosquito "kingdom" and its Sambo sovereign'.[13] On board a crowded *Prometheus* with the coast of Central America in view Mitchel and Smyth wished for the Americans to remove the British and his 'Mangy Majesty' from Greytown; and sell him to a sugar planter.[14] The Mitchels and Nicaragua Smyth sailed first for Cuba and then New York. At Havana, on the 22 November, Nicaragua took young John and James to the opera. The following day Mitchel, Nicaragua and an American passenger enjoyed visits to tobacco stores, a fine restaurant and conversations that compared Cuba, under Spain, to Ireland under Britain. To Mitchel's embarrassment, and probable agreement, the American suggested, with a racist nuance, that only the Irish 'amongst the white inhabitants of the earth' would 'lie down and die of hunger by myriads and millions, save only the natives of that gem of the sea'. Uncharacteristically, Mitchel made no reply and bit his tongue.[15] As the journey north continued Mitchel thought of a future in the USA and wondered, 'If I am to regard myself a "martyr" has my martyrdom done any service for my cause or the reverse … Shall I do good or evil in my generation?'[16] He had yet to embrace his second cause, yet to fatally engage his family in a war.

On 29 November 1853, on the Vanderbilt pier at New York, John Mitchel met his brother William and Thomas Francis Meager. His mother was waiting in Brooklyn where she had acquired and furnished a house 'so that on landing from the steamer we had only to hang our hats and we were home.'[17] Almost as soon as John had been exiled, William, an inventor seeking business opportunities and his widowed mother, expressed a desire to emigrate to the United States.[18] After moving to New York William found employment as a clerk in a merchant's office, at $500 per annum.[19]

As in San Francisco John was feted as New York welcomed the great 1848 hero. Jenny, Nicaragua and the children followed in a carriage and their new Union Street home filled with friends and admirers. At dusk, as they dined, they heard music. 'To my great amazement, Union Street is quickly filled up with ranked men, glittering bayonets and waving banners. Civic societies and military companies are here pell-mell. All coming to welcome me to a land of liberty …'[20] John and Jenny Mitchel were heroic celebrities. Jenny, as she had in Dublin, greeted rows of marching men. She was a political hostess again. Pleased, she wrote to Mary Thompson: 'For the first week we never got to our beds before two or three in the morning – serenades every night.'[21] Jenny's home was the centre of excited debate as exiles and New Yorkers discussed Ireland and the major issues of the day; the developing tension between the north and the south; the 1854–1856 Crimean War. High political debate featured in a house that drew water from street pumps and which, unlike Nant Cottage, was frequently burgled. Mitchel lost a new overcoat on the day he bought it. In a rage he complained to the police chief who smiled and took notes – and the robberies stopped.[22]

If petty criminals did not respect John Mitchel the rest of Brooklyn adored him. He was lavishly entertained. He thought the adulation absurd but he enjoyed it anyway. In a carriage with the Mayor of Brooklyn, he 'proceeded in a grand state ... beautiful women waved handkerchiefs from windows; some threw bouquets into the carriage ... Good God! What is all this for?'[23] There was no clear answer. He was later also honoured in New York City Hall and in the Broadway Theatre. John Mitchel renewed his strong friendship and revolutionary ardour with Thomas Meagher. Together they set up a newspaper, the *Citizen*, but Mitchel found himself increasingly at odds with northern opinion on both the Crimean War and slavery. When first hearing of the Crimean War Mitchel proclaimed. 'Czar, I bless thee. I kiss the hem of thy garment. I drink to thy health and longevity. Give us war in our time, O Lord!'[24] Although this is perhaps a recognition that Irish rebellion would have a much better chance of success if England was already involved in a conflict, and not a general exultation of war, it was in Yeats' *Under Ben Bulben* that Mitchel's war cry laid claim to being 'one of the most notorious lines in Irish poetry'.[25]

Likewise, when in 1856, he heard of the eventual peace Mitchel wrote to Miss Thompson in bitter humour. 'I am in bad spirits about Irish affairs. This peace ruins my peace of mind ... everything points to peace ... Oh the madness of sinful men to rush so blindly into the horrors of peace!'[26]

Mitchel did visit the Russian ambassador to invite him to back a Russian invasion of Ireland and, perhaps because of this, the *Newry Telegraph* picked up a story, from the *New York Herald*, that John Mitchel had gone to Russia in support of that country's war effort but then had to apologise.[27] Mitchel would not have been surprised at the mistake. He thought the New York press reproduced 'English insolence about Russia' in a 'most docile spirit'.[28] For Mitchel it was impossible for the British Government 'ever, by accident or design to be on the same side with justice'.[29] Again in a letter to Miss Thompson Mitchel gave a clear insight into his principle governing variable. Jenny also in writing to Miss Thompson revealed her feelings about wanting a war. When her husband expressed his disappointment that the next mail might bring 'news of the prospect of peace' Jenny guardedly wrote, 'I hope not. Yet I am not a blood thirsty person.'[30]

Mitchel's writing in the *Citizen* also angered his former friend, and foe, Gavan Duffy. In response to an attack by Mitchel on his character and nationionalist credentials Duffy, in turn, accused Mitchel of being hypocritical. In escaping from Van Diemen's Land, Mitchel had broken his parole and 'Nobody has ever used the censor's pen more unsparingly than your self. The writing of McGee, Reilly and Doheny had been habitually docked by you.' Duffy attacked Mitchel for opposing the emancipation of the Jews. In anger he asked, 'Good God! Could you find no worthier employment, after defeat and exile, than in reviving the jealousies of the past? Was it against me 'The Citizen' was established, not against England?'[31] Initially the *Citizen* prospered but Meagher's 'dashing pen'[32] had moved on, both physically and politically. Even

Meagher, had lost hope for Ireland. Jenny complained, 'Mr. Mitchel has never given up the old cause although many of his companions of '48 have.' Following her experience of the base value of solemn pledges in both Dublin and Newry, Jenny remained skeptical, even cynical. 'There are many very warm Irish hearts in America, and some very brave ones too, still out of the thousands who profess willingness to die for their country, we must never count more than a hundred to fulfill that promise.'[33] For Jenny, real patriots were few in number. Few had answered her husband's call from the dock.

Political ideals did not protect from disease, domestic responsibilities and chores. Jenny wrote of being the only member of the family to catch cholera and of being 'dangerously ill for one night.' The children got measles. 'Hentie was the worst … I had all the others in bed at the same time, and I can assure you one cannot make much spare time with five children to be nursed...'[34] She added that young John was about to make his own way in the world. Beyond the family John Mitchel's stance on slavery saw friends, well-wishers and readers fall away. He wrote, ' … but from the moment I ventured to hold and to express any independent opinion the press here opened on me in full cry - not only a large section of the American Press but also Catholic Irish papers. So far has this gone that I am denounced from the altars of some catholic churches.'[35] His attack on the temporal power of the Catholic Church, his assertion that the citizens of Rome should have, like all other citizens, the right to change their government 'incurred the wrath' of Archbishop Hughes: with the withdrawal of Catholic support, the circulation of the *Citizen* fell sharply from its peak of fifty thousand. [36]

Fifteen years later, reflecting on his clash with Archbishop Hughes, Mitchel admitted that it was an 'unfortunate controversy for me, and for the purposes and objects of the *Citizen*.' However, although he might 'erase from the page and from all men's memory, about three-fourths of what I then wrote' he still considered that Archbishop Hughes 'deserved harsh usage'. His regret was about damage done to himself and the *Citizen*, not the prelate.[37] There is no doubt about John Mitchel's views on slavery, and the punishment of slaves. He was consistent both in public and in private. Publicly, in the *Citizen* he proclaimed, leaving no room for doubt: 'We are no Abolitionists, no more Abolitionists than Moses, Socrates or Jesus Christ. We deny that it is a crime, or a wrong, or even a *peccadillo* to hold slaves, to buy slaves, to sell slaves, to keep slaves to their work by flogging or other needful coercion.'[38] Mitchel engaged through newspaper columns, with the Revd Henry Ward Beecher whose sister Harriet had written *Uncle Tom's Cabin*. In contrast to the tolerant style of his father, when he debated with the Revd Bagot over the 'oneness of God', John Mitchel's exchanges with Beecher were both political and personal. He referred to Beecher as 'your facetious reverence' and of being stupid.[39] Beecher referred to Mitchel's 'amateur survey of Moses and the Prophets' and to his views as trash and rubbish.[40]

Mitchel called to his defence illustrious slave owners like George Washington and Thomas Jefferson. He pointed out that Moses and the Prophets sold beings with immortal souls and that St Paul had sent the 'absconding Onesimus' back to his master.[41] When Beecher suggested that we should do onto others as we would to ourselves Mitchel pointed out that Christianity was not opposed to slavery: that 'Do onto others as ye would what others would do onto you' simply meant an obligation to treat slaves humanely but humane treatment did not exclude the whip. Mitchel wrote: 'In fact I want to set down the principle as nakedly as possible – that it is not wrong to own a slave – from this principle it follows, that it is not wrong to make a slave work; and there is no way of making him work (in the last resort) but dread of the lash.[42] For Mitchel the slave owner was a 'true patriarchate', whose responsibility for the care of his salves was much higher than that of a factory owner who 'pays his workers on a Saturday night and dismisses them to the grog shop.'[43] However, although adhering to his belief, Mitchel conceded, 'on my side in this controversy everything sounds harsh and looks repulsive.'[44]

Beecher demonstrated courage and visited the Mitchels to reply in person to the above article but Jenny was not impressed and dismissed him as 'a canting fellow more like an actor than a clergyman in the pulpit.'[45]

In private, also, Mitchel was consistent and made no secret of his support of slavery; in a letter to his good friend Father Kenyon he placed his support of slavery within his desire for an inert, agricultural society:

> Well then, I consider negro slavery to be the best state of existence for the negro, and the best for his master; and if negro slavery itself be good, then taking the negroes out of their brutal slavery in Africa, and promoting them to a human and reasonable slavery here is also good.[46]

The reference to support for a reopening of the slave trade moved Mitchel even beyond the views of most secessionists. In a letter to Mary Thompson, of Ravensdale, County Louth, the close friend and confidante of both John and Jenny, and whose opinion both valued, Mitchel wrote, '... be perfectly assured as I am that you (and the majority of the civilised 19th Century world) are altogether wrong on the whole question, and I absolutely right on it ... '

He continued, and answered the question most people in the twenty-first century probably want answered; namely, how could an Irish Republican support slavery? '… and when any of your taunting friends ask you again (as you say they do) 'What do you think of Ireland's emancipation now? Would you like an Irish Republic with an accompaniment of slave plantations?' – just answer quite simply – Yes, very much. At least I would so answer … '[47] However, such was Mitchel's respect for Mary Thompson, that Jenny revealed Mary Thompson's arguments against slavery were, 'almost enough to make a man believe he is wrong.' Jenny hated the 'black question' not because she doubted her position: 'I hate it because it has vexed you and another dear friend of mine.'[48] The friendship survived the moral arguments.

Thus, in public pronouncements and in private correspondence, with friends and with enemies, there is no doubt that John Mitchel enthusiastically supported slavery and saw no dichotomy in an Irish Republican doing so. Jenny did not have the same public platform but in letters to the trusted and admired Miss Thompson she also is identified as a strong supporter of slavery. Ironically, in the middle of this controversy, Mitchel longed for the peace of Nant Cottage and Van Diemen's Land. Within a letter to her father he wrote to Mrs Williams, '… here in New York I often almost long for Nant Cottage. You will hardly believe this. But probably you have heard into how many scrapes I have already fallen.'[49] Mrs Williams probably would have heard; Mitchel was condemned as the 'Sham-Patriot Mitchel' by the *Sydney Morning Herald*, for his views on slavery.[50] If there is no doubt John Mitchel supported slavery the question remains, why?

- Mitchel hated both England (but, he claimed, not the English) and the utilitarian nineteenth century. Referring to the 'well beloved Gaelic' language, Mitchel proclaimed, 'there is no word corresponding with 'the masses,' or with 'reproductive labour'; in short, the 19th century would not know itself, could not express itself in Irish.'[51] He hated industrialization and conversely admired rural Gaelic Ireland. He had a romantic notion of both the Irish peasant and the southern plantation system, with its attendant slavery.

- He considered that workers in mills were more in need of emancipation than the slaves. He had a very gloomy view of modernity and progress. For Mitchel (the Roman engaged in his fight with the Carthaginians), other than technological developments, human thought had developed little since Classical times. As a 'Roman' Mitchel accepted hierarchy, hierarchy that not only included patricians, like himself, plebeians like his convict servants, but also slaves.

- Unlike Tone he did not see the struggle for Irish independence as part of a wider recognition of 'The Rights of Man'. He labelled 'the great nineteenth century of centuries' with its 'enlightenment' as the 'darkest of the dark ages.'[52] Many of the 'Know-Nothings' and anti-catholics of the Northern States, who attacked Irish immigrants, and with whom Mitchel crossed words, were abolitionists. On the outbreak of war the *Nation* was to observe 'we cannot but recollect that in the South our countrymen were safe from insult and persecution, while 'Nativeism' and 'Knownothingism' assailed them in the North.'[53] It was a generalized opinion of the South and even in Knoxville the Mitchels were to encounter the enmity of Know-Nothings.

- Mitchel had a very stoical, hierarchical, settled, view of society. He wrote disparagingly about his fellow convicts and, at one stage, would have been quite happy to have the gentry lead his rebellion. The lower orders and the slaves were in their place; but in that place they had the right to be treated properly. This was also the prevailing view of the Catholic Church, in the South, as it sought an accommodation with the prevailing political opinion. For the Catholic Church slavery, 'apart from specific abuses to human dignity, was not opposed to the divine or natural law.' [54]

- Mitchel liked the South, and was liked in the South. It had a 'rural' settled and hierarchical economy. The South's cause was his cause. In entering the South he thought he was joining the settled past; a place resistant to false perceptions of progress.

Why did Jenny support slavery? O'Connor suggested she was supporting Mitchel's view out of loyalty not conviction.[55] As with John, a private letter to Miss Thompson of Ravensdale provides an insight into her thoughts. There is a suggestion that her experience in the South modified her opinion. She begins by stating, 'Be not alarmed I am not likely to become ... the mistress of a slave household.' However, she follows up with:

> ... not that I would consider it a sin to keep a slave ...
> My objection to slavery is the injury it does to the white
> masters. You will find it difficult (as I did myself at first)
> but it is no less true that the negroes are happier in their
> state of slavery than when they get their freedom.

The reference to the 'white masters' and the slaves being happier in their state of slavery suggests Jenny shared John's views of the natural patriarchal hierarchy. She expected slave owners to treat slaves with kindness and considered, like her husband, that American slaves 'are treated with more care and kindness than many servants in Ireland.' [56]

Jenny confided in Mary Thompson. Her views, expressed above, are those of a feisty woman who crossed oceans and continents; who lived at a time when slavery was not yet almost universally condemned; who had no time for the Revd Beecher; who was uneasily aware of an alternative view; who admitted to modifying her mind on the topic. The doubt, the modification over time might suggest that Jenny arrived at her belief after thought and experience. She was to pay a very high price for her opinions.

Although becoming politically uncomfortable in Brooklyn, John and Jenny Mitchel were personally and socially happy. In fact, the Mitchels were so popular that they adopted 'the practice of the city' and named one evening for acquaintances to visit, leaving the rest of the week, especially Sunday, for a 'few private friends'; including John Blake Dillon, one of the three founders of the *Nation,* and his wife Adelaide. Following the failure of 1848, Dillon had escaped directly to the United States. With the end of the 'gay season … anyone who could afford it leaves the city for three or four months in the hot season.' [57] In the spring of 1854, following Jenny's bout with cholera, the Mitchels, in common with middle class New York, moved to the shore for the summer, to escape the oppressive heat of the city. Jenny was well again and, as in Carlingford, she enjoyed sea bathing. The children were also flourishing. The boys attended the best school in New York. The Mitchel aunts, in the USA with their mother, schooled the two eldest girls. There was the joy of Rixy, 'one of the sweetest and prettiest little girls I ever saw – 19 months old yet and a little unchristened pagan.'[58]

The Mitchels had a 'home-circle' made up of family and both Irish and American friends. John Mitchel confided to Miss Thompson that this was Eden after his years of bondage.[59] However, in that first year in the USA one of the Mitchels' good friends died before they could 'see once more the face of Thomas Devin Reilly.' His 'restless, fiery life was extingished…at thirty years of age.'[60] Mitchel praised Devin Reilly out of both brotherly affection and loyalty. Devin Reilly was one of the small number of Young

Irelanders who actively supported Mitchel at the time of the split with the Confederation Council. Jenny wrote affectionately about her young protector from those worrying times in Dublin. 'On Sunday last died at Washington one of the truest and best fellows I ever knew, our dear friend Thomas Devin Reilly. It was an illness of only a few hours and he left a widow and one child …' Jenny then provided a rare but telling insight into her relationship with her father: 'No death since my father's has affected me so much.'[61]

Jenny remembered Reilly's loyalty in moving with Mitchel to set up the *United Irishman*. His name was prominent, his pen present, in that first edition. As was John Martin's who, along with Smith O'Brien and Kevin O'Doherty, was released from Van Diemen's Land in 1854. All three were released on condition that they would not return to Ireland or Britain. Two years later in 1856 this condition was removed but Martin chose to live in self-imposed exile in Paris. There, perplexed and disappointed in his oldest and best friend, he wrote of the 'abominal quarrel' that had developed between John Mitchel and Charles Gavan Duffy.

He thought it probably had its origins in editorial disputes in the offices of the *Nation,* where Duffy being less militant than Mitchel had 'excised from a report in the Nation' one of Mitchel's more seditious speechs to the Confederation.

In his diary, John Martin reflected sadly on the dispute and on Mitchel's failings:

> Then there was also the distressing subject of his escape from V.D Land which was condemned as inconsistent with honour by some honest and friendly persons...I lost the confident hopes that I had rested upon him. I saw that his power for uniting and organising the Irish

patriots was gone, and the haughty violence he was displaying and the wrongheadedness I attributed to some of his acts made me dispair of his ever regaining his power. [62]

Terence Bellew McManus was also in despair about the feud between John Mitchel and Gavan Duffy. However, unlike Martin, he strongly supported Mitchel. On 3 June 1854 he wrote to Duffy, from San Francisco..

> It is I assure you, a source of deep and bitter regret to me to observe the suicidal – nay criminal – personal war that is still waged among my countrymen...You assert... John Mitchel commmitted 'a disgraceful breach of parole' in leaving Van Diemen's Land. How so?...I declare most solemnly that nothing can be further from the fact that he violated any obligation of honour in the course presumed by him to relieve himself from British thraldom.[63]

However, despite the backing of McManus, John Mitchel was aware of his diminishing status. He remained restless and wrote to Miss Thompson, of Ravensdale:

> Yet we often pine for the country. Beyond the Alleghanies are beautiful shady vallies, and cheap land. And if war turns out an imposter, and no brightening soon appears in the prospect of Irish Revolution – do not be astonished if you hear of our flying suddenly from the Altantic coast, and burying ourselves in the umbrageous West.[64]

Mitchel was turning his back on progress, on the nineteenth century and its technologies. His eyesight was already failing 'for the hard work of a newspaper.'[65] If he had been a richer man he may have taken his whole household to France but, for now, the South would do.[66]

Mitchel and most of his anti-modern views had been warmly received in the South where, in June 1854, he was invited to deliver the graduation speech at the University of Virginia in an atmosphere 'perfumed by a hundred bouquets and cooled by the fluttering of five hundred fans.'[67] He contrasted this with dark, sombre Trinity College, Dublin.

His main point on being asked to speak on 'Progress in the Nineteenth Century' was that there was no progress. Of course, Mitchel had thoughtful reason behind his audience-grabbing statement. Technological progress like 'gas, steam, printing press, upholstering and magnetic telegraphs could not be denied.' Individuals (perhaps like the Irish convicts who worked for him in Van Diemen's Land) could 'advance by high culture, by self denial and heroic energy and faith, to the loftiest heights of human intellect and virtue.' Empires will rise and fall, but 'man, the family or genus, never stirs a step, either backward or forward.' For Mitchel, history was cyclical; nations may rise, nations may wither but 'there is no progress making men wiser, happier, or better than they were thirty centuries ago...'[68] Mitchel, the student from Dr Hendeson's Classical School, perceived himself as Roman.

He thought his university audience unconvinced but the experience in Virginia pleased him. It was a memory he would hang up in the chambers of his memory 'framed with gold and wreathed with flowers.'[69] In the South he might feel more at home, especially in a rural location. Mitchel had made up his 'mind to quit the feverish atmosphere of New York and breathe the air of the mountain woods.'[70]

Before leaving the family enjoyed 'fragrant summer weather' with their friends, the Dillons, by the seaside, in a rented house in Stonington, Connecticut. Mitchel described Stonington as 'a place of intensely puritanical aspect, and anything more dreary than a Sunday in Stonington (Sabbath they call it) cannot be conceived.'[71] However, the seaside resort won praise from Mitchel for having repulsed a British battleship attack in 1814. Even Mitchel's casual travel writing drew from a deep ink well of anti-British sentiment. Considering New York too much an Anglo-Saxon city Mitchel tolerated one more 'polar winter' there.

In writing to Mary Thompson Jenny advised her of their proposed move to the wilderness.. After reading yet another critical comment in her morning paper Jenny complained to Mary, 'They are at war with him in Cinncinnatti, Ohio.' She wrote that because of such hostility, and John's failing eyesight, 'we are about to leave the city and make our home in the bush.'[72] John Mitchel passed the *Citizen* on to John McClenahan and made ready to leave.[73]

CHAPTER SEVEN
The Hoosiers Of Tennessee

In the spring of 1855 the Mitchels took leave of their friends. They boarded the steamship *Nashville* and sailed, for 47 hours, to Charleston, en route for Knoxville, Tennessee. Jenny described Charleston as a 'fine old city...the only one I have seen in this country that has the look of age about it.'[1] This time John Mitchel junior did not travel with the family. He stayed with his Uncle William in Brooklyn and was to become a civil engineer. Entering Charleston Harbour they passed Fort Sumter where the Civil War was to begin and the absent John Mitchel junior's life was to end. After Charleston they took the train, and then a very uncomfortable wagon, for the last twenty miles, to the the Lamar House in Knoxville. With characteristic understatement Jenny described the journey. 'From New York travellers generally come in four days to Knoxville, but on account of the baby and the young ones we came at a much slower rate.' Perhaps the piano, linen and other belongings also contributed to the slower progress.[2] On the last day of the journey Minnie and the baby took sick and 'were quite ill for a week after.'

Although he was welcomed by its mayor William Swan, who was to become a friend and partner in setting up the *Southern Citizen*, in which they would suggest the reopening of the African slave trade, Mitchel disliked Knoxville. One reason for disliking Knoxville was that, to Mitchel's unpleasant surprise, Know-Nothings were well represented in the town. However, he did express his satisfaction that 'several ladies have called upon my wife,'[3] and the Mitchels were befriended by some Swiss families. The girls had piano and French lessons but Jenny wished for 'three or four families of our acquaintance to come and settle out here.'[4]

John Mitchel who, in a letter to his sister Matilda, long before he had set foot in America, had once confidently advised his brother William that farming in the United States was, 'a glorious way of life within reach of the cities, yet on the borders of the wilderness with lots of bees and bears and wild turkeys in the woods,'[5] was about to try it himself. With his nostalgia for rural Van Diemen's Land, he was determined to once again take up farming and in May 1855 he moved the family another 32 miles deeper into the wilderness, to Tucaleechee Cove, one of the most beautiful and barbarous spots in the United States. Here the Mitchels had the highest farm in the valley, consisting of 132 acres, with 80 cleared and 'a multitude of pigs'. As well as returning to farming Mitchel was also turning his back on progress for which 'I have contracted a diseased and monomaniacal hatred.'[6]

Back in Ireland, in Newry, where the local papers kept watch on his movements, the *Newry Commercial Telegraph* expressed its pleasure that letters home told of 'Mr. Mitchel's settlement in the territory of Tennessee where he proposes to follow the peaceful and honorable occupation of a farmer.' It further commented, 'The friends and family, as well as his own personal well wishers, in the North of Ireland will be gratified by this announcement.'[7] Alas, Jenny did not share her husband's, or *the Newry Commercial Telegraph's*, enthusiasm for their latest move and John was aware of it. In a letter to Mrs Williams in Van Diemen's Land he wrote that his wife was 'malcontent, because the house is so wretched and we are otherwise so ill accommodated with the appliances of civilized life'.[8] The house was a two room log cabin with a loft. Although Jenny again had a fine chestnut horse, unlike in Van Diemen's Land, she rarely used it. Lonely, Jenny read and reread letters.[9] Henrietta had the good sense to stay in Knoxville with a Swiss family; as did the piano they had taken from New York.[10]

However in the letter to Mrs Williams Mitchel's own growing dissatisfaction with life in the log cabin also emerged. He decried a lack of suitable neighbours, of refined company. The local people, the 'Hoosiers', were 'excessively ignorant and cunning but civil and otherwise not intolerable.' Cunning and civility he found pleasing because he was sick of 'servile rascals and gentlemanly insolence' but the family was 'tenfold more isolated and lonely than we ever were in Van Diemen's Land.' John and Jenny longed for educated friends and 'Ratho near us.' In this letter to Mrs Williams, in the middle of family news, Mitchel broadened his critical focus from the Hoosiers to all Americans. He thought it strange that 'America's undeniably admirable institutions don't turn out pleasant people …If you prefer it the other way, then it is just as strange that people so unpleasant should have turned out such capital institutions'. Mitchel painted his judgments with a broad brush.[11] Although the 'Hoosiers' approved of Mitchel's 'conservative principles in the matter of slavery' they could not persuade him to take his 'esteemed lady' to partake of their hotel and hospitality at Montvale Springs in support of the southern cause.[12]

In December 1855, despite the rivers being dangerous and the tracks through the woods being blocked with snow, a lecture tour allowed Mitchel to seek more cultivated company, and extra income; a diversion not available to Jenny. He did not like lecturing and hoped he had left it behind but it was now preferable to and more profitable than farming.

Mitchel was delighted the 'Hoosiers' liked James. They liked James because he was a good shot and owned a fine rifle. James's manly ways meant Mitchel could go, less worried, on his lecture tour, leaving his second son to look after the women.[13] Jenny shared John's confidence in James. She wrote, 'James is now our great dependence in the bush, and fortunately for us has a taste for such a life.'[14] The technology, the progress, Mitchel hated meant his wilderness was only a few days from New York, and he needed to earn money.

By September 1856, the Mitchels were sufficiently concerned about the '…education and social advantages for the children …'[15] to move back to Knoxville. Having tried and disliked isolation, no surprise given gregarious memories of Loughorne, Ontario Terrace and Bothwell, Mitchel was also ready for a renewed social and political life. He bought three and a half acres of land in Knoxville on which he 'supervised the construction of a fine house, called "No Where Else", in a place of oaks, walnuts and cedars, on the bank of a little stream fifteen minutes walk of the centre of the town.' Typically, whilst Mitchel thought his new house and location 'pretty enough' he also thought it inferior to the place they had just left in the mountains. Aware of his inner restlessness he wrote, 'When I have built my house, I feel I shan't live in it long. Jenny might as well have married a Bedouin Arab.'[16] Jenny, who 'was sick and tired of this changing' and who had vowed to make no new friends because it was too hard leaving them[17] shared both her husband's admiration for the house and the irony of its name. 'The situation is very pleasant indeed and I believe I would be happy here as anywhere else in the country …but I can never feel sure of staying long anywhere.'[18] Despite her theoretical support for the institution of slavery Jenny would not have slaves in her house. Refusing to have slaves did not protect her from domestic friction but her reaction to it mirrored her husband's hierarchical view of society. 'I have had plenty of trouble with servants ...white servants consider themselves as good as you and I'.[19] However, she thought, like John, that those of inferior status should be well treated and a paternal hierarchical order was good for all. She expressed her admiration for 'the way her neighbour's slaves were looked after in old age'.[20]

In writing to Mrs Williams, in Van Diemen's Land, about his family, Mitchel thought 'Jenny was little changed since you knew her - but she is now exceeded in stature by three of her children.' and whilst playing the piano 'pretty well' Henrietta did not sing. Minnie was rather small.[21] Mitchel's letters to Mrs Williams, and other friends, were confessional, personal and then political. In a letter to Miss Thompson, in May 1857, he thought, only thought, of returning to the Law. In the same letter he confessed to being an unworthy pagan and provided an insight into his views on religion. Despite attending Presbyterian services, he wrote of his contempt for organized Christianity. 'There is no sect of Christians whom I might not be tempted to persecute, if I were in power, for their cup of balderdash is nearly full: except, however, for the present, the Catholic Church.'[22] In writing, Mitchel enjoyed the 'atrocious impiety' of his sentiments, but his conditional liking for the Catholic Church was to be a constant during his life and would be especially relevant when his daughters converted.

After her time in the wilderness the Southern Commercial Convention, in August 1857, lifted Jenny back into her role as political hostess, and as the patriot's wife. It meant a full house at 'Nowhere Else'. Rebecca O'Connor imagined Jenny working hard in oppressive summer heat and impressing visitors with her recipes,[23] as she had once impressed Thomas Carlyle. The convention wanted to establish direct links with overseas markets, cutting out the need to ship cotton through New York. In the fall, following the conference Mr Swan, who had welcomed the Mitchels to Knoxville, suggested that John Mitchel partner him in a new weekly paper, the *Southern Citizen*. It would be an organ of extreme southern sentiment and it would 'advocate earnestly the re-opening of the African slave trade.'[24] Mitchel's lobbying for the re-opening the African slave trade made him appear more extreme than most plantation owners.

Even some strong Southerners, like Edmund Ruffin, thought Mitchel's new paper, and his extreme views, more likely to harm their cause. After meeting John Mitchel, Ruffin wrote in his diary, 'Mitchel …goes fully for the rights of the South. I fear however that his having so boldly advocated the re-opening of the African slave-trade will prevent his paper being supported by the many southern men who still view that proposed policy as most objectionable & condemnable.'[25] Such was Edmund Ruffin's attachment to the Confederacy that when it was defeated he made his final diary entry on 17 June 1865, and shot himself.[26] Given this, his opinion of John Mitchel and his writing say much about the extremity of Mitchel's support of slavery. However, Mitchel's personal and family sacrifices were also to be extreme.

As his support for the South and slavery deepened, Mitchel again wrote to Mrs Williams, in Van Diemen's Land, telling her about establishing the *Southern Citizen*, and of that paper's support for 'a revival of the slave trade from Africa'. He would not apologize for his views but, recognizing their extremity, he did ask that she would not turn against him, 'but count me always your attached friend.' He also informed her that John Martin had remonstrated with him about his views on slavery but Martin 'might as well whistle jigs to a millstone.' Yet, he wished to see his old friend's 'long nose poking in at our door.'[27] Again a private letter to a woman he liked and whose opinion he respected casts a harsh, undeniably clear light on Mitchel's extreme views. James also exchanged the plough for a desk and became the *Southern Citizen*'s business manager.[28] A favourite theme for Mitchel in the *Southern Citizen* was comparing Britain's relationship with Ireland to that of the North's relationship with the South. It was a matter of a heartless, hypocritical, industrial power imposing its will on a charming, agrarian and, in the case of the South, gentlemanly culture. Mitchel stretched his imagination, further skewed his stereotype, to see the Southerner as a Celt:

> The Celtic is the far superior breed; of finer origin, more fiery brain, more passionate heart – less greedy, grabbing, gripping and groveling …In race being Celtic, in pursuits agricultural; in temperament pleasure loving, hospitable and indolent; in position defensive against the commercial spirit of the age – the South is a new Ireland; her rival another England. Can you wonder I am a Southerner?[29]

In reflecting on the developing North-South conflict Mitchel wrote, to John Martin, 'You see that I am narrating, in part, the history of Ireland.'[30] Such reasoning helps explain why John Mitchel was prepared to make great sacrifices, and was prepared to allow his family to risk terminal sacrifices, for a secondary cause. In Mitchel's thinking it was a proxy cause. In Knoxville Mitchel was attacked by the 'Know-Nothings' as the 'Irish Poltroon'. The Knoxville *Register* so annoyed Mitchel that, when he met its editor, John Fleming, on the street, he broke his cane on him. The incident was reported in the *New York Times* and both Fleming and Mitchel replied with letters in that paper. Mitchel accused Fleming of 'falsehoods' and offered him 'satisfaction if he has the spirit to seek it'. A letter from Mitchel's friend J.A. Mabry following an approach by him to Fleming, noted the tame end of the affair.[31]

Whilst deeply engrossed in American affairs a visitor to Knoxville reminded both John and Jenny of Ireland and her militant politics. In early winter 1858, in a drizzle, James Stephens, who had been Smith O'Brien's *aide-de-camp* at Ballingary and was wounded, reported dead, arrived at 'Nowhere Else'.[32] He wanted to enlist John Mitchel's support for the emergent Fenians. It was to be a cell based, secret organisation. In his diary, dated 21 October, James Stephens reflected on the meeting. He described Mitchel rising from his chair at the parlour fireside, 'pipe in fumes', to meet him. Stephens thought Mitchel failed. 'It was painful to look at him worn, pale, emaciated with a frown occasioned by his constant tension of his faculties and some defect of his sight …'[34] Stephens thought Jenny, in her mid-thirties, looked 'uncommonly well still and must have been very handsome.' [33] Both Stephens and his ideas for a rebellion were initially welcomed and Mitchel promised to write letters of introduction for him. Stephens also talked to Jenny of home and Ireland. Ironically, given that Stephens himself was to fall because of his unwillingness to 'unsheathe the sword', Jenny complained to him about the lack of physical support for her husband in 1848.[35]

In his diary, Stephens claimed he also discussed John's support of slavery with Jenny. He wrote, 'She herself could very gladly place herself at the head of a plantation, but though even if she had the means, she could not as you must be born to it, like pastry.' These diary fragments, from someone Mitchel grew to dislike, reflect Jenny's opinions on both verbose rebels and slavery, as expressed in the earlier letter to Mary Thompson. She did not condemn slavery, but keeping slaves was not for her. Stephens was impressed by the family in exile, by their cordial hospitality, by their fondness for each other. He noted that all the children were good looking 'as might be expected from such parents,' but he had special praise for Henrietta. 'The oldest daughter is as interesting, comely, gentle and intelligent a girl as I have ever met.' [36] As Mitchel learned more about both the Fenians, and especially their leader, the relationship between himself and Stephens was to sour.

Predictably, despite having called their Knoxville House 'Nowhere Else' the Mitchels were soon on the move again. In December 1858 they moved to Capitol Hill, Washington in the hope of gaining a wider circulation for the *Southern Citizen*. A *Washington Union* editorial welcomed Mitchel's talent but not his extreme views. It wished failure for his cause but success to the paper. 'Mr. Mitchel's is one of those peculiar minds, which brilliant and full of momentum, are ever inclined to fly at a tangent ... Though we cannot subscribe to the extreme views of the *Citizen*, or hope for their accomplishment, we at least wish well to the business enterprise ...'[37] In a letter to Mrs Williams, Mitchel recorded the family's joy at the visit of the pardoned Smith O'Brien to their Washington home, and how statesmen of all parties feted Smith O'Brien. Mitchel was pleased Smith O'Brien accepted an invitation to visit the South. 'That dreadful land of chains and cowhide whips - as it is generally imagined.' In the same letter he recorded that his own popularity was factional.

'A great many people regard me as an incendiary and madman; they don't wonder that the English Government found it necessary to get rid of me ... Many others, on the contrary, are my faithful disciples and zealous friends.'[38] These included the old Young Irelander, Dr Antisel, who, as a Union officer, was to be a very helpful friend after the war. Years later, Mitchel was to praise Dr Antisel 'as a genuine man of science' even 'if he does read Darwin'. This comment is hardly surprising from a man who rejected the Enlightenment. In evolution the human species progresses over time. For Mitchel there was no progress.[39] With Smith O'Brien, Mitchel met President Buchanan, but generally the Mitchels' social activity mirrored their political allegiance. They attended a grand party given by the wife of Senator Clay but otherwise, having few acquaintances, participated little in the 'wild and rabid gaiety of the session.'[40]

James continued to run the *Southern Citizen* and John junior, without a job, considered joining General Henningsen's expedition to Arizona. The other younger children were well and had many acquaintances that created a 'rush and a whirl all around us.'[41]

At this time Mitchel's attention returned to Ireland, to his premier cause. In a letter to his friend Father Kenyon he wrote that his interest in America was a mere shadow compared to his interest in Ireland.[42] France had declared war on Austria and Mitchel thought Britain might be drawn in. Perhaps, as in the late 1790s, if Britain was at war with France, an Irish rebellion might be feasible. Like Wolfe Tone, an exiled John Mitchel was going to France, to seek that country's aid as, hopefully, it warred with England. Although 'a heavy loser by our newspaper undertaking'[43] Swan supported John Mitchel going to Paris and they wound up the *Southern Citizen*. Mitchel wrote to his mother that he hoped to leave sufficient money from the sale of the *Southern Citizen* for his family to survive without him for a year or so. He also suggested that, 'all the boys must instantly get into the way of earning their livelihood.'[44] Whist away his two youngest daughters would stay in New York with his mother. In August John Mitchel sailed for France on board the *St Nicholas*. He was seeking a war.

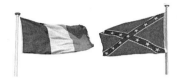

CHAPTER EIGHT

Tranquility in Paris

In August 1859 Mitchel arrived in Le Havre. He loved being where other Irish patriots had been before him. He especially associated his trip with that of Wolfe Tone, but in terms of persuading the French to arms in Ireland Mitchel was to be a failure compared to Tone. In Paris, Mitchel was able to meet old friends including his sisters, his brother William (who had travelled to Paris to promote a patent for his type setting machine) and especially John Martin, whom he had not seen since their parting in Van Diemen's Land. The two Mitchel men and Martin enjoyed talking, walking and smoking in France but once his friends left the winter was damp, dark and dreary. Mitchel was lonely, socially isolated and 'not in brilliant spirits.'[1] He wrote to Mrs Dillon, recently returned to Dublin from the USA. As with his other trusted female correspondents he is honest. '… the only formal written invitation I have received since I came to Paris was an invitation to an old lady's funeral, and that in the gloomiest weather. Is it not ghastly? If I were a woman, I would sit down and take a good cry …'[2] Whatever his emotional state if nothing happened on the political front he would re-cross the Atlantic, back to his family.

However a highlight of this time in Paris was when 1848 met 1798: John Mitchel met the eighty-year-old Colonel Miles Byrne.

Colonel Byrne was a veteran both from Ireland in 1798 and the French Army. He held the Legion of Honour. A warm friendship and mutual respect developed between the two patriots.[3]

At this time another old friend P.J. Smyth, Nicaragua, in a letter to John Martin, lamented the 'false impression' held by many of Mitchel's character and hoped that he would 'soon recover his position in the country.'[4] Mitchel's friends continued to be troubled by his extreme views and their impact on his status as a political leader.

In October 1859 Mitchel, in the Dublin *Irishman*, again tried to lay to rest the charge, resurrected in the *Nation*, that he had acted dishonourably in resigning his 'ticket-of-leave.' Mitchel pointed out that the only printed account of his escape was his own and that P.J. Smyth corroborated it. He accused Gavan Duffy, and the *Nation* of printing an anonymous accusation. 'His columns are open to the man without the name, for my injury; but not open to me for my defence.'[5] This disputed truth was yet another example of hatred between the two men.

With no immediate hope of a war between Britain and France Mitchel sailed back to the USA where, on 8 May 1860, he finally became a citizen[6] albeit a restless one. He returned to Paris, but this time with Jenny, the three girls and Willie. John and James remained in the USA, John as an engineer in Alabama and James as an insurance agent in Richmond.

Jenny was keen on the idea of going to Paris. She thought it would be a good place for the education of her daughters. The youngest, Rixy, Isabel, was certainly impressed with France. When the gendarmes boarded their ship in their bright uniforms she ran to the parents' cabin to 'announce that the Emperor was come to meet us.'[7] In Paris Mitchel worked constantly as a correspondent.

In October 1860 he wrote to his sister Mary that he had given up any idea of being a lawyer in America. He wrote to the Dillons that he had not given up hope of a war between France and Britain. He hankered to be like Tone, 'and the best thing I can think of now is to help stimulate the quarrel between France and England, with a view to having the chance of joining, before I die, in an invasion of Ireland.' For an exile, Paris was a 'hateful place'. He longed for Dublin, 'my real place of abode.'[8]

For the family the sightseeing novelty of Paris waned but they were comfortable and relatively well off. They settled into a pleasant, but cramped, life in accommodation on the Rue de L'Est, close to the trees of the 'Park of the Luxemburg'. The whole 'flat was not much bigger than our room in Tullycavine' (near Dromore, County Down). Once again, the piano had travelled with them; Willie was sent to a day school and the girls had a governess. Jenny regretted that she did not have better French with which to scold the servants.[9] Problems with servants were a constant for Jenny.

Mitchel wrote to his sister Matilda that life was quiet and they had 'good acquaintances'. In the same letter he revealed that the girls now went to the Catholic Sacre Coeur convent school and that Henrietta 'has been for two years a devout Catholic.'[10] When the family voiced concerns he scolded his mother. 'But it is not very kind of you to intimate that respect for my father's memory is anyway concerned for the matter. He vindicated the right of private judgment above all things. If one's private judgment leads him into the Catholic Church it is private judgment still.'[11] Mitchel wrote he had no religion of his own to 'inculcate'[12] but he did comment that there was 'a kind of hankering in all our family after the errors of Romanism'.[13]

Relations with Ireland were well established and the letter writing Mary Thompson, John O'Hagan and John Mitchel's two

best friends, John Martin and Father Kenyon, were all visitors to
Paris. It was a two-way process. Henty and Minnie were able to visit
their Aunt Matilda, Mrs Dickson, in 'Laurel Hill', Newry. In a letter,
Mitchel thought the invitation to his daughters kind, in the light
of past differences over his political stance.[14] Life improved again
when, in May 1861, they left 'the dungeon dark' Rue de L'Est and
moved to Choissy-le-Roi on the Seine. The cottage here had more
room and light, and was only fifteen minutes from Paris by rail and
half an hour from the Palais Royal.[15] Modern technology had its
advantages.

Jenny was at home in Choissy and, being semi-rural, young Willie
was able both to collect beetles and attend 'lectures by professors of
natural history at the museum of the Garden of Plants.'[16] The boy,
who may have to have been restrained by Nicaragua Smyth from
acknowledging his disguised father on the *Emma*, was growing up.

Mitchel went into Paris on a regular basis to read the papers,
'and follow with eagerness the progress of events in the United
States.'[17] One event, the outbreak of the American Civil War, was to
impact deeply and tragically on the Mitchel family. It was to bring
their last time of domestic tranquility to an end. John junior, who
had been working as a railway engineer, was already in action. He
was a volunteer Lieutenant with the Confederates, First Regiment,
South Carolina Artillery, when they shelled Fort Sumter, the action
that sparked the war.[18] James, the outdoors boy respected by the
Hoosiers in Tennessee helped recruit members for the 1st Virginian
Regiment; specifically the Montgomery Guards Company. The
Richmond Dispatch commented:

Attention, Friends of Liberty – We draw particular
attention to the advertisement under this heading

proposing the formation in this city of a new volunteer company, to be known as the First Regiment of Virginia, Virginia Volunteers. We understand that Mr. James Mitchel, a citizen of Richmond and a son of that distinguished son of the South, John Mitchel, the Irish patriot, is interesting himself in the formation of this company. This is not only a guarantee that the company will be speedily raised, but that they will be put on an effective footing. An invocation to the 'Friends of Liberty' from a son of John Mitchel cannot go unheeded.[19]

James joined the Virginia Volunteers as a private but was elected second lieutenant and then commissioned as a captain. The Montgomery Guards were an Irish Company who before the war organised a St Patrick's Day ball, paraded through the streets of Richmond under the harp, and wore green uniforms.[20]

However, before the reality of the Civil War had to be faced the Mitchels had another very welcome visitor to Choissy-le-Roi. In July Smith O'Brien, whose wife, Lucy, had died a month earlier, was in France to visit Marshal McMahon. He spent a day with the Mitchel family. In his Journal Mitchel recalled a delicious summer evening spent talking in the cottage garden, before being summoned to tea by Jenny. 'All in my little house idolised him.' With an ominous feeling that they would not meet again John Mitchel, and his youngest son Willie, left Smith O'Brien at the railway station where they parted with an affectionate benediction for and from 'the best and noblest of our generation.'[21] Despite differences on Ireland, slavery and the Confederacy, O'Brien returned the affection and admiration. After his 1859 visit to the Mitchels in Washington he had written to his wife admiring Jenny but also commenting upon Mitchel's darker side. 'She really is a charming person and though neither you nor I agree with the political views of Mr. Mitchel there are few persons more loved by his private friends and family than this formidable monster.'[22] Despite the extremity of his views, and a cane broken over an opponent, at a personal level most found John Mitchel charming.

In a January 1861 letter to his sister, Henrietta, Mitchel had confessed, 'John Martin is savage with me for my intolerant and reckless habit of denouncing everybody who does not agree with myself. I cannot help it.'[23] Obviously, John Martin and Smith O'Brien did not fall into this category. Despite overt political differences, the 'formidable monster', Jenny and their children loved both Martin and Smith O'Brien. Despite no news from, and concern for their two eldest boys, the summer of 1861 continued to be warm and pleasant on the banks of the limpid and beautiful Seine.[24] The Mitchels assumed John safe in the garrison of Fort Sumter but worried about James in the field.

It was a quiet time visiting friends and neighbours. The summer crept slowly into autumn. Henrietta, now a devout catholic, and 'extremely intimate with the ladies of Sacre Coeur', was preparing to go one step further and to enter their 'splendid convent'. Mitchel, who loved hierarchy and distrusted progress, was relaxed about his daughter's intention and 'offered not the least opposition'.[25] Perhaps this is not surprising, since he claimed to have 'never taught my children any religion, nor even spoken to them on the subject'.[26] Mitchel had no time for the pursuit of happiness. He thought we were here 'for the purpose of doing and suffering what it is our duty to do and suffer'.[27] It was a stoic creed he lived. However, it is similar to the Catholic theology of suffering; this is a 'vale of tears' and we accept our suffering as a cross. Although the unbelieving John Mitchel did not expect a reward in the next life - redemptive suffering was not for him – it may help explain, along with a reluctance to change and an acceptance of hierarchy, his affinity with Henrietta's chosen religion. Jenny also was at ease with Henrietta's conversion. Her tolerance was probably associated with a dislike of all organized religions, although she too had a soft spot for Catholicism and Isabel went to school in the same convent. Minnie took lessons in Choissy-le-Roi with 'M. Bayer, our worthy old neighbour.'[28] In both the spring and summer of 1862 John Mitchel went on walking tours; first in March through Normandy with his brother William and then, in July, in the south of France and Switzerland with both William and John Martin. They were most pleasant experiences. 'Travelling generally on foot and stopping at villages, we saw a great deal of the country people and liked the French extremely. We saw less of the Swiss, and candidly, liked them less than the French. At Lausanne however we got some very good wine.'[29] On this walk he saw 'pinching poverty' in Lyon but thought it did not compare with Dublin where he remembered 'alarming and heart rendering suffering ... with poor families lying down to die of hunger in the streets of the "liberty" and suburbs.' For Mitchel, 'France is one nation (since the revolution).' Ireland was two nations where the landlords preyed upon their tenants.[30] The landlord system in Ireland, with its intimate links to Britain, was one hierarchy Mitchel did not like. Back in Choissy-le-Roi, John Mitchel's desire to be with the Confederate Army meant that the family's last period of relative happiness was coming to an end. In 1864, reflecting on this earlier decision to go to the Confederacy, he returned to his adulation of war.

> The suspense began to be painful; for the host of confederates held some who were dear to me ... I felt the fullest confidence, why I know not, that Richmond would not be abandoned without a bloody battle; and I envied those who were on the spot – envied them for being alive with so passionate an excitement ... [31]

Even allowing for the 1864 need of the *Southern Illustrated News* to maintain the morale of the suffering Confederacy Mitchel was consistent in his view of war as exhilarating; especially since by then he had raw battlefield experience. In Paris, by August 1862, the war was disrupting communication with America and the Mitchels' income was falling. 'I receive a little money from these sources.' In addition, Mitchel felt 'finely cheated by the *Irishman* ... '[32] He claimed he was owed £60 and was advised not to have anything more to do with the *Irishman*.[33] Mitchel, who wanted to engage Presbyterians in his struggle with England, also disliked the 'religious aspect which the "Irishman" gives itself' and he did not 'relish the idea of helping to keep up a miserable rag like the "Irishman" in its present hands.'[34] With a declining income, Mitchel determined to join his sons in the fight for the Confederacy. His old, Young Ireland comrade; his fellow exile in Van Diemen's Land; his good friend in America, the Union Army's Thomas Meagher, honoured John Mitchel's Confederate sons. When recruiting for the Union Army's Irish Brigade, Meagher, who was to command that brigade, called 'for three cheers for the two sons of John Mitchel, who are fighting bravely on the other side.'[35] Given Meagher's friendship with the Mitchels, and his personality, this was not surprising. The eloquent Meagher sought to look at history, 'with the generous pride of the nationalist, not with the cramped prejudice of the partisan.' In a speech in Conciliation Hall in February 1846 he had proclaimed, 'We do homage to Irish valour, whether it conquers on the walls of Derry, or capitulates with honour before the ramparts of Limerick.' [36]

The visit of Father Kenyon in August 1862 heralded the break up of the family. Henrietta and Rixy, Isabel, would stay with the nuns in Sacre Coeur. Jenny, Minnie and Willie would return to Ireland. John Mitchel would run the Union blockade and enter the Confederacy. Willie, now eighteen, strongly objected and persuaded his father that he too should join the fight for the Confederacy. Reluctantly his parents agreed. It was a decision John and Jenny were to bitterly regret. Of this time Mitchel wrote, 'So there is another break up of our household. When shall we be at rest? Two trembling and saying their prayers in Ireland; two passing anxious hours in the Paris convent; two in camp and garrison beyond the Atlantic; and two making ready to penetrate the Yankee blockade in disguise, and by way of New York.' [37] He visited in their convent, 'the poor little girls everyday before leaving Paris.' [38] The Mother Superior tried to ease his worries but he would not see Henrietta again. In September 1862 John Mitchel and his youngest son Willie, under assumed names, sailed for America. [39]

CHAPTER NINE
The Deaths of Two Children

On 23 September 1862, having risked being arrested in a non-intended stop at Southampton, where they stayed in a small hotel, the disguised John Mitchel and his son, Willie, arrived back in New York. After moving between Baltimore and Washington they ended up in southern Maryland, staying with sympathetic planters and waiting for an opportunity to cross the Potomac River; it was patrolled by Union gunboats. The first attempt was betrayed but the Mitchels, and eleven other would-be Confederates, suspected the treachery and took to the woods rather than get into the boat. In the event the boat was boarded and the house where they had been staying was raided. Mitchel suspected the informer was a Dubliner from their party who had recognized and spoken to him. On the following night, a calm dark night, in an overcrowded fishing boat the party set off from the Union shore. Two thirds of the way across they ran under the bows of a revenue cutter, which alerted a gunboat, but they managed to make it to Mathias Point on the Virginian shore.[1] In Richmond they stayed with retired Major Dooley, whose two sons were still serving. Dooley had retired from the Confederate Army in 1862 and now commanded the Richmond Ambulance Corps. For Kelly O'Grady, 'The Dooleys were an Irish-American success story. Their stature in Richmond ... served as an inspiring example of the transformation of modest Irish immigrants to American respectability in the nineteenth-century South.[2] Such social and economic possibilities for the Irish was one reason John Mitchel preferred the South to the North.

Major Dooley was one of the founding members of the Montogomery Guard, called after 'Irish-born Continental Army General Richard Montgomery, who fell while leading a charge at the Battle of Quebec.'[3] The Montgomery Guards became the C Company in the 1st Virginian.[4] Willie followed his brother, James, into that company and regiment, as a private. John Mitchel, whose health would not allow him into the army, joined Major Dooley's Ambulance Corps. More significantly, he placed his pen at the disposal of the Confederate President Davis, a friend from Washington days. Mitchel became the editor of the pro-government *Enquirer*. The other major paper, the *Examiner*, was more critical of President Davis and his government.

Despite his pre-war reputation, as a great supporter of the southern cause, Mitchel's appointment was not universally acclaimed. The anti-Irish John Beauchamp Jones, a Confederate government official, wrote, contrary to the statistical evidence of forty thousand Irish having served in the Confederate Army[5]: 'There is no Irish element in the Confederate States. I am sorry this Irish editor has been imported.'[6] However, such views were not typical and, despite Mitchel's experience in Knoxville, Know-Nothing supporters had not made significant electoral progress in the South before the war. John Mitchel's work in the Ambulance Corps saw him both on armed guard duty in trenches and recovering the wounded after battles around Richmond. It was gruesome work. 'Pitiable and horrible cases of ghastly wounds are so frequent on these occasions that one might grow callous to the sight of human agony.'[7]

John Mitchel may not have fought but he was no stranger to the battlefield. He saw war. He saw its impact on bodies and minds. He did not lack courage and, as suggested in the above quote, empathy with soldiers suffering. In March 1863, his battlefield experience prompted Mitchel, in a letter to his brother William, to advise strongly against Jenny attempting to join him. He also described how his youngest son, still a private, had survived both the Battle of Fredericksburg and the bitter cold of winter.[8] Because he was editor of the *Enquirer* John Mitchel could get some extras, like coffee, for his sons. Before Fredericksburg, both Mitchel and Major Dooley had walked seven miles, from the railhead, to visit their sons, and to sit at the campfire with them.[9] They saw a Confederate Army in a 'wretched condition as regards tents, blankets, shoes and warm clothing.'[10] Many of the soldiers were barefoot and Willie shared blankets with his friends, privates John Dooley and 'Tantie' Jones. John Dooley wrote, 'Provided we all lie in the same position the blankets cover us snugly; but if one takes a different position from the other two, the blankets fail to accommodate all.'[11] In May 1863, James, who had lost an arm defending Richmond in 1862 was again in the thick of the action at Marye's Height, at the Battle of Chancellorsville. He was, again, badly wounded in the chest but recovered.[12]

Fort Sumter, in Charleston's harbour, situated between Morris Island and Sullivan's Island, was the key to the defence of the city. Although it was under constant attack John junior, now no longer a volunteer lieutenant but a captain in the regular Confederate Army, was safe. John Mitchel was proud of his eldest son's promotion, acceptance as a Southerner and his own status and influence. 'He is the only commissioned officer of foreign birth in the regular army of South Carolina, and it was regularly announced to me that the distinction was conferred on my account.'[13] However, John C. Mitchel was considered a good officer in his own right. Senator James Orr, in supporting a regular army commission for John C. Mitchel, wrote, on 17 April 1862, to the Secretary of War, G.N. Randolph, pointing out, that in his opinion, it was Volunteer Lieutenant Mitchel's eleven guns 'that fired the fort that led to its surrender.' If it was, it was done in the full view of the population of Charleston. 'All Charleston watched. Business was entirely suspended. King Street was deserted. The Battery, the wharves and shipping and "every steeple and cupola in the city" were crowded with anxious spectators. And "never before has such crowds of ladies without attendants" visited the streets of Charleston. "The women were wild" on the housetops.'[14] The *London Times* correspondent William Howard Russell, in *My Diary North and South*, provided a similar view of the early civil war as a spectator sport, both at Charleston in April 1861 and later in July 1861 at the Battle of Bull Run. Of Bull Run he wrote: 'The spectators were all excited, and a lady with an opera glass, who was near me was quite beside herself when an unusually heavy discharge roused the current of her blood – "That is splendid. Oh my! Is that not first rate? I guess we will be in Richmond this time tomorrow".'

However, Russell was soon reporting civilians being caught in a rout: 'But every moment the crowd increased, drivers and men cried out with the most vehement gestures. "Turn back! Turn back! We are whipped."'[15] Not surprisingly such reporting made Russell, who was anti-slavery and pro-Union, unpopular with the Lincoln administration. As early as December 1861, with the city under Union naval blockade and attack, the ladies of Charleston had a different view of the fort, and different opinions about the romance of war. Miss Emma Holmes recorded in her diary:

> As the fire rose so did the wind … hour after hour of
> anxiety passed, while flames raged more fiercely …
> throughout that awful night the flames leaped madly on
> with demonic fury and now the spire of our beautiful
> cathedral is wrapped in flames … at five am the city was
> wrapped in a living wall of fire.[16]

In early summer 1863, the news from Dublin was devastating.
Mitchel was sitting in his newspaper office when an officer came in
with a 'nervousness of manner'. The officer said nothing but handed
Mitchel a copy of the *Freeman's Journal* and left. When Mitchel
looked at the paper he learned that his eldest daughter, Henrietta,
who had so impressed James Stephens in Knoxville, had died in
her Paris Convent.[17] Jenny was in Drumalane, Newry, with her
sister-in-law Margaret, Mrs Hill Irvine, when news of Henrietta's
death arrived. She was ill and the family delayed telling her until
she was well enough to absorb the news. Jenny then travelled to
Paris, with the ever supportive John Martin to visit Henrietta's grave
and to bring Isabel home to Newry.[18] On the way home they visited
another loyal friend, the letter writing Miss Mary Thompson of
Ravensdale, County Louth. On hearing of the death of Henrietta
Mitchel worried about his three sons on 'the rough edge of battle'. [19]
John Mitchel had much cause to be worried. Both James and Willie
were at Gettysburg. News quickly came through that James had
survived the battle but Willie was missing in action. He was with
his friend John Dooley, now elected Captain of their company, in
Pickett's charge on the ridge of the aptly named Cemetery Hill. Of
that charge Captain John Dooley wrote, 'Now truly does the work
of death begin … Close up! Close up the ranks when a friend falls,
while his life blood bespatters your cheek or throws a film over your

eyes … while the bravest of the brave are sinking to rise no more.'[20] Willie was wounded but refused to stop. A hundred yards further on he fell, shrapnel in his stomach, clutching the regimental colours.[21]

Dooley was seriously wounded in Pickett's charge. Later as a prisoner of war he dreamed of Willie; of the young 17-year-old who studied bugs while they marched; who told his comrades of his exotic adventures in Australia; of recognising his father on board the *Emma*; of being held out the ship's state room window, 'over the dashing ocean's foam' presumably by Nicaragua Smyth and being told 'never to breathe his father's name whilst on that ship.'[22] According to Dooley William Henry Mitchel 'looked more like a schoolboy than any other member of the First Virginia's color guard.' [23]

Even in camp Willie had pursued his study of insect life, 'having a little manuscript book in which he entered all the discoveries he made with the aid of his microscope, describing minutely the figures and peculiarities of every unknown form of insect.'[24]

John Mitchel fretted for his youngest son. As time passed he grew more and more concerned. He knew Willie had fallen but 'nobody can tell anything of the nature or extent of the wound.'[25] It was another month, on 30 August, before John Mitchel had confirmation of the death of his youngest son. He wrote to John. 'I know poor Willie's fate at last. He was killed on the field at Gettysburg. It was only today I learned it from a gentleman in Philadelphia, to whom Mr. Dooley had written to make enquiries about his own son Jack…'[26]

John Mitchel worried about Jenny's reaction and reflected upon their fateful decision in Paris. 'Poor Willie's death will be a shocking blow to your mother and sisters, and I feel it very much too, because I might have insisted upon his remaining behind in Europe; but nothing would serve him except coming and taking his chances with his brothers.'[27]

Captain John Dooley in prison on Johnson's Island, Lake Erie, remembered his friend in verse:

> Bright in his genius and bright in his youth
> Gone to his grave!
> No Sisters to tend him, no mother to soothe …
> No arm to save.

> Died with the banner encircling his head,
> The staff by his side!
> Mid the smoke of the guns and strictly strewn dead
> His death moan was sighed[28]

In prison John Dooley wrote of a 'Yanko-Irish' soldier, from Lowell, Massachusetts, who made the (fanciful) claim that he had been 'a soldier under John Mitchel in '48'.

When young Captain Dooley asked him how 'he could crush a brave people asserting their right of self government' and what 'would Mr. Mitchel think of him? The poor fellow's eyes filled with tears.'[29] If we accept Dooley's account, such was John Mitchel's fame and authority among the Irish on both sides. The news of Willie's death was slow to reach his mother in Ireland. She lived in hope that it was a mistake and he would survive the war. Thus, in December 1863, mourning Henrietta and in hope of Willie's survival, Jenny made plans to join John and the rest of her family in the Confederacy. Letters were smuggled out of the Confederacy by sympathisers, and in one such letter to his daughter, Minnie, John

Mitchel had suggested that James might go to Ireland, as another officer had done, to escort the family through the Union blockade.[30]

Jenny would not wait. As O'Connor has suggested, as the mother of a fallen hero, of two Confederate Officers and the wife of a staunch supporter, with an international reputation, Jenny and the two girls were very acceptable as a passengers on a Confederate blockade-runner.[31] In December 1863, Jenny, Minnie and Isabel boarded the small, 425 ton steamer the *Vesta* in Falmouth. It was a twin screw, novel at the time for a merchantman but favoured by blockade-runners because it could reverse one engine and quickly pivot. The Mitchels travelled with all their worldly goods, family papers and a small quantity of gold from John Mitchel's brother, William. They sailed first to Bermuda, where, in 1848, John had nearly died, and had contemplated suicide. One of the passengers recorded what followed in the *Richmond Daily Dispatch*. On 3 January 1864 the *Vesta* left St. George, Bermuda and sailed for the Confederacy. The cargo included 116 boxes of bacon, three cases of whisky and a new uniform for Robert E. Lee. The Union Navy sighted the *Vesta* and the *USS Tuscarora*, *USS Keystone* and *USS Quaker City State* fired at her. As the Union ships turned to fire broadside, and shells fell around the *Vesta*, she made a run for it. Captain Eustice, an experienced blockade runner, ordered that both coal and the cargo of bacon be thrown into the *Vesta's* boilers. It worked, and the *Vesta* escaped with Union ships in hot pursuit. One shell passed through the *Vesta* but did little damage. The pursuit continued until nightfall when the *Vesta* was able to change course and shake off her pursuers. However, 'during the action Captain Eustice had visited the lockers a little too often and, just in the moment of triumph, became quite under the influence of drink.' He fell asleep on a chair on the deck. The first officer, Mr. Tickle, was 'completely stupefied with liquor.' The pilot was drunk and asleep, 'hopelessly so.' The second officer was left at the wheel, exhausted. When the pilot woke up he returned to the wheel, announced he knew where he was, and ran the ship aground. The passengers, including Jenny and the two girls, were put into a boat and set down on a sand bank. They were refused permission to get their belongings and had to watch as the *Vesta* was set on fire by its own crew, as the Mitchel papers, their trunks and Robert E. Lee's uniform were lost. [32]

The official Confederate account stated that the ship was bravely beached and destroyed to avoid capture. Whatever the truth, on a bitterly cold night, in the light and heat of a burning ship, the Mitchel women were shipwrecked. The male passengers, two confederate officers and an Englishman who eventually succeeded in finding a wagon, protected them. The conflagration attracted the Union cruisers but a boarding party was kept at bay, until 2 pm, by Confederate snipers. When the Volunteer Lieutenant Edward F. Devens, from *USS Aries*, finally boarded the *Vesta* it was a wreck lying in five feet of water. Its boats, which had ferried the Mitchel women, 'lay on the beach badly stove.'[33] Having survived a transatlantic journey, a sea battle and a shipwreck Jenny, Minnie and Isabel made their way to Smithfield. They then took a steamer to Wilmington, Virginia. A telegram informed John Mitchel that the family he thought safe in Newry, had once more crossed an ocean to be with him, this time under fire. As he had done in Van Diemen's Land, Mitchel described another reunion with his now depleted family. 'No more destitute refugees ever came to Richmond, even in these days of *refugeeing*, than my wife and two little girls after the burning of all the cargo of the ill-omened ship the *Vesta*.' [34]

During the late summer and autumn of 1863, whilst news of Willie's demise and bravery was filtering through, in Charleston

Harbour Captain John Mitchel was defending Fort Sumter. His courage was mentioned in the South Carolina Legislature. This pleased his father, as did the praise heaped upon Captain James Mitchel. In a letter to his eldest son the proud father regretted that neither John nor James had been promoted to major. 'Everybody speaks highly of James and, like you, he gets every luck except promotion.' [35] Beyond the natural pride a father takes in his sons' careers their promotion would have meant much to John Mitchel who valued hierarchy, and enjoyed it when his own superior status was recognized, be it on the poop deck of a prison ship or in the drawing rooms of Richmond 'belles'. Upon the arrival of the remainder of the Mitchel family in Richmond the much-praised Mitchel officers got leave to visit their mother and sisters. This reunion, in the house at the corner of Fifth Street and Carey Street, Richmond must have been a sad occasion without Willie and Henrietta.

By the time Jenny had arrived in Richmond John Mitchel, the constant rebel, had been reflecting on the course of the war. He had grown more critical of his friend President Davis 'for his failure to practice retaliation sternly'[36] and had resigned as editor of the pro-government *Enquirer*. He joined, as leader writer, the more critical *Examiner*, owned by another friend, John Moncure Daniel; a colurful 'polarizing' native Virginian who had served as a minister at the Court of Victor Emmanuel in 1853 in Turin and was 'a known racist and supporter of slavery.'[37] It tells us much about John Mitchel's opinions that he thought John Moncure Daniel the '...most accomplished – American whom I have ever yet known.'[38] As he reflected on the tide turning against the Confederacy John Mitchel doubted the commitment of the ordinary people, the ordinary soldier, to the cause:

I am quite sensible that there is one vice in this Confederacy; one weak spot in its harness – namely that the poorer people – the mean whites – have not the same interest in the contest which wealthy planters have … They say to one another, indeed that they must not be beaten, that it will never do to give the thing up; but they do not always mean it now when they say it.[39]

Perhaps John Mitchel had identified the major flaw in his classical stoicism; the major flaw in his advocacy of an almost inert social hierarchy. Others, the great mass of the people, would not suffer as he did, as his family did. People aspire to more than the place assigned to them by patriarchs, like John Mitchel, with romantic visions of both war and society. John Mitchel may have delighted 'in the spectacle of a people roused in this way to a full display of all its manhood … stripped for battle and defying fate.'[40] His 'mean whites' were losing patience enduring the hardships of 'a rich man's war'.

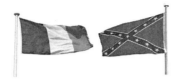

CHAPTER TEN

Scarlett Who?

Despite differences with President Davis the Mitchels enjoyed a social life close to the heart of government and were often guests at the President's home. Mrs Davis, like the other *belles*, admired John Mitchel. He was at ease in the company of women, including Miss Mary Pegram who provided William Dillon with a description and assessment of John Mitchel. Dillon, the son of John and Jenny's close friend and co-founder of the *Nation* John Blake Dillon, was John Mitchel's first biographer. Mary Pegram, who was to marry Confederate General Anderson, was warm in her praise of John Mitchel. She wrote of an unselfish, kind, courteous and broken-hearted father who always had time for the invalided soldier and the bereaved.[1] However she also referred to his consuming anti-British feeling, even when speaking of literary matters. 'Of English writers he could not give an unprejudiced opinion. He rarely spoke of them without some tinge of political feeling and he always protested against classing his favourite Scotch or Irish writers under the generic term *British*.' Alas, for Mitchel, Walter Scott whose stories of Scottish adventure provided solace in a Bermudan prison hulk, was eager to be identified with the British Crown. However, Mitchel did admire the conservative views of the Englishmen Thomas Carlyle and John Ruskin, the artist and, for some, reactionary art critic. Mitchel's tendency to classify people by perceived race and disputed nationality was common in the nineteenth and early twentieth centuries. The subtleties of ethnicity had not yet been fully recognized.[2] When visiting English Officers met John Mitchel, they were uneasy and embarrassed. Mitchel was formal and polite and they also found him charming and when he left 'said nothing uncomplimentary about Mr. Mitchel personally, but of course, denounced his efforts in Ireland.'[3]

Another Richmond lady remembered a mild-mannered courteous gentleman with blue eyes and clear-cut features who was pointed out to her as 'the famous John Mitchel'. Her 'principal remembrance of his talk was that it largely related to his children, to whom he was tenderly devoted.'[4] It is doubtful if Jenny, now in her forties, was as well received as her husband. O'Connor suggested that although she played her part in looking after the wounded, and was the mother of heroes, Jenny was suspect because she did her own housework and 'did not have slaves as servants.'[5] As the war closed in around Richmond Jenny still had some gold given to her by John's brother William. It must have been of great value as the Confederate currency tumbled. During the summer of 1864 as Lee desperately tried to defend Richmond, John Mitchel and his son James were close to the fighting. John continued to serve in the Ambulance Corps and James's horse was shot. Mitchel was often away from Jenny to whom he telegraphed, and wrote, assuring her that although James was in the thick of the fighting he was all right. In a letter to Jenny he described a scene of filth, horror and anguish 'receiving the wounded and putting them on board the trains. Half of us up and working all night, all of us busily engaged all day. I cannot yet guess when we may get away and go home.'[6] John Mitchel, who suffered from asthma, slept on the ground.

In a letter to his brother William, in the summer of 1864, Mitchel mentioned his sons. He wrote with pride that John, still a captain, was now in command of Fort Sumter. 'John is in command of Fort Sumter, with seven companies of artillery; it is a command higher than his grade…All this is a very great satisfaction to me and therefore I cannot help telling you about it'. Touchingly, he remembered Willie and referred to the entomological 'manuscript book' his youngest son compiled on the battlefield. 'I have a little book of entomological memoranda and drawings, that he kept in his knapsack, and one of his comrades sent to me afterwards'. In the same letter he reaffirmed his faith in the Confederate public but acknowledged the increasing isolation of the Confederacy and a world losing faith in its cause. They were, '… isolated from all other people, and without a friend in the world'.[7] The Mitchels had friends in the outside world who were concerned about them and, to a degree, shared their political views. From Rostrevor, County Down, 16 July 1864, writing to Eva, the poetess and wife of Izod O'Doherty, with whom he and Mitchel had shared exile in Van Diemen's Land, John Martin expressed his support for the Confederacy. He hoped 'the people of all the Northern states will at last come to the conclusion that it is best to let the Southern people alone'.[8] Fighting for independence and not the defence of slavery, was the editorial message Mitchel's *Richmond Examiner* wanted to get out to 'foreign nations'. 'The question of slavery is only one of the minor issues; and the cause of the war, the whole cause, on our part, is the maintenance of the sovereign independence of these states … '[9] However, Mitchel had been, and would be again, robust in his defence of the 'minor issue'. John Martin too recognized the 'South' as an independent cultural and political identity, a rural economy with the plantation system, and slavery, at its heart. However, Martin scolded Mitchel for his extreme views on slavery, but so had the ultra Confederate, Edmund Ruffin. How far did Martin's support of the Confederacy extend?

John Martin argued, in print with Meagher, like Mitchel, comparing the United States to the British Empire; if Ireland had the right to remove the 'yoke' of the Empire the Southern states had the right to secede. He tried to discourage Irishmen from enlisting to fight for the North. He helped Father John Bannon, the Confederate agent in Ireland, to garner support for the South.[10] However, James Quinn, managing editor of the Royal Irish Academy's *Dictionary of Irish Biography*, and a biographer of John Mitchel, in personal communication with the writer wrote:

> I think we can say that Martin didn't approve of slavery, but didn't think it was worth fighting a bloody war that would cause immense suffering to slaves and non-slaves alike. I think his idea would have been to leave well alone and eventually slavery would just wither away.[11]

Whatever their political differences, in the letter to Eva, John Martin also wondered if like 'poor Billy' the Mitchels were already dead. He was right to fret for just three days later, on 20 July, the Mitchels were to suffer again.

John Mitchel had just put the *Examiner* to bed and was chatting to its proprietor, and his friend, John Moncure Daniel, when a telegram arrived, from Major General Jones in Charleston. It announced the death of Captain John Mitchel, the commanding officer of Fort Sumter. The last line may have been some consolation to his father: 'The shot that removed him has deprived the country of one of its most valuable defenders.'[12] The twenty-six-year-old Captain John C. Mitchel died bravely, exposed on the battlements of Fort Sumter, the iconic fortress he had helped capture at the beginning of the civil war. He was 'struck on the left hip by a fragment of a mortar shell, which shattered his thigh, inflicting a mortal wound.'[13]

Captain Mitchel was highly respected by his officers. Speaking to the Survivors' Association, Charleston District in 1890, Captain Mitchel's senior, First Lieutenant Courtenay, referred to 'the most remarkable man I have ever known.' John Mitchel's teaching in Van Diemen's Land must have been good because Courtenay spoke of an 'accomplished mathematician … a wonderful historian' and a man who 'could make himself understood in three or four languages.'[14] He was also a man of action and was involved in offensive as well as defensive operations. On 30 January 1863 he was a key officer in a 'secret expedition' organized to attack an enemy gunboat on the Stono River. The *Isaac Smith* was disabled and her crew, of eleven officers, one hundred and five men and three slaves captured. Along with fellow officers and men, Captain Mitchel was commended for bravery and firing from a position 'entirely exposed to the enemy's fire within 200 or 300 yards.'[15]

Although Captain C. Mitchel was an artillery officer, Brigader General Ripley recognized him as a competent engineer. In May 1863, and without sanction from Headquarters, Ripley sacked the engineers under Captain Langdon Cheeves, and ordered Captain Mitchel to finish the batteries on Morris Island. Sadly, on 16 July1864, four days before John C. Mitchel was mortally wounded General Ripley had requested that his polymath officer be promoted to major.

I have the honor respectfully to request that Capt. John C. Mitchel First Carolina Artillery (enlisted), be appointed a major of artillery … Captain Mitchel has served with energy and fidelity since the war commenced. He is now and has been for some months commander of

Fort Sumter, for which position his experience and qualifications peculiarly fit him ... It is proper that this important position should be commanded by a field officer, and I think that Captain Mitchel, by months of ceaseless vigilance and activity therein, as well as previous service, has fairly earned his promotion.[16]

In his journal the bereaved father described how he took the long way home with the terrible news before entering the parlour where Jenny and the two girls were sitting.[17] As he walked did John Mitchel reflect on reason number five for not committing suicide; 'I hope to do my children some good before I die'?

The young officer from Newry received a hero's funeral in Charleston Cathedral and General Beauregard wrote a glowing letter of condolence to his famous father. He is buried in Magnolia Cemetery, Charleston, in the old city that, at first sight, had impressed his mother. The words 'I willingly give up my life for South Carolina; Oh! That I could have died for Ireland' are carved on his gravestone. After the war it was surrounded with a border in the shape of the Fort Sumter battlements. A second Mitchel son had died bravely in a secondary cause. The third surviving son was battle scarred, equally brave, and in constant danger. He was removed from immediate danger on 6 October 1864 when he was appointed Assistant Adjutant General of Brig. Gen. Evan's Brigade.[18] It is assumed James was given a staff job because his family had suffered enough. John Mitchel carried the order into the Shenandoah Valley.

Given that Jenny had lost two sons and a daughter, that all were now in danger from the war, it is strange that Mitchel sought a duel with Senator Henry S. Foote, of Tennessee who had 'insulted' him in the Confederate Congress. Before the war Foote tried hard to keep the

Union intact and was instrumental in creating the 1850 compromise between North and South that had delayed hostilities for a decade, after California was admitted to the Union as a free state. Foote hated President Davis and now sought peace with Washington. He twice refused Mitchel's card, 'saying Mitchel was not a gentleman.'[19] The incident highlights both Mitchel's personal courage and his heightened sense of honour; his wish to be perceived as a gentleman and as a Patrician. As with John Fleming, in pre-war Knoxville, the affair petered out. This had not been the case two months earlier in August 1864 when the owner of the *Examiner*, John Moncure Daniel's anti-government writing had so annoyed the Confederate Treasurer, Edward C. Elmore, that he challenged Daniel to a duel. John Moncure Daniel, a former confederate officer, had a damaged right arm and had to hold the pistol in his left hand. He was wounded and although he survived the duel he was to die three days before the end of the Civil War.[20] Unlike Mitchel, John Moncure was not popular with the *belles* who thought him to be 'a social sphinx.' Mitchel was held to be 'the humanizing element' of their newspaper partnership.[21]

The pressure on Richmond was now very severe as Grant continued to press Lee's depleted and poorly equipped army. However, there was denial in Richmond. Perhaps because, as Mitchel noted, despite the bitter fighting around it 'nothing can be quieter or more regular than the aspect of the town – the markets supplied as usual, every railroad leading to Richmond … carrying its trains outward and inward with punctuality.'[22] In the dying capital, 'Expensive parties, balls, private theatricals and other amusements abounded. Richmond was never gayer than during the winter of 1864–65; so much so that the clergymen of the various denominations felt called upon to remonstrate from the pulpit.'[23] Clergymen had been vocal throughout the war and ironically, in 1863, the pastor of the First Unitarian Church, the Church of John

Mitchel's father, the church of John Mitchel's childhood, 'was arrested and sent north under a flag of truce', because of his abolitionist activities. It had also been the church of Mitchel's friend, and owner of the *Richmond Examiner*, John Moncure Daniel.[24]

With high casualty rates and morale ebbing away it is not surprising that the Confederate government considered desperate measures. But from Mitchel's perspective, what desperate measures! On 20 February 1865, the Confederate House of Representatives passed a bill allowing black men to join the army, but only with the permission of their masters. General Lee endorsed this proposal but in letters to General Richard Ewell regretted that landowners were not allowing their slaves to enlist.[25]

In contrast, Confederate soldiers, including Captain C. Mitchel, had been fighting black regiments since the 1863 battle for Fort Sumter and its islands. The entrance to Charleston Harbour was 'the testing ground for African American troops whose fine performance against Battery Wagner convinced the Northern government to expand its recruitment of black soldiers.'[26] Black soldiers taken prisoner created a problem for Confederate General Beauregard. Initially they were treated as slaves or as free men fermenting revolt; execution was the fate of the latter. However, after President Lincoln threatened retaliation for the execution of black soldiers, Beauregard 'did realize that the war had taken another step, and they reluctantly had to recognize the legitimacy of the North's Sable Arm.'[27] For some, the war was changing attitudes, if not convictions.

This was not the case for John Mitchel. Despite recognizing that 'given the North's greater manpower such brutal arithmetic would eventually mean defeat for the South'[28] John Mitchel did not support the proposal to allow slaves into the Confederate Army. A year earlier in February1864, Irish Confederate General Patrick R. Cleburne had been silenced for making such a suggestion. However, Cleburne, Ireland's most successful Confederate General, had gone beyond attempting to solve Mitchel's arithmetic problem. He had suggested slavery was both an 'embarrassment and inherent weakness' for the Confederacy. President Davis, whilst not overtly disciplining his general, pulled him back into line. General Cleburne was killed in November 1864 at the Battle of Franklin.[29]

Now with his family decimated the 'vapourous drop profound' from his unnerving experience in the landscape of Van Diemen's Land was about to fall into the certainty of Mitchel's classical mind. Unlike Cleburne, and, probably, his own friend John Martin, Mitchel saw support for slavery and support for the Confederacy as indivisible. He especially hated the idea, allowed for in the eventual Confederate Act of Congress, that freedom could be, with the master's permission, a reward for war service. John Mitchel declared, 'Now, if freedom be a reward for negroes – that is, if freedom be a good thing for negroes – why, then it is, and always was, a grievous wrong and crime to hold them in slavery at all.' More tellingly, and with devastating clarity, Mitchel continued, 'If it be true that the state of slavery keeps these people depressed below the condition to which they could develop their nature, their intelligence and their capacity for enjoyment, and what we call "progress," then every hour of their bondage for generations is a black stain upon the white race.'[30] Presumably in his consternation Mitchel did not intend an ironic pun. For Mitchel, the hierarchy of the Confederacy was right, good and inert. The slave was a slave because he was not capable of being free. For Mitchel, if this was not the case then slavery was immoral, and his family would have been sacrificed on the wrong side.

Few moral questions have a clear right or wrong answer. Mitchel posed such a question, he did not concede the case. He could not concede the case. His neural patterns, his admiration for the classical world and the ultimate sacrifice of two of his sons would not allow him the alternative answer to his own question.

Arthur Griffith defended Mitchel's views, in his 1913 preface to Gill's reprinting of the 1854 version of *Jail Journal*. 'Even his views on negro slavery have been depreciatingly excused, as if excuse were needed for an Irish Nationalist declining to hold the Negro his peer in right.'[31] Griffith, like John Mitchel, was clear on the correct order within the cultural, and natural, hierarchy. William Dillon pointed out that for Mitchel the solution to cruelty was legislation 'to prevent and punish ill usage',[32] not emancipation. Perhaps, just as for Mitchel, the solution to the Irish Land problem was *tenant right* not revolution. For the conservative John Mitchel, change should only happen within the existing social edifice. However, preventing ill usage did not exclude beatings. Mitchel thought pysical punishment on the plantation was necessary. 'Severe measures are sometimes needful in subduing a young negro. What then? Is the colt not to be broken because he is vicious?'[33] John Mitchel consistently supported slavery, the plantation system and beatings.

However by this stage, for the dying Confederacy, the argument about slaves and free slaves in the Confederate Army was becoming academic. Grant was taking Richmond. On Sunday 2 April 1865, the Confederate government abandoned the capital.

Jenny, Minnie, who was unwell, and Isabel remained in the city as James retreated with the army and John followed the government, and the story.

Harper's Weekly provided a contemporary account of the fall of Richmond. The city was in flames, not from Union artillery, but on the orders of the retreating General Breckinridge. 'The torch had been applied to all public buildings from the Tredegar Works on the canal above the city, to the Navy-yard at Rocketts a distance of two miles – including the laboratories, artillery-shops, arsenals, Franklin paper-mill, the Petersburg and Danville depots, all the Commissary and Quarter-master buildings on and near Fourteenth Street, Rahm's Foundry and other buildings. By seven o'clock A.M. nearly the whole city south of Main Street between Eighth and Fifteenth streets was one great sea of flame.'[34]

Initially, Jenny and the two girls, in their house on the corner of Fifth and Canal Street, might have feared drunken looters, the ungodly and the wrath of freed slaves as thousands of Richmond's own citizens robbed shops, emptied warehouses and fled from the advancing Union troops. But as Jenny and others waited for the inevitable, in boarded up houses, the fire and exploding Confederate arsenal became their main concern. The house opposite was destroyed in flames. Jenny's windows exploded and shrapnel, from the thousands of exploding shells, fell flaming on the roof. Jenny Mitchel was experiencing, in reality, what *Gone with the Wind* would bring to the screen over seventy years later. In life she demonstrated courage and determination similar to that of the fictional Sacrlett O'Hara. Although the conflagration consumed John Mitchel's *Examiner* office, his house and family survived.

The walking and retreating John Mitchel, fourteen miles away on the road to Danville, heard the arsenal explode and immediately erroneously exclaimed, 'Can the Yankee villains be bombarding the defenceless city?' He described 'a dull red glare on the eastern sky, which was not the dawn of a spring morning. We knew that the city was burning.'[35]

The Civil war was over and again the Mitchels were on the losing side, this time, as they came to terms with defeat, they did so without three of their children.

CHAPTER ELEVEN

Martyrdom – It Is Quite a Bad Trade

John Mitchel had done the Union troops an injustice. Constance Cary Harrison, a member of the plantation aristocracy, wrote to her mother saying that her family was treated 'with perfect courtesy and consideration' by the Union soldiers. There was looting. 'Some negroes of the lowest grade, their heads turned by the prospect of wealth and equality, together with a mob of miserable poor whites, drank themselves mad with liquor scooped from the gutter.'[1] Sally A. Brock Putnam remembered:

> The roaring, the hissing and the crackling of the flames were heard above the shouting and confusion of the immense crowd of plunderers who were moving amid the dense smoke like demons, pushing, rioting and swaying with their burdens to make a passage to open air.[2]

However, General Weitzel's federals, both white and black, restored order and fought the fires, not the people. Weitzel was particularly proud of Colonel Adam's 'fine regiment of colored men' who 'made a very great impression on those citizens who saw it.'[3] One such citizen commented, 'very agreeable was the disappointment at the behaviour of the victorious army.' The seventeen-year-old Miss Lelian M. Cook welcomed the return of order:

> Tuesday evening. We spent a very quiet night. I have never known Richmond to be as still. A great many persons went down after a guard but General Weitzel, I think, said he would not give them all a guard but there would be one at every corner and a strong patrol out all night.[4]

The Mitchel women were grateful for the offer of a Union guard on their house.

Although thankful for the guard Jenny shunned union officers, blamed England for the defeat and thought that the negroes could not cope with their freedom.[5] She, and the daughters left to her, had now survived being fired upon, a shipwreck and the taking of the Confederate capital.

As Richmond tried to recover John Mitchel and his remaining son, James, returned to 'a gaunt and ghastly sight'. So many buildings had collapsed that they 'became confused among the ruins, and had to stop and take an observation of distant buildings still standing to make sure of the street we were walking on.' However, they found their own house with shattered windows but generally intact.[6]

Typically Mitchel's sympathies lay with his class and the 'disbanded Confederate officers ... their four years of the best of life thrown away.' He too now conceded that the Union soldiers exercised little harshness 'against these forlorn fellows.'[7] Minnie was not well and needed to be removed from the smoke of the fallen city. She was sent to friends in the country and on 28 April, Isabel was sent to a Jesuit Convent in New York.[8] Jenny remained with James in Richmond and John went to New York, seeking newspaper work. The staunchly southern New York *Daily News* employed him, as editor. Mitchel worried about his mother in Ireland. He wrote to his sister. 'And now, my Margaret, I am almost afraid to ask after my friends, and especially my dear mother.' Mary Hasslett Mitchel, who had travelled to New York and was there to greet her eldest son in 1854, died in Ireland on 8 April 1865, aged seventy-nine. John Mitchel would learn of her death in a Union prison. In the same letter to Margaret he worried about his injured surviving son. 'I don't know yet what James will do with himself. He is deeply distressed and humiliated … '[9] However, for James life was improving. He was courting Elisabeth Mosley, a young *belle* from Buckingham County, and had got a job in insurance with the National Express Company. He decided to stay in Richmond.[10] Both Dillon and O'Connor make reference to a donation to Jenny from friends in New York. Dillon suggested it was anonymous. O'Connor identified the Jesuit priest Father O'Hagan as the source of $400. She claimed Jenny told John it was only $200.[11] If so, it could be an indication of a changing balance in their relationship, as John's health and status declined.

Jenny made ready to travel to join John in New York. She was to be disappointed.

In the New York *Daily News* Mitchel had continued to justify the Southern cause. He feared 'a bitter and mean and cowardly spirit of revenge' might lead to the arrest of General Lee. He considered that he was in some danger and wished he might flee, with his family, to France. Mitchel continued to place himself in danger by writing in defence of President Davis and as he wrote to his sister Margaret, 'several of the more violent newspapers called for my arrest'.[12] He was warned to desist by an officer from General

Dix's staff, who advised a friend to tell Mitchel to tone down his criticisms. Mitchel continued and ignored a second warning, this time from a visitor to his newspaper offices. General Ulysses S. Grant took the view that if John Mitchel was so concerned about the welfare of President Davis then he should join him in Fortress Monroe. On 6 June Grant signed the order for Mitchel's arrest, and his transportation to Fortress Monroe. It was carried out on 14 June 1865. Mitchel again provided an account of his own arrest. Just as he was about to invite Jenny to come to New York an artillery officer, two soldiers and three detectives 'hustled' him out into a carriage. 'Blinds were drawn down, and we started at a very rapid pace.' [13] As in Dublin, in 1848, John Mitchel was being rushed away from his family, through a city's streets to a waiting ship.

The journey, in the steamer *Burden,* to prison in Fortress Monroe, must have felt horribly familiar. As he was being transferred Mitchel reflected, with some pride, 'I suppose I am the only person who has ever been a prisoner-of-state to the British and American Government one after the other.'[14] For Mitchel, it was indicative of his being in the right; the British government needed to create a law to imprison him; the American government did not even bother with such a pretext. He was pleased to be the victim of the two greatest examples of progress in a century he despised. However, Mitchel was to discover that there was a clear distinction between the two governments. After he was landed at Fortress Monroe, the Union, unlike the Carthaginians, would take no regard of his gentlemanly status.

Mitchel was kept in solitary confinement in a small dark cell with only a table and an iron bed. His food was placed on the dirty table without a plate or knife or fork. He was promised but was denied tobacco for a month. For two months he was not able to exercise and had no access to books.[15] He was denied his three favourite pastimes of smoking, talking and walking. His health deteriorated. General Miles, the commander of Fortress Monroe, visited him, interviewed him and appeared to be uncomfortable with Mitchel's treatment, but nothing changed. On one occasion an Irish soldier, Mike Sullivan from Fethard in County Tipperary, bought and smuggled a comb, a toothbrush and an orange into John Mitchel. The Irish soldier offered to bring him a pencil and paper but that was his last night guarding John Mitchel. The kind gifts Mike Sullivan brought also brought a tear to the ill John Mitchel's eye.[16] Throughout his term Mitchel refused to complain to General Miles. After two months on 10 August a doctor examined Mitchel. He certified that if Mitchel's conditions did not change he might die. From then on the Union prison became more tolerable and Mitchel was even able to exchange greetings with President Davis in the exercise yard.

On the outside his family fretted and laboured to get John released. The *New York Times* reported James going to Fortress Monroe and being refused permission to see his father. [17] Dr Thomas Antisel, a Lieutenant Colonel, medical officer, Young Irelander and old Washington friend, contacted the War Department but his request that Jenny be allowed to visit John was turned down. In a letter to John, dated 28 August, Jenny expressed her satisfaction at the exercise concession, but she had only learned of it through the newspapers.

> Dear John,
> I see by the newspapers that our application was made and was granted to permit you to take exercise, the exercise that is granted to other prisoners …

She wrote of the improved health of his two daughters and of James leaving a parcel with underclothes and tobacco with General

Miles.[18] In a letter to Jenny on 1 September Mitchel asked about 'his two dear little daughters', complained little but did mention the return of his asthma.[19] His health continued to deteriorate. He was in physical decline, beyond his years. Jenny was again without her husband; Mitchel was again a martyr and the American Irish were again interested in the services of John Mitchel.

This time it was the Fenians who lobbied for his release, which was announced, to loud cheers, at their Philadelphia Congress on 21 October. A deputation from the Congress sought, and was granted, an early audience with President Johnson. They addressed the President thanking him for restoring 'freedom to a man whom they love and venerate for his self-sacrificing devotion to his native land.' They remembered 'nothing of JOHN MITCHEL's American career.' The President also chose to forget Mitchel's American treason and replied:

> As you, Sir, delicately remarked, we could not remember Mr. MITCHEL's American career; but we were anxious, as a mark of respect and compliment to the larger section of our countrymen, with whom Mr. MITCHEL was previously identified, to yield to their wishes in that regard.[20]

The Fenian Congress may have cheered Mitchel's release but the *New York Times* warned them to be careful of Mitchel. 'John's past history has demonstrated whatever he touches politically, he kills ... Mr. Mitchel's touch is fatal.'[21] As with Young Ireland and the American Confederacy, the Fenians too were to be defeated. Within the Fenians Mitchel's touch may not have been fatal but he was consistently critical and rebellious. Cut off in the Confederacy, and later incarcerated, Mitchel wrote that he was not aware of the growth of the Fenian organisation, 'and when it broke upon me here it loomed large and imposing'. He 'became excited like the rest' at the prospect of a Fenian-led alliance between hardened Irish American veterans and 'large forces of the peasantry'.[22] He was further encouraged since, at first, the American government was ill disposed towards Britain, following the fitting out of Confederate cruisers in British ports. There was also increasing tension between Britain and France. He wrote in November 1865, 'In short, if this gallant game is to be set afoot I must have a share in it.'[23] In prison, John Mitchel was not yet a Fenian but as he explained to General Myles, who now frequently conversed with him, his interest in helping his 'countrymen in Ireland someday to shake off the British domination' had not waned.[24]

As the Fenians were negotiating his release, Mitchel suggested to General Miles that he would be prepared to leave the country. Miles thought this 'a good method of getting rid of the incendiary ...'[25] In the event, on 31 October 1865, Mitchel was released, without conditions. Before he left prison he was able to visit ex-President Davis.

Mitchel had spent over four months in a Union prison. He suffered more in those four months than he had in five years with the British. There was no wine at the Captain's table, no ticket-of-leave, no conversations with friends – old and new – and no comfort from Jenny. Today there is a large plaque at Fortress Monroe to a 'fearless and courageous southern journalist, staunch supporter of the Confederacy'. The *New York Times* provided a description of John Mitchel on a wharf in transit to Richmond. It also speculated on his future.

> JOHN MITCHEL, in an unpretending manner, with simply a light thin overcoat thrown over his shoulders,

and a small carpet-bag in hand, was walking up and down the 'Baltimore' wharf with impatient, restless steps, and his long, thick hair brushed carelessly back from his forehead, his heavy beard slightly sprinkled with gray, recognized in this comparatively unnoticed personage the notorious Irish chieftain, ex-rebel, and one who is doubtless destined, in the anticipated future Fenian movement, to play no inferior role, or second part in the Fenian drama of 'Ireland for the Irish'.[26]

John Mitchel never fully recovered from his imprisonment in Fortress Monroe. It was a physically much-diminished fifty-year-old John Mitchel, with a hacking cough and graying beard who returned to Jenny in Richmond.[27] 'His figure, formerly so erect and even military in its carriage, was now stooped a little, and the shoulders stooped in a way that suggested a weak chest.'[28]

Jenny did not have him for long. Once released from prison Mitchel did what the New York Times had suggested he would do. He met with the American Fenian leaders, including John O'Mahony, a rebel from 1848, who with James Stephens had formed the Fenian Brotherhood. The Fenians wanted Mitchel to go to Paris as the agent 'for the safe transmission of funds to Ireland'. Excited by their plans to use Civil War veterans against England Mitchel accepted the commission and joined the organization.[29] On 7 November 1865 John Mitchel complied with President Johnson's 29 May 1865 Proclamation of Amnesty and Reconstruction, which allowed a pardon and restoration of citizenship to former rebels and, for the second time, swore allegiance to the United States.[30] Three days later he sailed, from New York, for Paris as a Fenian agent.

That Mitchel would travel alone may suggest his lack of commitment to the Fenian cause; perhaps he thought that his stay in Paris might be short; perhaps Jenny was more concerned about the other needs of her depleted family. She would never again cross an ocean with him, or be with him. With Mitchel in Paris, the family, in recovering Richmond, was relatively comfortable. Mitchel had a decent salary from the Fenians; Jenny had money from friends in the north and some gold remaining from William Haslett Mitchel; James had a job, unlike many other ex-Confederate officers. As time passed, more defeated soldiers straggled past their house.

Jenny still hoped young Willie would be among their number. Even the return, from captivity, of Captain John Dooley, Willie's friend, who heard of him fall with a gaping stomach wound, did not convince Jenny. She continued to live in hope that Willie had survived. 'I got it into my head that he had been taken prisoner and carried off a long distance – but that he would make his way back home.' She was finally convinced of his death by a Mr Joyce who described how, after the Battle of Gettysburg, he and three other soldiers had found Willie's body rolled in a blanket, with his face washed. Pinned to the blanket was, 'W.H. Mitchel, son of the Irish Patriot.' In a letter, to her son James, Jenny recorded how Willie's body was buried 'on the banks of a stream, near a small cabin, so close that no plow could ever disturb it.'[31] Jenny wanted to find and visit Willie's grave. She never did. John arrived in Paris on the 23 November 1865. Despite spies, whom he confronted, he diligently discharged his duties as the Fenian's financial agent; but he had little heart in it. He believed a rebellion could only succeed if Britain was involved in a war.

He distrusted and disliked both secret organizations and James Stephens. Stephen's reports of the exaggerated presence of rebellious fervor in Ireland, and the Fenian split in America, further disheartened John Mitchel. In March 1866 he wrote to John O'Mahony:

> I need not tell you, dear O'M-, how bitterly I have been grieved by the shameful break up of the F.B. [Fenian Brotherhood]. Its worst effect was not cutting-off money supplies; it was the deconsideration of our cause in America…I have doubts about the propriety of remaining as a financial agent in Paris. For the next three months, of course, I will remain at my post, and carry out any instructions and dispositions with regard to funds…that will give both you and me time to convince ourselves of the real history and present situation of affairs in Ireland.[32]

In this letter Mitchel was serving notice of his intention to leave the Fenians, expressing his disappointment at disarray in the movement and suggesting his distrust of the optimistic reports he was getting from Stephens in Ireland. In *Jail Journal* he recorded that he relied more on letters from his friend Father Kenyon as to the true state of affairs in Ireland.[33] In an earlier letter O'Mahony hoped Mitchel might 'at your own judgment and discretion' interest the French government in their cause.[34]

Although he claimed to be on good terms with both the Private Secretary of the Emperor, M. Pietri (who was also the Prefect of Police), and the French government John Mitchel's efforts to involve them in the cause of Ireland ended 'in a position of utter nullity.'[35] Also in March, Mitchel wrote to his son James pointing out that because of Stephens's activities his 'arrangements with the FB are of a very precarious nature'.[36] He resigned from the Fenians on 22 June1866. He survived by writing for the New York *Daily News*.

John Mitchel was lonely in his chambers at the top of a long flight of one hundred and five stairs on Rue Richer. He missed his family and especially regretted that Rixy, Isabel, had not written to him. 'I am beginning to think she hates me.' But earlier at the end of 1865

> … One damp and dismal evening I entered my lodgings about eight o'clock, intending to have the wood fire lighted in my small room and to read. I opened the door with my key and was surprised to find my rooms already flaring with light, a fire blazing in the hearth and a candle burning on the table. Two ladies and a gentleman rose upon my entrance. I took my hat off and bowed and stared; the dazzle of light and my own defect of eyesight prevented me from recognizing anyone. At last both ladies laughed and then I knew – it was my two sisters and my brother William who had come over to visit me. Needless to say that this enlivened the dull hours and days for a while. [37]

Thus, despite political differences the wider Mitchel family remained close. However, the above passage also tells of Mitchel's failing eyesight, a terrible burden for a writer.

His general discontent, and genetic, nomadic tendencies, saw him move, in February, from Rue Richter to his old lodgings in 24 Rue Lacepede; in early summer from there to 186 Rue Rivoli and finally back to Rue Lacepede.

John Mitchel's ability to inspire deep and lasting friendship was further illustrated when in September 1866 his two closest friends, the ever-loyal John Martin, who had also visited Mitchel in January, and Father Kenyon P.P. of Templederry, County Tipperary, made the journey to Paris to be with him. On a previous occasion

Father Kenyon was with the Mitchels in Paris when they made the fateful decision to allow young Willie to run the blockade into the Confederacy with his father. Both visitors needed a holiday. Father Kenyon was ill and, in June, John Martin had written to the priest telling of his own depression. He understood William Smith O'Brien's gloom before he died[38] in Bangor, Wales on 18 June 1863. Mitchel was aware that the three men, growing old but still enjoying each other's company, were together for the last time. 'Over these pleasant days in Paris impends a kind of a shadow. We three old friends, when we part this time, will probably never meet again, altogether.' Father John Kenyon, 'as gay and jovial and witty as ever,'[39] was terminally ill.

Mitchel visited the Irish College with Father Kenyon, where he anticipated the president, Dr Lynch, might consider him 'a dangerous and ultra revolutionary character.'[40] However, he was delighted to be well received and to view 'a complete set of the Nation Newspaper, bound in green folio volumes, the gift of Colonel Byrne', the 1798 rebel. According to Mitchel's own account this was only the start. When Mitchel walked into the garden he found, 'all the students and professors ranged in two dense rows on either side … when I made my appearance, by the side of Dr. Lynch, three cheers long, loud and hearty, burst from the crowd … as Father Kenyon and I passed between these ranks, the cheer was renewed with wild energy.'[41] The occasion moved Father Kenyon to tears and John Mitchel, despite his views and activities in the Confederacy, knew he was still loved in Ireland. It was why the Fenians wanted the name of John Mitchel associated with their attempt to rebel in Ireland.

Mitchel often visited the widow of Colonel Byrne, 'Once of Oulart Hill'. He travelled to the Normandy coast where he stayed with Nigaragua Smyth, with whom he had shared so many Australian adventures.[42] Despite these distractions, Mitchel painted a miserable picture of his life in Paris. He missed James's wedding to Elizabeth Mosley and wrote to his brother William 'I am neither in good health nor in good spirits at all.'[43]

In a letter to his sister Matilda he wrote, 'I am solitary and spend most of my evenings smoking and reading by my little wood fire. You cannot imagine how I long for my little household, or the half of it which remains to me.' With a knowing irony he went on to point out, 'Not one of my children ever give me one moment's pain.'[44]

On the same day his reflective mood deepened; in another confessional letter to Miss Thompson he wrote, 'We have suffered heavily indeed ... by that Confederate business and although it was a good cause I must admit I grudge it what it has cost us - the lives of two of our sons in defence of a country which after all was not their own.'[45] This is faint and guilt-ridden praise for a lost cause; but, significantly, Mitchel now saw 'that Confederate business' as a lost cause. On 2 February 1866, he wrote to Jenny warning James to forget about the Confederacy and not to be a martyr. He added, 'I have been a martyr now for eighteen years, and it is quite a bad trade. I had rather be a farmer.' He asked Jenny to 'Kiss over and over again for me my two dear little daughters. My poor children – It is they who are the real martyrs.'[46] As he read the flames of his fire, did John Mitchel remember again that, on board ship in 1848, he had rejected suicide because he hoped to do his children some good before he died? Given what the war cost John and Jenny this reflection is sad, subdued and stoical.

In late 1866, John Mitchel decided to return to Jenny and his family; but he would leave one member of his family behind in Paris. Before he left, 'a lonely wretch'[47] he went to the grave of his eldest 'daughter Henrietta in the cemetery of Mount Parnase, wither I carry a *lauriertin,* in a large pot, and place it on the tombstone, and

Adieu![48] John Mitchel was suspicious of progress; he sought and experienced lasting values. Throughout his life, and especially in France, he enjoyed loyalty, friendship and deep family relationships that transcended, and survived, political differences. These were constants in a life of personal tragedy and political failure. Three times he went to France to try and emulate Wolfe Tone by involving the French in action against England. He knew he would not try again.

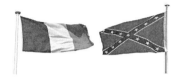

CHAPTER TWELVE

Professor Cornelius O'Shaughnessy
in Decline

John Mitchel sailed to New York and then travelled on to be with his family, including his new daughter-in-law, in Richmond, which was still under military control. Without a job, in a city of unemployed soldiers, Mitchel was glad of a commission, from the New York publishers Sadlers to write a *History of Ireland from the Treaty of Limerick*. Written in a year it was mainly a compilation of some of his previous work and, not surprisingly, a 'denunciation of centuries of British oppression in Ireland.'[1] Athough he purposely stopped short of the most recent events he could not resist commenting on the Fenians. With reference to their recent failures, including the June 1866 invasions of Ontario and New Brunswick, he wrote:

> It maybe said, however, that a powerful illustration has been thereby given to the fact, that while England is at peace with other powerful nations, it is extremely difficult, if not impossible, to make so much as a serious attempt at a national insurrection, in the face of a government so vigilant and so well prepared.[2]

It is therefore not surprising that when, in February 1867, he received a telegram offering him the leadership of a reconciled Fenian movement he refused and reiterated: 'I disbelieve in the existence of any fighting in Ireland, and in the possibility of making any fight there, while England continues at peace.' Although both wings of the Fenian movement had offered to unite under John Mitchel's leadership he was unequivocal in his response. 'I do not wish either your branch of the organization, or that of Mr. Roberts, to use my name in any manner whatsoever.'[3] He had to refuse again before February was out and in March he wrote to the editor of the *Richmond Times* denying he was 'Chief of the Fenians either in England, in Canada, in Ireland or the United States.'[4] Mitchel did write of his support for the Fenians but objected to calling on the people for large contributions of money for immediate military operations under the delusion that anything important could be affected either in Ireland or in Canada as long as England was at peace with France and the United States.

In concluding his history he made an indirect derogatory reference to James Stephens and the Fenian leadership in Ireland. He lamented that the Fenians, without directly naming them, in Ireland, 'all seemed to break and dissolve away in the very hour of highest hope and resolve.' He was not criticising the 'gallantry of the peasants' or the courage of those civil war veterans who had travelled to Ireland. 'All honour to the men who made the daring effort and staked their lives upon it.'[5] More directly, and humorously, in a letter to John Martin he both attacked the Ruritanian pretentions of the Fenians, and provided an insight into his own, singular, character:

> Constitutional questions would have raged all around
> me ... a constitution is in itself ridiculous and I being
> acutely sensitive to ridicule, would feel ashamed of

occupying a position in which I would be expected to carry on the sham of a provisional government, and to commission generals for an imaginary army ... So I would have begun by abolishing that 'constitution', by dismissing all secretaries of state, disbanding all paid 'organizers', cancelling all paid 'commissions' to officers, extorting the circles everywhere to keep their money within their own power ... – and *to wait*.[6]

John Mitchel believed in one leader, one voice – his voice. He realized he did not have the patience, the empathy or the ability to compromise, to belong to (even for a short time), or to lead a political movement – armed or unarmed. Mitchel's rejection of the Fenians, and their 'doings or misdoings ... either on the side of Canada or the side of Ireland ... '[7] did not mean he disagreed with their objective and he hankered to be a newspaperman again, writing about Ireland. It was time for the *Irish Citizen*. The place to do it was New York, not Richmond. The family, especially Jenny, agreed; she would love to return to Brooklyn.

John Mitchel had missed his son's wedding, but in October 1867, before the Mitchel's travelled back to New York, Minnie was married to Roger Jones Page, a Confederate Colonel, in St Paul's Church. The groom's father, an Episcopalian minister, performed the ceremony. In a defeated Confederacy the wedding, which five years earlier would have been a major social occasion, was a small affair.[8] Mitchel's report of the wedding, on 3 October to his sister Margaret, Mrs Irvine, was skeletal – as was his comment on his new son-in-law. 'So there, in a few words, you have the bare facts. Page, I suppose you know, is a young lawyer with nothing but his profession ... '[9] If defeated Richmond was experiencing shortages and humiliation, victory brought New York growth and opportunities. In Brooklyn the technological progress John Mitchel disliked allowed his eldest son, James, to open a lithography shop in Duane Street. Compared to a defeated Richmond New York was both developing and accessible. Old friends, who had helped in times of need, were now close by.

This time, however, there would be no welcome from Thomas Francis Meagher. Although he had only been a nominal partner in the 1854 *Citizen* and they had been on different sides during the civil war, and earlier, in the Irish Confederation, Thomas Francis Meagher was a loved constant within the Mitchel family. Before the war, Meagher had visited, lectured in and supported the South. He recognized the dark side of slavery, would have preferred to get rid of it but had not called for abolition. In 1856 he wrote, 'Slavery like every other social institution has its dark side, and it would be well, perhaps if we could get rid of it. But we can't in our time, and therefore should confine our effort to alleviating the evils that accompany it.'[10] Both Mitchel and Meagher wanted to alleviate the suffering of slaves but Mitchel, within his classical world view saw this as an end in itself. Meagher saw it as a step on the road to abolition in the future. When war came Meagher deliberated then joined the Union army but it was not until 1863, in a letter to P.G. Smyth, Nicaragua, was it 'unmistakably clear that Meagher was against slavery.'[11] He rose to command the Irish Brigade. Like Mitchel, Meagher emerged from the civil war damaged. Following the battles of Antietam and Fredericksburg, where the Irish Brigade suffered severe losses, Meagher's military career faltered. He was tainted by rumours of drunkenness.[12] On 1 July1867, whilst acting governor of Montana, he fell overboard from the steamer *Thompson* and was drowned in the Missouri. For John and Jenny another link with 1848 was gone.

After Minnie's wedding Mitchel set up his final paper in New York. It was first published on 19 October 1867. Initially the *Irish Citizen* did well and the whole extended family, including both sets of newly-weds, was able to take a house in Fordham, a pretty village eight miles outside New York.[13] Although it was obviously crowded, following his lonely exile in prison and in Paris, John Mitchel was as happy as a man who had lost half his family, and was in declining health, could be. Perhaps he remembered that he and Jenny had been welcomed in his father and mother's house, in Dromalane, after their own wedding. In Fordham he enjoyed the garden and the company of close friends.[14] Anything else now taxed the sociable John Mitchel.

His energies were focused on his work, on his paper. As befitted an Irish paper it backed the Democrats who before the Civil War had favoured slavery and after hindered Reconstruction. Democratic politicians consistently told immigrants, including the Irish, that freedom and rights for the black man would weaken their chances of employment and even endanger their wives. Frederick Douglass, an escaped slave who, 'perhaps more than any other man of his race, was instrumental in banishing the color line',[15] in a speech in New York in May 1853 referred to the relationship between the Democratic politicians and the Irish as follows:

> The Irish people, warm-hearted, generous, and sympathizing with the oppressed everywhere, when they stand upon their own green island, are instantly taught, on arriving in this Christian country, to hate and despise the colored people. They are taught to believe that we eat the bread which of right belongs to them. The cruel lie is told the Irish, that our adversity is essential to their prosperity.[16]

Although John Mitchel had let the Confederacy go, he held to his thoughts on slavery. Emancipation was a 'monstrous crime'; former slaves wanted a return to the security of the old system.[17] John Mitchel the Roman was holding on to his hierarchy. Losing both a war and two of his sons did not change his perceived truth.

On Ireland too, the aging Mitchel differed little from the young Mitchel. Although his rescuer, Nigaragua Smyth, and his good friend John Martin were moving towards Repeal and Home Rule, accepting an Irish Parliament under the British Crown, Mitchel would have none of it. In the *Irish Citizen* his political honesty alienated both Fenians and the emergent Home Rulers. The paper struggled.

However, the increasingly divergent political opinions of John Mitchel and John Martin did not diminish their friendship. Ties were strengthened in 1868 when Mitchel's best friend married his sister Henrietta; Professor Cornelius O'Shaughnessy (Mitchel's literary pen name in the *Irish Citizen*) looked forward, with relish, to a visit from the mature newly-weds. In September 1868 John and Jenny became grandparents, when Minnie gave birth to John Mitchel Page. The little boy brought joy, especially to his grandfather, who played games with him and allowed an access to his desk denied to others. The great Irish rebel, the scourge of the Carthaginians, hid bananas for little John, nicknamed Buffer, to find.[18] He now fawned on Buffer as he had done, and still did, on Isabel, Rixy. Like her sister, Henrietta, and Minnie before her marriage, Isabel was a catholic, which may help explain why Professor Cornelius O'Shaughnessy wrote a tolerant article about the recent visions and Bernadette in Lourdes. 'And this, in the latter half of the nineteenth century! Yes, even so; and better might it be for the said century if these things did not seem so incredible and grotesque.'[19]

Perhaps implicit here is Mitchel's consistent dislike of the Enlightenment, science, utilitarianism and progress. Mitchel did not accept the observable, the physical world as the grounds for reasoning. He rejected empiricism. 'The truest text is the one with the least connection to the physical world, leaving the writer in a universe of textuality.'[20] Thus wrote Chris Morash, when commenting upon Mitchel's imaginative meandering through *Jail Journal*. For Yeats, when John Mitchel 'thundered from his convict hulk' he was communing with 'the great Gods'[21] – Mitchel's text, his 'savage prose'[22] was instinctive and passionate. It was inspired rather than *enlightened*. William Carleton from County Tyrone, who wrote intimately about the Irish county life of tenant farmers, referred to a 'ferocious and brutal violence of language; not the language of common sense or common feeling, but of political insanity.'[23] Insane or not Mitchel agreed with Dickens in rejecting utilitarianism; in rejecting the Gradgrindian statement, 'You can only form the mind of reasoning animals upon Facts.'[24]

Mitchel's refusal to dismiss the stories coming from Lourdes would have pleased his old friend Father Kenyon, who died on 21 March 1869. Commenting on how John and Jenny would miss the priest, John Martin praised him. 'It is a huge piece of our lives is cut off … I could not, with hard trying, note down half the qualities that made him so charming and so dear to us.'[25] In the autumn of 1869 when Mr and Mrs John Martin finally arrived for a visit Mitchel had tired of living so far out of the city, at Fordham, and the family had returned to Brooklyn to Carleton Avenue. Although the fifty-five year-old John Mitchel was in declining health he was greatly cheered by, and enjoyed, the visit of his sister and his very old friend and new brother-in-law. William Dillon described their friendship well.

> Mitchel and Martin had the same interminable talks and smokes of old. They disputed over Irish politics;

could hardly ever agree, abused one another, and loved one another as much as ever.'[26] As in the County Down of their youth, they still loved walking, talking and smoking.

One dispute over Irish politics centred on John Martin's desire to become a member of the British parliament; a desire expressed in an earlier letter to John Mitchel. 'To say the truth I wish some constituency would select me on my own terms for its M.P. I would go to London and I would speak in their parliament.'[27] But the Home Ruler John Martin and the Republican John Mitchel united in their support of the memory of the Manchester Martyrs. They both attended, and spoke at, a meeting in aid of the Manchester Martyrs, William Philip Allen, Michael Larkin and Michael O'Brien, in the Cooper Institute, New York in the winter of 1869.[28] Allen, Larkin and O'Brien were hanged on 23 November 1867 for alleged involvement in the rescue of two Fenians, Thomas Kelly and Timothy Deasy, in Manchester. A police officer was killed during the rescue.[29] Nationalist Ireland held that the three men were innocent and it was John Martin who had given the oration at their mock funeral (they were hanged and buried in England) on 8 December 1867 in Glasnevin Cemetery. He proclaimed:

The three bodies that we would tenderly bear to the churchyard, and would bury in consecrated ground with all the solemn rites of religion, are not here...they were not murderers. These men were pious men, virtuous men - they were men who feared God and loved their country...It was as Irish patriots that these men were doomed to death...[30]

The widespread support across Irish nationalism for republicans who were executed by the British or died seeking political legitimacy for their armed struggle was repeated after the 1916 Rising and during the 1981 Hunger Strikes. Both produced great subsequent electoral success for republicanism.

In New York in 1870, John and Jenny were cheered by the presence of old, dear friends. The declining Mitchel were even ready to succumb to the joys of whist. Such was their sadness at the imminent leaving of the Martins that they were persuaded to 'postpone their departure for one more week.'[31]

Theirs was not the only departure to sadden John and Jenny Mitchel. 'Our dear Minnie and her department of the household are to go uptown in New York, which vexes us.'[32] The vexed Mitchels moved from Carleton Avenue to Lafayette Avenue in Brooklyn and a very hot summer that yielded a great abundance of grapes, peaches and oysters 'and what more would people have?'[33] Perhaps the answer was security. In contrast to Van Diemen's Land where he employed and was surrounded by felons, Mitchel now reported ghastly, nightly murders. He continued to travel and to write 'odious articles'. When his brother William suggested he might return to Ireland and live quietly he dismissed the idea. What would he live on? He would not return a penitent.[34] Minnie and his grandson moved even further away to West Virginia. 'My poor Minnie is all alone beyond the mountains, six hundred miles from here, in a little town upon a river which runs Mississippi-ward. Yesterday we had a letter from her, with likeness of her famous little boy, who is certainly a first rate buffer.'[35] The division of opinion over future direction in Ireland was evident in correspondence with old friends. Mitchel attacked John Martin and P.J. Smyth, Nicaragua, for considering standing for the Westminster parliament. However, in a 1871 letter to Smyth he was keen to separate a growing political difference from old friendships and loyalty. Having stated his objection to his friend's constitutional ambitions Mitchel wrote, 'Yet I would expect you and do expect you to take all that as implying no hint of a selfish or unpatriotic purpose.'[36] He went on to recall thoughts,

> ... of old times, and of the shores of Lake Sorel, and of Bothwell, and of San Franscisco, and later still of the last time you and I met – travelling together on the top of a diligence from Bernieres to Caen – and though I thought that you had been too abrupt with me I never thought of you with less regard ... [37]

In May 1872, the Mitchels moved again to Long Island and the seaside. For most of this summer they had their beloved Minnie and Buffer, John Mitchel Page, with them. However, John's eyesight continued to decline. With a poor circulation and his own difficulty in reading and writing, John Mitchel closed his last newspaper. The final edition of the *Irish Citizen* was dated 27 July 1872. Perhaps with less stress, with his grandson close and walks along the seaside John's health and temperament improved and to those around him he seemed happier and in better health during the fall of 1872 than he had been for several years before.[38] The arrival of another grandchild, a daughter for James and Elisabeth, also helped lift his spirits. With the summer over they left the seaside and moved to West Fifty Sixth Street, New York. In a letter to John Martin, Mitchel described a comfortable, French style apartment, 'including a good kitchen, spacious bathroom, the whole heated by steam heaters which we find very satisfactory. And we have an "elevator" or dumb waiter for bringing up all parcels. In short housekeeping is here reduced to its minimum of botheration and of uncleanness.'[39] This is an aspect of progress, of modernity of which John Mitchel obviously approved. Given Jenny's housework in Richmond one assumes she also heartily approved.

Mitchel described himself, to Martin, as a 'penny-a-liner', for the *Irish American*. He found such writing 'irksome' and admitted only doing it for the money. To increase his income he would use long words where a short one would suffice; 'for every letter counts.'[40] However, passion rather than income was to the fore when Mitchel entered into a personal and political duel with 'the scoundrel Froude'.

James Anthony Froude was an English historian who like Mitchel admired Thomas Carlyle and the role of the hero in history. However during a tour of America, although he delivered his lectures with charm and style Froude demonstrated a 'prejudice against the Irish' and the *Irish American* employed Mitchel to respond.[41] Again, John Mitchel made no effort to distinguish between the issue and the man. To Mitchel, James Anthony Froude's views on Irish history were 'odious' and he attacked them with 'vindictive spite'.[42] He wrote, 'We have enough of Froude. He is already a notoriously convicted imposter and no historian, and it is making too much of him to pursue him in this way.'[43] What annoyed the Presbyterian-born Mitchel most was Froude's claim that 'the cause of the Catholic religion and Irish independence became inseparably and irrevocably one.'[44] Given that as far back as 1848 he had warned of the need to involve and welcome the 'Saxon Irishmen of the North'[45] into the national movement Mitchel's reaction was predictable. Although Wolfe Tone and John Mitchel were very different, with Tone's Republicanism a product of the Enlightenment, and Mitchel's ideas owing 'more to an austere classical republicanism,'[46] Aidan

O'Hegarty argued that they were the only nationalist leaders who had attempted to reason with Ulster Protestants.[47] Naturally Mitchel thought he won his duel with Froude.

With the family growing up Jenny had more time, and a companion in Isabel, who had grown into a beautiful young woman. However, she also had mounting worries about money and John's health. She knew he was becoming increasingly nostalgic for Ireland. In a letter to his sister Matilda, Mitchel wrote, 'I do hate this city and this country and would like nothing so well as the chance of spending the remainder of my days amongst my own people … I wish I were at Tullucairne, and could stroll down the Lagan and wade a little.'[48] However, he also suggested that if he were in Ireland he would soon get into trouble by opposing Home Rule. He wondered how he ever stayed out of a French gaol.[49] This letter, to Matilda, is indicative, not only of nostalgia for his youth, but also of an increasing interest in Ireland and her affairs. Interest in America was waning. During the summer of 1873 fate had more bitter blows ready, especially for James who had suffered enormously during the war. His wife, Elisabeth, died and within a few days his young daughter also died. Faithful James, much admired by the Hoosiers and the Confederate military, bore his loss with a stoicism inherited from his father – a father who also had to bear the sudden loss of a much-loved granddaughter and daughter-in-law. John Mitchel's health declined further.

Without a newspaper, with sickness limiting lucrative lecturing opportunities and with James finding it difficult to get work, the family's income was declining. They moved again to cheaper homes, ending up on Clinton Avenue, Brooklyn. Their friends, especially John and William Dillon (Mitchel's first biographer), the sons of John Blake Dillon, were aware of the Mitchels' reduced circumstances and a testimonial fund from Ireland provided $10,000. John was embarrassed and he wrote to his brother William, 'and I need not tell you how humiliating to me is this "testimonial" movement.'[50] John Mitchel preferred to keep his troubles to himself or, as he wrote to William, 'consume his own smoke.'[51] Given what we now know of the dangers of smoking, it could be a metaphor for his unwillingness to contemplate any ideas but his own, for the consequences of his decisions.

The winter of 1873–4 was a bad one for John Mitchel. He was very ill for weeks. The visit of Minnie and her son cheered him up and by the spring he was feeling much better. Jenny, who would find him looking at the map of Ireland, 'from top to bottom, from side to side'[52] and twisting his now grey lock, knew he had to go home.[53] It was more than sentiment; John Mitchel had a lingering thirst for Irish politics. He had mixed feelings about John Martin's Home Rule election victory, for the Meath constituency in January 1871. He was glad his friend was successful and consoled himself that Martin was still, at heart, a republican who would not take his seat. Alas, for Mitchel, Martin was now a confirmed constitutionalist.

Mitchel's own first foray into Irish electoral politics, during the 1874 general election, was at a distance and was a failure. He stood in Cork as an independent nationalist, with no intention of taking his seat and the Home Rule candidate soundly beat him.[54] John Mitchel finished last. However, the *Nation* suggested that this was because 'it was not universally believed at the last election that the candidature started in his name had Mr. Mitchel's sanction.'[55] Despite the Cork result, John Mitchel had announced he was back in the game; and that game was becoming more interesting. In November 1873 a meeting in the Rotunda, in Dublin, where Mitchel had spoken passionately as a Young Irelander, had brought

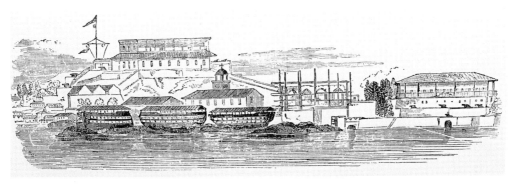

19. Prison hulks in Bermuda: the *Dromedary* is to the right and is where Mitchel contemplated suicide. 'I hope to do my children some good before I die.'

20. Mitchel's childhood home: his children were staying here when he wrote 'It is deep in the night … we are not far from the meridian of Newry, though six thousand miles to the South and I know that this white disc struggling here through Atlantic storm clouds is the very globe of silver that hangs tonight between the branches of the laurels of Dromalane.'

21. John Martin was helpful, loyal and sometimes insulted, but remained a lifelong friend.

22. Meagher's Cottage: Mitchel's sketch of Meagher's Van Diemen's Land house.

23. Isabel (Rixy) Mitchel was born in Van Diemen's Land. 'The dearest, sweetest, loveliest child that ever a mother's heart could desire.' (Courtesy Pat Brown)

24. Nicaragua (P.J.) Smyth: an agent of the Irish New York Directory, sent to aid the escape of John Mitchel.

25. Nant Cottage: as Mitchel was escaping he passed by Nant Cottage, his 'little quasi-home … with all its sleeping inmates lulled by the murmuring Clyde'.

26. Young Ireland and Fenian Monument, Glasnevin: Terence Bellew McManus, a hero of 1848 who escaped from Van Diemen's Land and died in the USA, is buried here. His funeral did much to excite interest and passion in the Fenian cause.

27. The *Cortes*: the ship that took the Mitchels from San Francisco to San Juan del Jour. (O'Connor Papers)

28. Mitchel Sign in Tennessee: although still remembered in Tucaleechee Cove, Mitchel was keen to leave the wilderness and return to a Knoxville of 5,000 people.

29. John Mitchel: the southern gentleman much approved of by the Hoosiers. This is the volatile Mitchel who broke a stick on a rival editor. (Courtesy Pat Brown)

30. Edmund Ruffin was an extreme Confederate who liked Mitchel but thought his *Southern Citizen* newspaper so extreme that it could harm the southern cause. (Library of Congress)

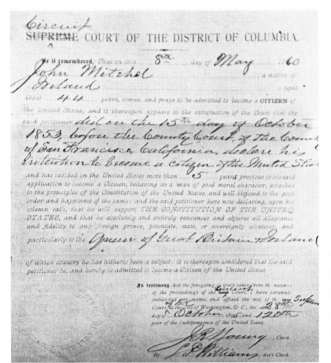

31. Naturalisation Certificate: in May 1860, before he returned to Paris with Jenny and the younger children, John Mitchel became a citizen of the United States. (O'Connor Papers)

CAPTAIN JOHN E. DOOLEY, C.S.A.

John Dooley
Confederate Soldier
HIS WAR JOURNAL

Edited by JOSEPH T. DURKIN, S.J.
Professor of American History,
Georgetown University

Foreword by
DOUGLAS SOUTHALL FREEMAN
Author of *R. E. Lee*, *Lee's Lieutenants*, Etc.

GEORGETOWN UNIVERSITY PRESS
1945

The Sitterding Foundation

32. Captain John Dooley was an Irish Catholic who recorded the death of his friend, Private Willie Mitchel. His father, the retired Major Dooley and John Mitchel, went into the Confederate camps to visit their sons. It was Major Dooley who finally broke the bad news of Willie's death to John Mitchel.

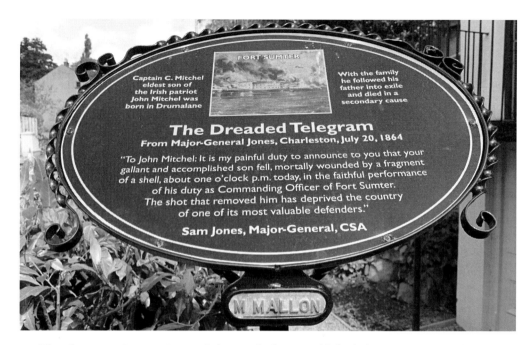

FORT SUMTER

Captain C. Mitchel
eldest son of
the Irish patriot
John Mitchel was
born in Drumalane

With the family
he followed his
father into exile
and died in a
secondary cause

The Dreaded Telegram
From Major-General Jones, Charleston, July 20, 1864

"To John Mitchel: It is my painful duty to announce to you that your gallant and accomplished son fell, mortally wounded by a fragment of a shell, about one o'clock p.m. today, in the faithful performance of his duty as Commanding Officer of Fort Sumter. The shot that removed him has deprived the country of one of its most valuable defenders."

Sam Jones, Major-General, CSA

M MALLON

33. The plaque to Captain C. Mitchel, outside his grandfather's home, is surrounded by the laurels mentioned by his father in *Jail Journal*. It was erected to commemorate the 150th anniversary of the young captain's death.

34. Captain C. Mitchel: in 1896 Jenny presented her eldest son's sword, and the flag that flew over Sumter on the day he was killed, to Charleston Museum.

35. The plaque commemorating John Mitchel's imprisonment in Fortress Monroe. (Courtesy Kelly J. O'Grady)

36. Three Old Friends: John Martin, John Mitchel and Father Kenyon. 'Over these pleasant days in Paris impends a kind of a shadow. We three old friends, when we part this time, will probably never meet again, altogether.' (Courtesy Pat Brown)

37. Dromalane houses: in his absence, John Mitchel's brother-in-law Hill Irvine added the dressed granite house to the back of the Revd John Mitchel's older house. John Mitchel died in the room to the left of the laurels. (Courtesy Hannah Russell)

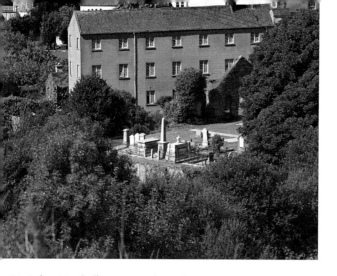

38. John Mitchel's graveyard, High Street, Newry: Mitchel lies with his parents in the tomb to the left of the obelisk. Jenny's tribute is to the far left. (Courtesy Hannah Russell)

39. Jenny's tribute: it is not the Celtic c she originally wanted.

40. A 1970s political protest at Mitchel's statue, but not against his involvement in slavery. Few people were aware of that aspect of his politics. They were protesting against Ireland's membership of the Common Market.

41. The statue of John Mitchel: he stands, confide with his books, demanding to be heard. It is statue to a man who was heroic; to a man wh more than any other writer or politician, defin the nationalist perception of the Great Famine. is a statue to a rebel. It is not a statue to a gre revolutionary. (Courtesy Hannah Russell)

together the Land Party, the Catholic Education Party, the remnants of the Repeal Party, and the Fenians with a view to nationalist unity. Such unity needed strong, much-admired candidates. Despite many differences with very many people, Mitchel, because of his consistent integrity, had grown into an elder, nationalist statesman. He wrote to John Dillon, who had helped organise a fund for him, about a possible return to Ireland to stand for parliament.[56] After negotiations about standing in Tipperary, the *Irish American* announced, 'we are authorized to state that not only will Mr. Mitchel accept the candidacy thus tendered ... but that he will at once go over to Ireland and if elected will represent his constituency.'[57] After twenty-six years, John Mitchel was returning to Ireland.

For Jenny it raised questions. She knew John needed to go home but was he fit for it? How would the British react to him? He was still an escaped felon and even a more lenient British jail term would kill him. How would his potential supporters, many of whom his caustic pen had insulted, react to him? Would the people be interested in a man from another age, from 1848? Should she go to Ireland with him?

The family discussions yielded the following result. John would go to Ireland. Isabel would go with him and Dr William Carroll would be on hand to look after health issues. Jenny and James would remain in Brooklyn. It would be mainly a private rather than a public visit, testing the response of his fellow countrymen and the willingness, or otherwise, of the British to reopen old wounds. There were several reasons why Jenny did not travel, She was now middle-aged and had responsibilities in America, was always seasick and they had very little money.

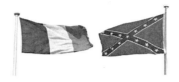

CHAPTER THIRTEEN

How Pleased My Poor Wife Will Be

On 1 June 1848, having said goodbye, four days earlier, to Jenny and his young sons, John Mitchel was taken from Cork. In late July 1874, twenty-six years later, he returned to Queenstown (Cobh) with his beautiful, young daughter Isabel and Dr Carroll. He was returning with failing vision and in poor health. Given the adventures, tragedies and deaths it was an emotional return but John Mitchel was able to raise a smile. 'I left Queenstown twenty six years ago in a shower I see it hasn't stopped since.' He was well received in Cork and it lifted his spirits. On 27 July John Martin received a letter from his sister Mary, the wife of Professor Simpson, University College Cork. Maxwell Simpson, Professor of Chemistry, was a childhood friend of both Mitchel and Martin from their days in Dr Henderson's Classical School, Newry.[1] In the letter to her brother, Mary provided a hopeful description of the returned exile: 'He was so glad to see me and so kind. He is splendid still; there is any amount of life in him. It is said that he is broken down by the journey; but he is vastly better of it and has no look of sickness or delicacy ...'[2]

However, the *Freeman's Journal* did not agree. It wrote of 'a prematurely aged, and enfeebled man.'[3] After a few days to recover from the journey John Mitchel headed for the north and on 30 July

1874 he arrived back in Newry, the town he loved, the town where he met Jenny. He arrived by rail, which had not existed before he left. 'A large crowd had assembled at Dublin Bridge Station to welcome the popular "48 man" and the moment he alighted from the carriage the cheering was tremendous. Mr. Mitchel acknowledged this compliment but excused himself from making a speech, owing to the delicate nature of his health. He was met at the station by his brother-in-law, Mr Hill Irvine J.P. and proceeded to that gentleman's residence, followed by a large number of persons cheering enthusiastically.'[4]

The 'gentleman's residence' was John Mitchel's boyhood home. It was still surrounded by the laurels, mentioned by John in mid Atlantic, as in the moonlight, he thought of his children. It was extended by Hill Irvine when he built Dromalane linen spinning mill. With cotton's availability reduced on the world market by civil war, with the death of the Confederacy, the production of more expensive linen expanded. Newry, with an enlarged and extended ship canal, with several new mills and workshops, was sharing in this prosperity. When the news spread that John Mitchel was back, thousands of people assembled at Fathom at nine o'clock 'and proceeded in a torch lit procession around the main streets of Newry. The steamer *Alphine,* then lying in the Albert Basin, fired rockets and its guns at regular intervals.'[5] John's sister, Margaret, warmly welcomed him and Isabel. There followed days visiting old friends and favourite places. After Newry John and Isabel moved to Dromore and his sister Matilda, Mrs Dickson. Here he could fulfill the wish, expressed in an earlier letter to Matilda, and walk along the banks of the Lagan at Tullycairn. They returned to Newry and on 3 September John wrote to Jenny. It was Isabel who had been doing most of the writing. He told Jenny of going to a gentlemen's dinner in Warrenpoint and he speculated about putting his oar into 'the puddle of Irish politics'. Although he professed reluctance he did suggest that if 'an opening should be made for me to stand for the representation of some county or borough, then indeed, I would "sail in", and you might pray for me.' It was an indication of his serious intent that in the same letter he asked Jenny to put James on standby to come to Ireland to help him campaign.[6]

With Mitchel opposed to both the Fenians and John Martin's Home Rule how could he re-enter Irish politics? As he prepared to go back to Dublin from Newry, a letter written to P.J. Smyth, Nicaragua, provides an insight into his thought. It is dated 3 September 1874 and in it he declared, 'I will be the guest of no "Home Ruler" in Dublin, not even John Martin. In fact I am savage against that hapless, driftless concern called "Home Rule" and nearly as vicious against your simple repeal.' However Mitchel goes on to say that if he 'were under any obligation (which I am not) to enter Irish politics I would prefer to do so simply seeking the repeal of the Act of Union.'[7] Before leaving Ireland he would agree to stand for the British parliament on the understanding that he would, under no circumstances, take his seat. When he got to Dublin John Mitchel wrote again to P.J. Smyth reinforcing the message. 'I keep myself very aloof from Home Rulers and such species of folks ...' but he did invite his old rescuer to visit him.[8] In Dublin, whilst staying with his sister Mary, John Mitchel and Isabel were celebrities. Old friends, including the Martins, visited him. Old dead friends, from three continents, were remembered. John Mitchel travelled much, in and around the Dublin area, but due to his poor health, he accepted few dinner invitations. One exception was a visit, with Isabel, to 1 Merrion Square, the home of Oscar Wilde's mother – *Speranza* the poetess from the *Nation,* and she whom Meagher had called his Lake Sorel boat after.

As an eighteen-year-old Anglo-Protestant Miss Jane Francesca Elgee, later Lady Wilde, was 'quite indifferent to the national movement and if I thought about it at all I probably had a very bad opinion of the leaders. For my family was Protestant and Conservative, and there was no social intercourse between them and the Catholics and Nationalists.'[9] However, after reading the *Nation* she was enthused by Gavan Duffy and radicalized by John Mitchel. She became his 'whole hearted disciple'[10] and in an article *Jacta Alea Est* (The Die is Cast) on 29 July 1848 she 'urged armed revolt in the cause of Irish freedom.' Such was her popularity that, even after she had married William Wilde, later Sir William, she was cheered as she was driven through the streets to functions in Dublin Castle.[11] By 1874, the widow of Sir William Wilde was also short of funds but remained a leading figure in the social, artistic and literary life of the capital. John Mitchel and Isabel enjoyed a memorable and pleasant dinner. In a letter, following the evening, Lady Wilde referred to Mitchel's 'sad, brilliant life of genius, pain and suffering' and to 'his lovely daughter'. For Lady Wilde Isabel was the *Angel of the Captivity*; for her father she was *Isabel of the Fetters.*[12]

Appropriately, given its role in the literary life of Dublin, it was opposite Lady Wildes's house, 1 Merrion Square, by the railings of Merrion Park, that 30 years later James Joyce waited to meet Nora Barnacle, for their first date. Nora did not show up. Mitchel and Joyce shared an admiration for, and wrote about, the Young Ireland poet James Clarence Mangan who lived a short tragic life, dependent upon alcohol and narcotics. He was found dying in a cellar in Bride Street. T.F. O'Sullivan commented that for the author of *Dark Rosaleen*, 'Misery and despair were his portion not only for a day or for a week, but during almost the whole of his forty six years.'[13] After the split in Young Ireland Mangan supported the *United Irishman* and Mitchel rejoiced in Mangan's Irishness, in his anti-Britishness. In the introduction to an 1866 American edition of Mangan's poetry he declared:

> For this Mangan was not only an Irishman - not only an Irish papist, - not only an Irish papist rebel; - but throughout his whole literary life of twenty years, he never deigned to attorn to English criticism, never published a line in any English periodical, or through any English bookseller, never seemed to be aware that there was a British public to please. He was a rebel politically and a rebel intellectually and spiritually – a rebel with his whole heart and soul against the whole British spirit of the age.[14]

In 1897 the critic Louise Imogen Guiney thought Mitchel strongly overestimated Mangan's dislike of Britain; 'that, whilst he mocked the English from time to time, he espoused no cause and was a man of characteristically gentle judgement...'[15] More recently Andrew Gibson has suggested that 'Joyce's Mangan', as portrayed in his 1902 lecture to the Historical Society at University College Dublin, lacked the 'anguish and rage' of 'Mitchel's Mangan'. However, in sounding archaic, it did connect 'Joyce more generally with a Mitchelite tradition...in commentary on Mangan.' For example Joyce wrote 'All his poetry remembers wrong and suffering and the aspiration of one who has suffered and who is moved to great cries and gestures when that sorrowful hour rushed upon the heart.'[16]

Whilst Mitchel was an influence on Joyce's work on Mangan in 'Under Ben Bulben' W. B. Yeats made a more direct literary reference to John Mitchel, quoting him as he sought a perspective on the 1916 Rising:

> You that Mitchel's prayer have heard,
> 'Send war in our time, O Lord!'
> Know that when all words are said
> And a man is fighting mad,
> Something drops from eyes long blind,
> He completes his partial mind,
> For an instant stands at ease,
> Laughs aloud, his heart at peace.
> Even the wisest man grows tense
> With some sort of violence
> Before he can accomplish fate,
> Know his work or choose his mate.

Malcolm Brown, in a critical review of Mitchel, suggested that Mitchel's famous war cry referred to his hope that Britain would not remain at peace and Ireland's opportunity would come sooner rather than later. Alas for Mitchel, Pax Britannica would last ninety-nine years 'between Waterloo and Ypres.'[17] For Mitchel, this was not something to be celebrated. This was not progress. This was 'the canker of peace' that will 'kill the soul of nations and of men.'[18] Although Mitchel wrote these words in 1854, and war would decimate his family, he did continue to support physical force, but only when the timing was right.

More recently, 'written in the wake of the Hunger Strikes of 1980–1981'[19] Paul Muldoon's poem *Yggdrasil* makes an 'opaque' reference to both Mitchel's inverted prayer and its Crimean War context:

> for a legend:
> It may not be today
> Or tomorrow. But sooner or later
> the Russians will water
> their horses on the shores of Lough Erne
> and Lough Neagh.[20]

With a setting contemporaneous with the Great Famine Brian Friel's play *Translations* echoes John Mitchel's political thought: ' ... the idea of the beautiful failure of the Irish interest in the culture of the ancient Romans and Greeks, as against the crude success of the British interest in imperialism, commerce and trade.'[21] In support of this idea Kieran Bonner quotes the hedge schoolmaster Hugh, admitting his ignorance of English Literature to the British officer, Captain Yolland: 'Wordsworth? ... No. I'm afraid we're not familiar with your literature, Lieutenant. We feel closer to the warm waters of the Mediterranean. We tend to overlook your island.'[22]

After Dublin John and Isabel, with different family members, at different times, visited Killarney and Cork before they returned to America. During his visit to Ireland the Carthaginians kept an eye on Mitchel but did not impede his progress. He had caused them legal difficulties before and they knew he was now a weak, sick and aging man. Doing nothing was the better option. Mitchel left John Martin the promise to return, and an election address, to be published in the *Nation,* if a suitable vacancy arose. As he sailed from Ireland on the *Minnesota,* Mitchel wrote to his sister Matilda. 'Now that it is all over the two months seem like a vision of the night but a very pleasant picture on the whole – or rather a succession of pictures. I will hang them in the gallery of my memory and imagination, framed in gold … '[23] That image 'framed in gold' was the one Mitchel had used to express his 1854 joy at the reception he received in Virginia University.

In October 1874, Jenny welcomed back a reinvigorated man. He had enjoyed his visit, and his status as the elder statesman of Irish nationalism. In this role, in December 1874, John Mitchel addressed the Cooper Institute in New York.

The audience included O'Donovan Rossa, who was to play a similar role to that the deceased Terence Bellew McManus played in November 1861, when the emergent Fenian movement sent his body to Dublin for a funeral to promote their cause. In 1915, O'Donovan Rossa's body was also sent across the Atlantic for a mass funeral in Glasnevin. Here Pearse declared, 'They have left us our Fenian dead, and while Ireland holds these graves, Ireland unfree shall never be at peace.'[24] Thus, O'Donovan Rossa's presence in Mitchel's audience in 1874 was to be a link between 1848, 1866–7 and 1916.

In his lecture *Ireland Revisited*, in front of prominent Irish Americans, John Mitchel reflected upon his visit. Whilst in Ireland, Mitchel declared, 'My mouth was shut, my eyes and ears open.' In his speech he dismissed his friend John Martin as being naïve, attending Westminister as 'a demoralizing practice' and he condemned Home Rulers as foreign rulers. However, he also suggested, to loud cheers, that England needed to be 'beaten to her knees' and the Home Rulers were representing the I.R.B. (Irish Republican Brotherhood) and a 'great mass of silent, quiet power now holding itself … ready should an opportunity arise.'[25] Such sentiments suggest the aging Mitchel had changed little from his *United Irishman* writing. He avowedly hated progress. He was not for transformation. Bitter personal experience of the battlefield, and of loss, had not diluted his physical force ardour, had not significantly transformed his analysis of Ireland's problems.

In contrast to Mitchel, when visiting Wexford on 15 May 1865, D'Arcy McGee, then a Canadian minister, declared,

> I was one of the Young Ireland fugitives in 1848. I am not at all ashamed of Young Ireland – Why should I? Politically we were a pack of fools, but we were honest in our folly; and no man need blush at forty for the faults of one-and-twenty, unless, indeed he still perseveres in them, having no longer the fair excuse to plead youth and inexperience.[26]

The Fenians did not agree. On 15 April 1868 D'Arcy McGee fell to an assassin's bullet, possibly a Fenian's, on Sparks Street, Ottawa; after he had bitterly attacked the 1866 Fenian invasion of Canada; after he had promoted 'unity in diversity'; after he had played a major role in helping create the Canadian confederation; after he had compromised with the Orange Prime Minister, John A. McDonald and after he had crossed the floor to serve in a conservative cabinet. McGee paid the ultimate price for his transformation, from 1848 Irish physical force rebel to Canadian Loyalist. Honoured in Canada, in Ireland he was swept aside by the flow of Irish history and rarely mentioned, until 2012 and the Canadian Embassy's promotion of the D'Arcy McGee Summer School, in Carlingford, where McGee was born. Also, in contrast to Mitchel, the previous year, in 1873, his old enemy, Gavan Duffy accepted a British knighthood after serving as Prime Minister of Victoria 1871–2. In *Four Years of Irish History*,

Sir Gavan Duffy reflected on 1848; the year, which A.B. Hamilton suggested, 'sent a electric thrill through discontented Europe', and when 'successful rebellion seemed practicable and easy'.[27] In his reflection, Sir Gavan Duffy regretted his, and Young Ireland's 1848 sudden, heated conversion to supporting armed rebellion. With reference to the Confederation he wrote:

> We can now perceive that their first work was their wisest and best, and that Irish nationality would have fared better if there had never been a French Revolution in 1848. That transaction arrested a work which was a necessary preliminary to social or political independence: the education of a people long depressed by poverty or injustice, in fair play, public spirit, and manliness. All that had been achieved up to that time was swallowed up by famine, emigration, and unsuccessful insurrection.

However, this older Duffy, who had proudly held 'the highest office of state in a community which was English and Scotch, by an overwhelming majority', also wrote that he would not exchange the memory of his rebellious involvement for 'anything that parliaments or Sovereigns can give or take away.' He insisted, 'for though men fail, and means and agencies are modified, a true cause is immortal.' Duffy ended *Four Years of Irish History* by suggesting that the English eventually come to understand Irish rebellions. For example, 'Lord Holland, a cabinet minister under William IV, declared that the government of Ireland, in the eighteenth century, justified Lord Edward Fitzgerald in appealing to arms.'[28] Duffy hoped history would say the same of Smith O'Brien's 1848 rebellion. His own experience, when an Australian Victorian parliament of

English and Scotch accepted him and refused to condemn his past rebellious actions, suggested this might be the case. Thus, playing the long game and engaging with the British system was a better way. A constitutional approach was superior and ultimately more successful than physical force. Whilst Mitchel had no doubt as to the immortal nature of Ireland's cause, a transformation that left an Irishman sitting in a British parliament, no matter where, and accepting high office and honours, was not the honourable way to achieve freedom. The political journeys of Young Ireland, following 1848, were as diverse as their personalities and their geography.

Alas, John Mitchel's asthma was as constant as his attitude to Ireland's problems and he became too ill to lecture, too ill to visit 'My dear and darling little daughter Minnie' and his grandson, John Page, in Louisville. However, on 6 February 1875 he wrote to Minnie to tell her he was going back to Ireland to fight the Tipperary election. He told her James was going with him and abandoning 'his position in the Photo-Litog, not very eminent or lucrative, indeed, but something.'[29] He knew that with James and he in Ireland Jenny and Isabel would be 'two lonely birds'. He ended the letter with a poignant, 'And so, my darling Minnie, adieu.'[30] Again, Jenny who had crossed oceans to be with him, let John go back to Ireland without her. Having nursed him through the winter she must have known he was very sick, but in the nature of his illness he had down times followed by periods of improved health; and he had survived his last visit to Ireland. Having watched John and her family suffer so much for Ireland she would have strongly agreed with John Martin. 'No living Irishman better deserves the highest political honour his country can bestow.'[31] This, at last, was an opportunity for a political victory. Mitchel left for Ireland, with the unselfish James, on 6 February 1875.

In the election address, left behind with John Martin, John Mitchel had skillfully used his pen to take two positions at once; two positions that would ironically allow him to be presented as a unity candidate. He stated, 'I am for Home Rule – that is the sovereign independence of Ireland.' Further down the document after, among other things, calling for the disestablishment of the Church of Ireland, tenant rights, free choice in education and the release of Fenian prisoners he baldly stated, 'Lastly as well as firstly, I am for *home rule*.'[32] But in his initial comments he had already qualified the statement. However, in a letter to Charles J. Kickham, who had been with Smith O'Brien in 1848 and was sentenced to fourteen years as a Fenian leader in November 1865[33]; John Martin advised Kickham of Mitchel standing for the British parliament but that he was in no doubt his friend was 'neither impartial nor friendly' towards Home Rule.[34] As we have seen, upon his return to the USA, John Mitchel had been direct in is condemnation of Home Rule, and insulting to John Martin. However, although Mitchel's 'disrespectful remarks' hurt John Martin, and robbed him of any hope Mitchel might embrace Home Rule, Martin did ask Mitchel to treat Home Rule 'with neutrality, not quite a respectful neutrality at the first, but still a fair neutrality.'[35] John Martin, Duffy's peacemaker in Bryansford in 1845, remained tolerant of his friend John Mitchel to the end. After an eleven-day voyage John Mitchel MP landed in Queenstown as a member of the British parliament. As he was crossing the Atlantic, he had been returned unopposed. However, Prime Minister Disraeli, whose novel the *Young Duke* John and Jenny were reading when the unfortunate Captain James Verner discovered them in Chester, asked the House, to which Mitchel had just been elected, to disqualify him. He was still a convicted and not fully unpunished felon. At Westminster, despite the best efforts of

John Martin and other Irish members, the writ for a new election was issued.

Mitchel responded to the news of his election and disqualification by heading by train for Tipperary. Crowds met him at each station. From Limerick Junction bands and banners escorted him into Tipperary town. It was a very tired and very sick John Mitchel who, in the presence of Mr and Mrs John Martin, P.J. Smyth and other old friends, made his final public speech. In this humorous speech he referred to Disraeli, among other things, as a novel writer.[36] Perhaps, he had a particular novel in mind. The transatlantic journey and electioneering had taken much out of John Mitchel. At Clonmel and Cork, despite huge crowds and great expectation, he only managed a few words. Very weak, he wanted to return home to Newry. On the 9 March he left Cork, with his sister Henrietta Martin, and headed first for Dublin and then Newry. From his wife, Henrietta, John Martin learned that his friend, John Mitchel, was dying. 'Poor Mitchel is nearly through his tumbled earthly career. He is very feeble … He is not likely - from what Mrs Martin writes me – ever to appear on a public platform again.' [37] As in 1848 when Mitchel was being exiled from Dublin it was women who came to his aid. According to the local press the women of Tipperary pledged, 'we will never walk with, talk with, cook for, wash for, court, marry, or countenance, but let live and die as they like any man who will not vote for and support John Mitchel.'[38] Perhaps the threat worked. On 12 March the news came that John Mitchel had beaten the Tory candidate Captain Stephen Moore by 3,114 votes to 716, in the second Tipperary election. Mitchel proclaimed, 'How pleased Jenny will be to hear all this; how pleased my poor wife will be.'[39] The Mitchels were finally on a winning side.

Although confined to his bed, in his old room in Newry, there must have been no immediate concern for Mitchel's health as he insisted James return to his mother in New York. However, when word was then sent to Jenny that he was 'sinking' Jenny readied to go to Newry.[40] Perhaps, as often before, Mitchel thought he was again recovering when he told his brother William, 'I feel better this morning; I think I will soon rise.'[41] They were his last words. John Mitchel fell asleep and, in contrast with his life, died peacefully. It was 20 March 1875. Jenny received the news with a mixture of grief and pride. She did not travel to Ireland.[42] James learned of his father's death when he landed in New York.

CHAPTER FOURTEEN

Jenny Without John

Over twenty years earlier, in letters to female friends, John Mitchel, conscious of his growing unpopularity in Australia and Ireland over his pro-slavery stance, had requested that they did not judge him too harshly. Miss Thompson of Ravensdale, to whom both John and Jenny revealed much about their lives and attitudes, especially on slavery, retained an admiration and affection for John Mitchel. In a poem, *In Memoriam (On the death of John Mitchel, 20th March, 1875)*, she wrote of his sacrifice for Ireland, of his rejection of personal ambition.

> But Mother Eire ne'er appealed in vain
> To heart like his – he chose the thorny path,
> Beset with danger, and like valiant knight
> Faced it for her – nor stayed his swerving course
> To grieve o'er his decision – bearing all
> The pains and penalties his fealty bought …
> With uncompromising manhood, till the hair
> Of raven blackness turned to silver grey … [1]

John Mitchel would have been pleased with Miss Thompson's verse. He would have been very pleased with his funeral. Jenny was pleased with his funeral. The conservative *Newry Reporter* numbered the crowd at ten thousand representing 'the commercial, manufacturing, professional and working classes of the town … '

Business was completely suspended and 'many humble men who could ill afford to lose a day's wages stayed away from work in order to follow the remains of John Mitchel to their last resting place. The vessels in the quay had their flags hoisted at half-mast and everywhere throughout the town might be seen the indications of mourning.'[2] His massive oak coffin, with several immortelles on the lid, was placed 'in a plain hearse drawn by four horses in their sable trappings.' Four mourning coaches drew up and the cortege, led by catholic clergy, moved slowly and quietly through the town, taking a longer route than was necessary.[2] The Revd J. Craig Nelson delivered the oration from John Mitchel's father's pulpit, which had been left in the little graveyard after the Unitarian Congregation moved to a new church in William Street. Revd Nelson, whilst not agreeing with Mitchel's views, recalled that he had never examined a student 'exhibiting more marked talent or greater breadth and depth of mind.'[3] John Mitchel was very well read but given his linear obsession with the evils of England and his focused classical world view, perhaps 'breadth of mind' was too strong.

The death of such an important and well-known international personality unleashed a huge number of obituaries, from foe and friend. Obviously, such a controversial character attracted criticism but all had an element of admiration. The *Freeman's Journal* commented, 'A remarkable man has been removed from the stage of Irish politics … The brave man struggling with the storms of fate lived long enough for consolation if not for success.' [4]

The *Irish Times*, no friend of John Mitchel, wrote:

> No one who is not blinded by the most lamentable prejudice can refuse to join with the Rev. Nelson in according to John Mitchel the most thorough uprightness and sincerity of character ... Honest and sterling as steel – the possessor of rare intellectual gifts ... His outrage outran all prudence ... Had John Mitchel no other title to distinction than the efforts which he made to promote religious tolerance among his countrymen, it might be safely said of him that his name was not writ in water.[5]

The *New York Times* praised John Mitchel's 'undaunted courage' but 'outside his ability as a writer of the English language, he processed no attribute which would entitle him to rank as a leader of the people.' [6]

The *London Times* was more sympathetic as it picked up on the dichotomy between Mitchel's angry public words and the affection he both gave and received from family and friends.

> The man who was feared and hated with an intensity which only terror could produce was endeared to those who knew him intimately as an affectionate relative and a sympathetic friend. His public life has been a terrible mistake, unfortunate for his country and still more calamitous to himself.[7]

However, this obituary ended by referring to Jenny as 'a niece of Sir William Verner, who for many years represented the County of Armagh ... ' The Verners, who had objected to John Mitchel being treated on board ship as a gentleman, were not going to let that pass. Jenny was not the genetic daughter of James Verner. The *Times* of 24

March 1875 carried a letter of rebuttal from Sir Edward Wingfield Verner, which politely suggested that Jenny was illegitimate. 'The lady, though a step-daughter of the late baronet's brother, was no relation to the Verner family.'[8] For Jenny who loved her father Captain James Verner and was proud of his name, this was a bitter, but expected, additional blow.

John Martin, who had spoken in support of his friend days earlier in the Carthaginian parliament, collapsed at John Mitchel's funeral. He too had bronchial asthma. He too was taken to John Mitchel's old house in Dromalane where he died, on the 29 March 1875. After a huge funeral from Dromalane, through the streets of Newry, he was buried in his own townland, Loughorne, where he and the young, married Mitchels had spent many happy hours. By birth, and in his disposition, John Martin was an unlikely rebel. In his concern for justice and the welfare of others he was a very likely rebel. Mitchel's words, written in 1848 at that time of great personal and political flux, focus on the truly Christian nature of Martin's character: 'John Martin is my staunch and worthy friend … my fellow felon. What a mild and benevolent looking felon! The convict Jesus was hardly purer, meeker, truer more benignant than this man is.'[9]

Although we tend to think of Martin as the nationalist moon to Mitchel's republican sun, in many ways the asymmetrical relationship between John Mitchel and John Martin was skewed in favour of the less flamboyant Martin. John Martin was more tolerant of diversity, more generous, more forward thinking, politically more successful, less cantankerous, less volatile and, perhaps most significantly, no danger to those he loved.

The garden memorial, erected in Newry, on the two hundredth anniversary of John Martin's birth, is appropriately understated and reflective, but Smith O'Brien's words, written on granite, leave the visitor in no doubt as to the noble and unselfish character of Honest John Martin. 'I have never met in private life so unselfish a man as you; and I am inclined to believe that in the public affairs of nations, there never appeared on earth a patriot more single-minded and disinterested. I feel assured also, that when we differ you will state frankly your reasons for disagreement without bitterness or ill will.'[10] Given Mitchel's aggressive relationships with Duffy and political opponents the last sentence best highlights the difference in character between the two men. Probably the last thing John Martin ever wrote, after viewing Mitchel's corpse, was an affectionate, succinct and partial summary of his best friend's career:

> The face, as I looked at it last night, had a wondrous beauty, both of features and expression. This morning it had a beauty still, but it seems to me of a graver sort and not the almost smiling grace that beamed on it last night … John Mitchel has died well – at home in Ireland, in his father's house, surrounded by his loving brother and sisters and other friends; after a nobly consistent life, crowned with the affectionate of the people he loved and served, triumphant in every respect but material force over his enemies.[11]

Mitchel was consistent in his hatred of those enemies; in his lack of transformation; in his affection for family and friends; in his stoical acceptance of a series of tragedies. He was a remarkable man, a flawed man – given his consistent support of slavery - a remarkably flawed man. Whilst the *New York Times* was critical of John Mitchel and his support of slavery, William Dillon wrote that all the United

States paid tribute to John Mitchel, but especially Virginia. Governor Kemper wrote to Jenny, 'As a tribute of Virginia's admiration, affection and sympathy, the assemblage and its proceedings were all your own heart could have desired.'[12] Such sentiments were welcome and meant a lot, but Jenny was an impoverished widow. In John's final years, as his eyesight was failing, the Mitchels were struggling financially. However, with John's death money worries eased as the Irish community provided Jenny with a fund of $30,000 dollars.[13] With money to develop the lithographic and photographic business, the surviving Mitchels, at last, had financial security. As one small firm was prospering in New York another large industry was declining in Newry. With cotton returning to the world market, after the upheavals of the civil war, linen production was suffering. Dromalane Mill's owner, Jenny's sister-in-law Margaret's husband, Hill Irvine, was bankrupt. Indeed, between 1876 and 1882 Dromalane Mill was to change hands three times because, 'of a depression in trade that did not make it a profitable undertaking.'[14]

The house where John grew up, with its dressed granite extension from which John Mitchel's and John Martin's remains were removed, to their respective graveyards, was sold. The Hill Irvines moved to Dublin and, like the Mitchels before them, down the social scale. Hill Irvine died 18 February 1878, his wife ran a boarding house and the children emigrated to Australia where William Hill Irvine, junior (1848–1943) was to become Prime Minister of Victoria.[15] Before that Jenny was able to repay some of the kindness Margaeret had shown her, by sending money for Margaret to join her sons in Australia.[16] She died in Melbourne 22 July 1904. William Haslett Mitchel, who had many patents to his name and who had been involved in designing the machinery for Dromalne Mill, was again a shipping clerk. Ironically, he was also a trustee of the Quinn

Charity, which was set up ' … for the maintenance and support or
benefit of such indigent persons, male or female, for the time being,
residing within the district as shall have formerly lived in a better or
superior class of life … '[17] Henrietta, John Martin's widow became a
peripatetic teacher, moving from Hampstead to Italy.[18] She died in
Dublin on 12 July 1913 and was buried with the Mitchels in Newry;
not with her husband, of their mature years, in Loughorne.

After John Mitchel's death his wife and children predictably got
on with their lives. As in Dublin in 1848, when Jenny was taken
to Newry and Carlingford, friends moved to help. The lawyer
Richard O'Gorman's family offered refuge at Sands Point, Long
Island. [18] O'Gorman, born in County Clare in 1826 was the son of a
United Irishman and was another Young Irelander who had fled to
America after the 1848 Rebellion. He rose to become a Judge of the
New York Supreme Court.[19] After comforting her mother Minnie
returned to Paris, Kentucky and a struggling marriage with money
problems.[20] Ex-Confederate Colonel Roger Page found it difficult
to work as a lawyer. Isabel moved with Jenny to a better house in
Lefferts Avenue, Brooklyn.

Isabel married Dr Thomas O'Connor Sloane, a gasworks
superintendent, in front of Cardinal John McCloskey on 18 Sept
1877. The couple were unsuited and the marriage was not happy.
According to O'Connor, Dr Sloane's scientific innovation included,
the properties of illuminating gas and 'the wearing of rubber gear
as a guarantor of good health.'[21] John Mitchel's other daughter's
marriage, also in trouble, required Jenny's financial support. Minnie
left Colonel Roger Page and returned to New York to teach and
support her son John Mitchel Page's education. Widower James
married Mary Purroy, whose family the Mitchels had known, and
liked, since arriving in New York in 1853. Whilst coping with the

needs of her domesticity Jenny also had an eye to the past and the grand politics of her late husband. She wanted a Celtic cross as a suitably Irish memorial on John's grave. However, William Haslett Mitchel advised against it. He wrote to Jenny, from Newry, on the 18 March 1879, pointing out that a cross may not be suitable because 'John, never that I know of, distinctly professed himself a member of the Christian Church', and 'There is still existing a certain amount of stupid prejudice among a certain class.'[22] In a divided town a Celtic cross could be vandalized. Jenny, therefore, accepted a simple obelisk with the following inscription.

> After twenty seven years spent in exile for the sake of Ireland, he returned with honour to die among his own people and rests with his father and mother in the adjoining tomb. Erected by his widow.

Tragedy was again a premature visitor. Isabel, John Mitchel's little girl, born in Van Diemen's land, gave birth to a boy, Thomas O'Connor Sloane. Isabel, who had charmed Ireland in 1874, was now sick and very unhappy. Soon afterwards 'Isabel of the Fetters' was released from her mortal misery. Thereafter, Jenny had limited contact with her grandson. According to O'Connor, Jenny's friend, the poet Mary Jane Serrano, blamed Thomas Sloane for Isabel's death:

> *To a Husband*
> *A flower crushed beneath thy heel,*
> *Fast withering she lies;*[23]

Thomas O'Connor Sloane remarried and continued to experiment and invent.

On 19 July 1879 another John Mitchel entered the world. John Purroy Mitchel was born to James and Mary. By this time Jenny had built a new house and was close by in Fordham. Minnie and John Mitchel Page lived with her. She received friends and visitors. It was in James' shop in 1883 that Charles Russell, future defender of Parnell, future Lord Chief Justice of England and old Newry, Queen Street, neighbour, visited a stouter, greyer Jenny; a contrast to the beautiful, but he had thought fragile, young woman he had known in Newry. He recorded the meeting with Jenny in his diary:

> I found Mrs. Mitchel looking stronger and stouter than I had ever seen her before. Trouble had indeed silvered her head; but considering the sorrows, which have been crowded into her life, she seemed in good spirits. To look at her you would hardly imagine that, friendless, she ran the blockade (of the Confederacy) to join her husband and sons in the south.

Russell thought James 'a little resembles his father in the placid expression of his face, in his voice, and in his absence of colour. He has not the strong masterful expression of his father.' [24]

Given James's war record and subsequent forbearance, Russell's curt perception probably did not do him justice. On 12 January 1885, John Mitchel's friend and rescuer, P.J. Smyth, Nicaragua, died at the age of sixty-four. Politically, he had become almost as individually cantankerous as Mitchel. Smyth was estranged from Home Rule, quarreled with Parnellites and referred to the Land League as the 'League of Hell'.[25] Like Mitchel he was MP for Tipperary; however, unlike Mitchel he moved towards Dublin Castle and accepted 'the office of Secretary to the Loan Fund (Ireland) Board' at a salary of

£300 per annum. The Dublin *Freeman* was inclined to be charitable: 'Not withstanding the political shortcomings of his later life, the Irish people have never forgotten in Mr. Smyth's regard the sacrifices which he made and the risks which he ran for them in the generous days of his youth.' It suggested Nicaragua had become a 'government placeman' pleading the same 'excuse of Shakespeare's apothecary'.[26] P.J. Smyth needed the money. He died before he could collect his first salary.

In 1890 The Survivors Association remembered Jenny and her sacrifices for the Confederacy. Captain Courtenay, Captain Mitchel's lieutenant in Fort Sumter, addressing the chair praised Mrs Mitchel. 'There lives in a distant city a venerable matron, with brow frosted by time, whose gracious smile is a benediction, and whose thoughts instinctively wander back to this Southland. She gave three sons to the war … '[27] On 26 July the Association sent Jenny a letter and a book, *The Defence of Charleston Harbour*. There was also an ornate, metaphorical tribute to her son, Captain C. Mitchel:

> … we gratefully and sorrowfully remember that your noble son, Captain John C. Mitchel, while at his post of duty as commander of the proudest citadel of our harbor, was stricken down by the foe and borne back from the forefront of battle upon his equally bright and untarnished shield.[28]

Jenny was pleased and replied. 'If anything could compensate me for the heavy losses I have sustained, it would be the knowledge that there are many who shared my grief with me.' In the same letter Jenny wrote that one of her most treasured possessions was a pencil sketch, sent to her soon after Captain John's death, by Captain

Johnson, her son's friend, and author of the book the Survivors Association sent as a present.[29]

On 23 January 1891 William Haslett Mitchel died. In February 1885 he had written to James Mitchel and explained he was living in Newry because nobody in London 'was ready to give me £100 a year.'[30] In a letter to Mary Thompson, thirty years earlier on 21 March 1855, Jenny, referring to her brother-in-law, noted he was 'quite a successful inventor, and probably will be a rich man in a short time.'[31] William did have several patents to his name and in 1860 returned to the United States from Paris, not only having visited John but also, according to the *Boston Pilot*, having attempted to perfect 'his ingenious type-setting machine by having one constructed on French soil.'[32] Alas, despite his inventiveness Jenny's hopes for William's future prosperity were not to be realized.

In 1896, indicative of a continuing pride in the sacrifices of her family, Jenny presented Captain C. Mitchel's sword, and the flag that flew over Sumter on the day he was killed, to Charleston Museum. They are still there. The 1890s meant Jenny was in her seventies and life moved on. Her grandson, Mitchel's little Buffer, became an Episcopalian priest. Her last surviving son, James the Confederate war hero, became Fire Marshal of New York[33] and his son John Purroy Mitchel, aged only thirty four, was elected mayor of that city from 1914–1917. John E. McClymer has suggested that whilst the Purroy family's history of political success was an important factor in John Purroy Mitchel being elected, 'even more valuable than the Purroy connections in the New York politics of early twentieth century was the Mitchel name.'[34] Although John Purroy Mitchel had the reputation of being both a young reformer, and a good mayor, like his grandfather, 'he trod upon the toes of group after group.'[35] It was claimed he lacked political savvy and 'the loose cog in the wheel happened to be the fact that he held a political position and was a thousand miles away from being a politician.'[36] However, unlike his grandfather Purroy Mitchel was accused of repudiating his own background, 'politically as well as socially, for in Mitchel's hands municipal reform became explicitedly anti-Catholic and anti-Irish.'[37] Whatever the truth of it this is an accusation that could never have been laid against his grandfather John Mitchel. The young mayor lost his 1917 bid for re-election by a record margin. He then joined the Army Air Service and at thirty nine, with the rank of major denied to his uncles, he died in a military training flying accident on 6 July 1918.

On the last day of the nineteenth century, at 10:30 pm, Jenny Verner Mitchel died peacefully. As the world celebrated progress, she slipped into the past, where John was always happiest.

Jenny Verner Mitchel was a remarkable woman, beautiful and sociable. Although devoted to her husband much of her courage, in his causes, was independently displayed: as when, with her children, she crossed oceans and ran a blockade – significantly without John's knowledge. Her private letters, especially to Miss Thompson, tell of a resilient, well-read woman, ready to accept the challenge of farming in an unknown country. She travelled on horseback and covered wagons through a Central American jungle and through the American wilderness. She lived in a log cabin. She was tolerant of ethnic differences. She accepted the conversion and death of her eldest daughter in a Catholic convent. She stoically accepted the loss of her sons in a secondary cause. She lived bravely in a city under siege. Jenny was loyal. She was especially loyal to family and close friends. She was kind to many, including the wounded John Martin and the Hill Irvines. However, she was of her class. She disapproved of Meagher's Tasmanian marriage, travelled with piano and servants, whom she expected to know their place. Politically her views were skewed towards the extreme. She supported an armed rising in Ireland, she suggested members of the legal establishment, who supported banishing rebels, should be shot and if she objected to slavery it was because of the damage it did to slave owners. O'Connor, who as well as writing an affectionate biography of Jenny placed a valuable archive in the National Library of Ireland, has suggested that Jenny reluctantly supported slavery because her husband did so.[38] Her private letters would suggest otherwise. In April 1854 she wrote from Tennessee to Mary Thompson:

> By far the greater number of them are very helpless when left to themselves, suffer miserably, and die off quickly. Nor is it true that there are one hundred tyrants for one humane master. The contrary is the fact. It is in the interest of slaveholders to treat with kindness and care their slaves, and I am sure with few exceptions they are treated with more care and kindness than many servants in Ireland are.[39]

Jenny lies in Woodlawn Cemetery under the Celtic cross denied to John. She lies with the unselfish, brave, cavalier Captain James, who died on 6 October 1908. She lies with her daughter Mary, who was the last of their children to die. The *Irish Monthly* recorded Mary's death and the high esteem nationalist Ireland held for her father at the beginning of the twentieth century:

> The intelligence of the death of Mary Mitchel Page, the last of John Mitchel's children, will be received with deep regret wherever her father's memory is honoured and

preserved and honest hearts still beat with sympathy for the sacrifices of a heroic patriot, and of his noble wife and children who share, and supported him, in his exile, his trials and vicissitudes.[40]

Minnie rests as Mary Verner Mitchel. The inscription recognizes her other grandfather. The last of John Mitchel's troubled immediate family was dead.

CHAPTER FIFTEEN

Less Revolutionary than the Average English Shopkeeper

The lives of John Mitchel and Jenny Verner were remarkable. In terms of nineteenth-century travel, adventure, war, sacrifice and a lifelong fidelity their story is almost incredible. For many, that they were rebels, Irish nationalists and part of the centuries-old struggle against England and empire; that part of their sacrifice involved the violent deaths of two of their children, with one maimed, in a secondary cause; that they encouraged freedom of thought and religion and practised this when their daughters converted to Catholicism; all combine to make them a fascinating and attractive couple. In the century after John Mitchel and Jenny Verner Mitchel were lowered into their respective graves republican Ireland rebelled. As the young Irish Free State and emergent Republic, struggled to a find an identity, independent of its historical entanglement with Britain; struggled to metaphorically widen the Irish Sea; the Mitchels' consistent support of physical force and their condemnation of British involvement in Irish affairs were in synch with first the 1916 rebellion and then the aspirations and actions of the new state.

In 1875, the *Irish Times* had suggested that Mitchel '... descended into the grave without bringing the shadow of a stain on the fair name of his ancestors'[1] and until the 1950s, this may have been perceived to be the case. However, now in the twenty-first century, with Ireland at peace, with President Obama in the White House, and given Mitchel's support not only of slavery but also the reopening of the African slave trade, the dark stain of prejudice is seeping through his legacy, obscuring his influence on the birth and early development of the Irish State and weakening admiration for his life of adventure, hardship and sacrifice with Jenny. There is an irony in it. Both John and Jenny supported a cruel institution neither was ever going to be part of, or materially benefit from. They never owned slaves and, other than in humorous riposte to a Mr Haughton, of Dublin '...we for our part wish we had a good plantation, well stocked with healthy negroes in Alabama.'[2] never had any desire or intention of doing so. If there was a time when John Mitchel was aware of a moral, social and historical fragility to his position it was when the Confederacy, in desperation, considered allowing slaves into the army. Alas, his reasoning doppelganger, with whom his more instinctive Ego had argued on board the *Dromedary* prison hulk, remained silent. Perhaps, given his sacrifices, any deviation from his chosen route would have been too painful to bear. He continued to hold to his creed, as expressed to Father Kenyon in 1859: 'It is good in itself, good in its relations with other countries, good in every way'[3]

Probably in ignorance of the full extent of his support for slavery on 8 March 1965 a statue of John Mitchel was erected, by public subscription, in John Mitchel Place, Newry, yards away from the site of Dr Henderson's Classical School where John Mitchel first met John Martin. Mitchel's statue stands, ironically, given Mitchel's rigid stance on most issues, as a compromise. With the fiftieth anniversary of 1916 approaching, the local nationalist community had wanted to erect a Republican Cenotaph, but at the time, in Unionist-dominated Northern Ireland, this was not politically acceptable. However, given that Pearse had declared *Jail Journal* to be 'the last of the four gospels of the new testament of Irish nationality, the last and the fieriest and the most sublime'[4] a statue to the physical force republican, John Mitchel, was viewed favourably by nationalists in Newry. In reports of the planning and of the unveiling of the statue there was no mention of John and Jenny Mitchel's support of slavery.

Mitchel's statue in Newry is a fine statue, in Kilkenny limestone on a plinth of Newry granite. He stands, confident with his books, demanding to be heard. It is a statue to a man who was heroic; to a man who, more than any other writer or politician, defined the nationalist perception of the Great Famine. It is a statue to a rebel; to a man who lived in a furnace of rebellion, its flames, fuelled by a loathing of the British government, consumed his political ties with Daniel O'Connell, the *Nation*, the Irish Confederation, the United States government, the Confederate Presidency and finally the Fenians. It is a statue to a complex man who lost his home and freedom writing for what he believed in; a man who made great sacrifices for not one, but two lost causes. However, his 'shade' would surely draw solace from the course of Irish history, in the early and mid–twentieth century – Pearse and de Valera were disciples and up until the 1960s the name of John Mitchel was revered in his hometown, and in nationalist Ireland.

Mitchel had not been interested in social, political and economic revolution. His fight was against England, and for Ireland – a rural, hierarchical Ireland, peopled with fair landlords and well-treated tenants, an Ireland where crime and misdeeds were to be punished with the lash, if necessary. In *Jail Journal* Mitchel imagined his Ireland. He venerated the unquestioning

...independent farmer, cultivating his small demesne – a rural *pater familias*, who aspires to no lot but labour in his own land, and takes his hat off to no 'superior' under Almighty God. Tenant-right, fee-farm call his tenure what you will...Such a farmer as this though his acres be very few can generally bring his children forward in a life of honest industry...never troubling his mind about the progress of the species not knowing in the least what that phrase means. I have loved to see...the smoke of the homesteads of innumerable brave working farmers rising from a thousand hills...[5]

This was the Ireland imagined and articulated by De Valera on St Patrick's Day 1943, as:

...the home of a people who valued material wealth only as a basis for right living, of a people who, satisfied with frugal comfort, devoted their leisure to the things of the spirit – a land whose countryside would be bright with cosy homesteads, whose fields and villages would be joyous with the sounds of industry, with the romping of sturdy children, the contest of athletic youths and the laughter of happy maidens, whose firesides would be forums for the wisdom of serene old age.[6]

Both Mitchel's and De Valera's romantic visions saw contentment in stagnation. Beyond not allowing for a human aspiration to improve one's own lot, and that of our children, they did not acknowledge the plight of sons, and daughters, who could not inherit a tenancy or own the small farm. Emigration was a major feature of the Irish economy in the early to mid-twentieth century. Sixty thousand were leaving annually.[7] James Quinn summed it up in writing that nationalism in the early twentieth century was 'often characterised by an introspective and backward-looking romanticism that saw little of value in contemporary industrial society and despised the modern preoccupation with material comfort and prosperity.'[8]

Yet, even as the nationalist citizens of Newry were placing John Mitchel's statue and life on a pedestal Sean Lemass and T.K. Whitaker were dismantling 'De Valera's dreary paradise'.[9] Lemass was Taoiseach from 1959 – 1971 and Whitaker was the secretary of the Department of Finance who warned in the mid 1950s that very aspect of the economy including 'low living standards (half those of Britain), high emigration, low production output, low output from land, savings not being used to best use, inflated wages levels out of line with the cost of production, state funding being expended on non-productive schemes...'[10] all meant 'it would be better to make an immediate move towards re-incorporation in the United Kingdom rather than wait until our economic decadence became even more apparent.'[11] In rescuing the Irish economy, by opening it to foreign investment, by turning it outwards towards Europe and Britain Whitaker was recognized in 2001 as 'Irishman of the Twentieth Century'.[12] A truncated republic, minus six counties, seeking progress, embracing change and welcoming investment, even from Britain, was not one John Mitchel would have been happy with. Increasingly nationalist Ireland was unsettled by John Mitchel's ideas. From the 1960s Mitchel's name, if spoken, was softly spoken in political, even republican circles. Articles and books from academia became more critical. '...he became a bête noir for many historians.'[13] Mitchel's statue in Newry is therefore not a statue to a great revolutionary, in thought and deed he was no Wolfe Tone. He failed to interest the French in an invasion of Ireland and other than seeking humane treatment for the lowly, his ferocious, political pen had little interest in the *rights of man*. He thought it impossible to enslave negro slaves, 'or to set them free either; they are born and bred slaves.'[14]

Yet, in 1848, Mitchel's choice of title for his last Irish newspaper, *United Irishman*, harked back to the 1798 Rebellion, and paid homage to the actions of Tone, and the other leaders, to their hope that all Irishman, of all religions, would unite in rebellion. However, beyond the use of physical force and a desire for ethnic unity, Mitchel had very limited sympathy with the wider egalitarian ideals of the United Irish. For John Mitchel history was cyclical not linear. Empires come and go. There is no progress. He rejected the Enlightenment, empiricism and utilitarianism. Thus, when the nineteenth century writer Emile Montegut claimed Mitchel had no 'democratic sentiments'[15] and that he was 'less revolutionary than the average English Shopkeeper'[16] there was truth in it. Montegut further claimed Mitchel had 'no political opinions' only sentiments and instincts.[17] He suggested Mitchel was 'revolutionary on the surface, in his accent and expression, but not in spirit or in principle.'[18] However, racial stereotyping was not unusual in nineteenth century Europe and Montegut's myopic views of the Celts were hardly any less instinctive and racist than Mitchel's view of the English. He proclaimed the Celtic clans, which by then no longer had any political relevance, had the 'power of a half savage aristocracy tempered by the religious fevour of the priest.'[19] For Montegut, in terms of British and Irish, Mitchel had just got it the wrong way round.

However, given his contemporary national and international reputation; given his influence on the early development of the Irish state; as an Irish rebel, if not as a political revolutionary, John Mitchel, Smith O'Brien's 'formidable monster'[20], has claimed his place in history. Initially when the new, fragile Irish state uncritically accepted its heroic origins Mitchel was revered politically and in biographies. From the mid-twentieth century, with a growing economic confidence, a more cordial and productive relationship with Britain and a greater measure of political stability in the north, Mitchel has suffered from a revision of his, and the state's, heroic narrative.

At a personal level, John Mitchel's statue, in Newry, is a statue to a loving father, who encouraged in his children, both boys and girls, freedom of thought but, most tragically of all, saw two of them killed, and one maimed, because he perceived slave-owning plantations as the antithesis of steam driven factories. Mitchel in relentlessly goading the British probably made his own sacrifice, and that of his wife and children, inevitable but without complaint he accepted the awful family and personal consequences of his decisions. He obviously enjoyed being with his friends and family, especially with John Martin at Loughorne; with Young Ireland in fierce political debate in Dublin; with Jenny in the landscape of Van Diemen's Land; with friends and family in Paris; but, in this life, he did not expect happiness.[21] He probably did not believe in a next life. As with the kangaroo mother he saw his dog viciously kill, in a brutal world the best we can do is struggle and, ironically, hope to do good for our family. Given his life, his decisions, his actions; given his hatred of 'lunatics' and, ironically, his Trevelyan-like view that epidemics rid the world of the weak and sick[22] it is hard not to agree with Quinn that Mitchel's thought was centred 'on a stern, stoical, classical republicanism.'[23] At the end of his two-volume biography Dillon returned to Mitchel's speech from the dock and his view of himself as Mitchel the Roman. Dillon wrote, 'The virtues which attracted Mitchel most strongly, and which were most conspicuous in his own character, were precisely those upon which men set most store in the best days of Greece and Rome.'[24] Such stern virtues saw John Mitchel seek nothing more than improvement in the living conditions of both the Irish peasant and the American slave. There is no paradox between Mitchel's wish to ameliorate the suffering of the Irish peasant yet keep the American black man as a slave. John Mitchel was consistent in his classical world view. The peasant was a peasant who deserved better land tenure. He would remain a peasant. The slave should be treated fairly within slavery, and this could include beatings where necessary. For Mitchel he would always be a slave. This belief and Mitchel's rejection of progress mean that few, in this decade of commemorations, are keen to acknowledge the two hundredth anniversary of his birth.

Jenny Verner emerged from doubtful, obscure, Orange, Ascendancy origins to live a life beyond the imagination of the most romantic novelist. Elopement, rebellion, emigration, Paris, war, blockade, siege, shipwreck, tragedy and loss are the key words in Jenny's story. She was beautiful, courageous, loyal and stoic. She organized global journeys and travelled with her family, in ships, on horseback, in covered wagons, over oceans, through jungles and into the wilderness, she breached military blockades. She too bore life's cruellest blows with an incredible fortitude. Reared, if not born, to privilege she was adaptable and took to the tactile chores of a farmer's wife with zeal. She was both sociable and snobbish. She loved and at times longed for the company of cultivated friends. It was not the log cabin and rural hardship she rejected in Tennessee. It was the isolation and uncouth ways of the Hoosiers. If the testimony of her friend, Mary Jane Serrano, is to be believed Jenny's 'devotion to her husband and the cause to which he had dedicated his life was absolute and unquestioning, both while he lived and afterward ...' [25]

She shared Mitchel's hierarchical views of society, including the perceived benefits of slavery, for both slave and master. On the steps of 8, Ontario Terrace, Dublin she supported a violent rising and later scorned those who spoke and wrote of rebellion but failed to act. Her views on slavery place her legacy beside that of her husband; from a modern perspective stranded in a moral desert from which the waters of justification have long evaporated. Yet in any century her story, her travels, would be remarkable. In the nineteenth century they were heroic.

Given that so much of their tragedy stemmed from one source, Mitchel's hatred of the English government, the passionate, flesh and blood Mitchel, whose statue stands defiant, on the streets of Newry, bears comparison with the fictional Lear. It was his hatred, it was his pride, it was his belief in his own righteousness, it was, especially, his anger – that could not be diluted –that led Mitchel, and his family, into a proxy and fatal war. However, this 'sinner' was also a kind, loving father, husband and friend; a socially charming patrician with a distant, removed, love of Ireland and her peasants; a brave man who helped the dying on the battlefields around Richmond. It is unlikely he was 'more sinned against than sinning' but, unlike Lear, Mitchel did not rage against the fates. He, bravely, accepted the consequences of his skewed, unreasonable, 'even repugnant'[26] thought and actions.

For romance, for adventure, for suffering for what they believed in, for improbable tragedy the story of Jenny Verner and John Mitchel, soured by their rejection of progress and especially their extreme support of slavery, is global in its geography, universal in its appeal. Over the last four years a musical entertainment telling the story of Jenny Verner and John Mitchel has played in catholic, dissenter and protestant halls across Ulster. Such is the appeal of their story.

Notes

Chapter One

1. I.J. Bourke, *A Genealogical and Heraldic History of the Commoners of Great Britain and Ireland Enjoying Territorial Possessions of High Official Rank; But Uninvested with Heritable Honours, Vol. 4* (London: Colburn, 1838), p.56.

2. Ibid.

3. Quoted in J. Kerr, 'Churchill – Home of the Verners', *Journal of the Craigavon Historical Society*, 6: 3 (Apr., 1992).

4. Irish National Archive, Rebellion Papers [hereafter INA], 620/24/37, letter from Ogle to Cooke, 15 July 1796.

5. Kerr, 'Churchill – Home of the Verners',

6. Ibid.

7. P. Townend (ed.), *Burke's Peerage and Baronetage, 105th edition* (London: Burke's Peerage, 1970), p.2704.

8. C. Russell, *'Diary of a Visit to the United States in the year 1883'* (New York: U.S. Catholic Historical Society, 1910), pp213–15.

9. N.J. Curtin, *The Origins of Irish Republicanism:The United Irishmen in Dublin, Vol.1* (Dublin: University of Wisconsin,1988), p 49.

10. A.T.Q. Stewart, *The Narrow Ground: Patterns of Ulster History* (London: Faber and Faber, 1977), p.83.

11. Personal Communication, Revd John Nelson, Historian of the Non-Subscribing Presbyterian Church. Interviewed by the author in Linenhall Library, Belfast on 10 December 2013.

12. Ibid.

13. Ibid.

14. W. Drennan, *Glendalloch and other Poems(with additional poems and memoir by his sons William Drennan and John SwanwickDrennan)* (Dublin: Robertson, 1859), p. xii.

15. Quoted in P.A. Sillard, *Life of John Mitchel* (Dublin: Duffy, 1908), p.47.

16. R.S. J. Clarke, *Old Familiies of Newry and District* (Belfast: Ulster Historical Foundation, 1998), p.122.

17. W. Dillon, *Life of John Mitchel, Vol. 1* (Dublin: Kegan, Paul, Trench & Co.), p.15.

18. W. Porter, 'Obituary, Revd John Mitchel', *Bible Christian*, 2: 4 (May 1840), p.105.

19. Ibid.

20. Ibid.

21. Revd J. Mitchel, *Scripture Doctrine of the Divinity of Our Lord Jesus Christ and other subjects connected therewith* (Newry: Greer, 1828), p. viii.

22. D. Bagot, *The Trinity: A Reply to the objections to that Doctrine* (Newry: Keene & Sons, 1831), p. vi.

23. Dillon, *John Mitchel*, p. 34.

24. Ibid., p.7.

25. Personal Communication, Nelson.

26. J. A. Crozier, *The Life of the Revd Henry Montgomery* (Belfast: E.T. Whitfield, 1875), p. 434.

27. National Library of Ireland [hereafter NLI], Hickey Papers MS 3226, letter from Mitchel to Revd John Mitchel, 17 July 1834.

28. NLI, Hickey Papers MS 3226, letter from Mitchel to Matilda Mitchel, n.d.1834.

29. Dillon, *John Mitchel*, p. 24.

30. R. O'Connor, *Jenny Mitchel Young Irelander: A Biography* (Dublin: O'Connor Trust, 1988), p. 3.

31. Dillon, *John Mitchel,* p. 27.

32. *Dublin Mail*, 16 Nov. 1836.

33. Dillon, *JohnMitchel*, p. 28.

34. G. MacAtasney, *The Dreadful Visitation: The Famine in Lurgan/Portadown* (Dublin: Beyond the Pale, 1997), p.101.

35. NLI, O'Connor Papers, copy of untitled certificate, not catalogued.

36. Miss Martin to Jenny Mitchel, n.d. 1870 in Dillon, *JohnMitchel*, p. 46.

37. Mitchel to Martin, n.d.1844 in Dillon, *JohnMitchel*, p. 54.

38. Dillon, *John Mitchel*, p. 45.

39. Royal Dublin Show, *Past Membere William Verner* website http://www.rds.ie/ cat_historic_member_detail.jsp?itemID=1103426&item_name= (last accessed 27 August 2014).

40. *Belfast Penny Journal*, 19 July 1845.

41. Ibid.

42. Commission to inquire into the conditions of the Poorer Classes in Ireland 1833-1834,Appendixes D,E,FH.C. 1836 (36) xxxi.

43. Commission appointed to inquire into the Occupation of Land in Ireland 1843-845 (The Devon Commission,) H. C. 1845 (605) xix.

44. Ibid.

45. J. Mitchel, *Jail Journal, or Five Years in British Prisons* (Dublin: Gill & Son, 1913), p. xxxviii.

46. Ibid., p. 134.

47. Mitchel to Martin, 23 June 1844 in Dillon, *John Mitchel*, p. 54.

48. R. R. Madden, *The United Irishmen: Their Lives and Times* (Dublin: Duffy, 1846), p.548. On the 8 October 1797 'the son of a gentleman of good fortune from Newry' called with Lord Downshire at his London residence and told him the names of all the principal members of the Executive Committee of the United Irish and their proceedings over the previous two years. Turner's betrayal only came to light years later. For more information see W.J Fitzpatrick, *The Secret Service under Pitt* (Longman and Green, 1892) and the above reference. Fraser, Mitchel legal partner, lived in the Turner's old house.

49. Russell, *Diary*, pp. 213-15.

50. B. P. McGovern, *John Mitchel: Irish Nationalist Southern Secessionist* (Knoxville: University of Tennessee Press, 1999), p. 13.

51. T.F.O. O'Sullivan, *The Young Irelanders* (Tralee: Kerryman, 1945) p. 1.

52. J. Mitchel, *The Last Conquest of Ireland (Perhaps)* (Glasgow: Glasgow Cameron & Ferguson, 1861), p. 17.

53. Ibid.

54. James Quinn, *John Mitchel* (Dublin: University College Dublin Press, 2008), p.8.

55. McGovern, *John Mitchel*, p. 16.

56. M. Huggins, 'A Strange Case of Hero-Worship: John Mitchel and Thomas Carlyle', *StudiIrelandsi, A Journal of Irish Studies*: 2 (2012), pp. 329-52.

57. Duffy, *Young Ireland*, p. 191.

58. Mitchel to Martin, 23 June 1844 in Dillon, *John Mitchel*, pp. 54-5.

59. Mitchel to Duffy, 13 Sept. 1843 in Duffy, *Young Ireland*, p, 145.

60. Mitchel, *Last Conquest*, p.143.

61. Duffy, *Young Ireland*, p. 193.

62. Ibid., p.194.

63. Ibid, p. 193.

64. Ibid., p. 214.

65. Quoted in Thomas Bartlett, *Ireland: A History* (Cambridge: Cambridge University Press, 2010), p. 233.

66. O'Sullivan, *Young Irelanders,* p. 307.

67. Mitchel. *Last Conquest*, p. 82.

68. Duffy, *Young Ireland*, p. 21.

69. Sullivan, *Young Irelanders*, p. 134.

70. Sillard, *Mitchel*, p.44.

71. Mitchel quoted in Sillard, *Mitchel*, p, 45.

CHAPTER TWO

1. *Nation*, 7 Mar. 1846.

2. J. Mitchel, *Life and Times of Aodh (Hugh) O'Neil. Prince of Ulster* (Dublin: Duffy, 1945), p.ix.

3. Carlyle to Duffy, 1 Mar. 1847 website carlyleletters.dukejournals.org/cgi/content/full/21/1/lt-18470301-TC-CGD-01?maxtoshow=&hits=10&RESULTFORMAT=&fulltext=mitchel&searchid=1&FIRSTINDEX=0&resourcetype=HWCIT (accessed 19 June 2014).

4. T. Carlyle, and J.W. Carlyle, *Letters and Memorials of Jane Welsh Carlyle* (London: Longman & Green, 1883), p. 374.

5. *Nation*, 10 Jan. 1846.

6. *Nation*, 7 Feb.1846.

7. J. Mitchel, *The Last Conquest of Ireland (Perhaps)* (Glasgow: Cameron & Ferguson, 1861), p.151.

8. C. G. Duffy, *Young Ireland: A Fragment of Irish History 1840 –1850, Vol.1* (London: Cassell, Petter, Galpin& Co., 1880), p.554.

9. S. Kilfeather, *Dublin: A Cultural History* (Oxford: Oxford University Press, 2005), p. 124.

10. *Irish Citizen*, 2 Nov. 1867.

11. Mitchel to Martin, 23 June 1844 in W. Dillon, *Life of John Mitchel, Vol. 1* (London: Kegan Paul, Trench & Co., 1888), pp141–2.

12. J. Quinn, *John Mitchel* (Dublin: University College Dublin Press, 2008), p.16.

13. *Nation*, 7 Mar. 1846.

14. Mitchel, *Last Conquest*, p.148.

15. J. Mitchel, *Jail Journal, or Five Years in British Prisons* (Dublin: Gill & Son Ltd., 1913), p. 427.

16. Mitchel, *Last Conquest*, p.214.

17. Ibid.,p.213.

18. Ibid., p.219.

19. Ibid., p.216.

20. Ibid., p.151.

21. *Nation,* 18 Mar. 1848.

22. Mitchel, *Last Conquest*, p. 216.

23. *Newry Commercial Telegraph*, 13 Apr. 1847.

24. Ibid.,30 Mar. 1847.

25. Letter from Margaret Russell to Mr. Thompson, Chairman of main relief committee. Copy in possession of the author.

26.   Census of Ireland for the Year 1851. Available at Irish Studies Library, Armagh.

27.   *Independent,* 2 June 1997.

28.   B. O'Cathair, *John Mitchel* (Dublin: Clodhanna Teoranta, 1978), p.13.

29.   *Nation,* 8 Jan. 1846.

30.   Ibid., 5 Feb. 1848.

31.   National Library of Ireland, O'Brien Papers, MS 449, n.d. May 1848.

32.   C.G. Duffy, *Four Years of Irish History, 1845 – 49* (London: Cassell, Petter, Galpin, 1883), pp117–8.

33.   Mitchel to Lalor,4 Jan.1848 in J. F. Lalor, *James FintonLalor: Patriot & political Essayist 1807-1849* (Dublin: Talbot Press, 1918)pp120-1.

34.   Mitchel to Mrs. Mitchel, 12 Dec. 1847, in W.Dillon,*John Mitchel,* p.180.

35.   *Punch,* Vol. XIV,1848, p.51. websitehttps://www.google.co.uk/search?tbm=bks&hl= en&q=%E2%80%9CHow+many+disunited+parties+are+required+to+make+up+a+ United+Irishman%3F%22&gws_rd=ssl (accessed 21 June 2014).

36.   *Newry Examiner and Louth Advertiser,* 22 Jan. 1848.

37.   *United Irishman,* 12 Feb. 1848.

38.   NLI, MS 609/1, letter from Duffy to Mitchel, 12. Apr. 1854.

39.   S. R. Knowlton, 'The Quarrel Between John Mitchel and Gavan Duffy: Implications for Ireland', *North American Journal concerned with British Studies,* 21: 4 (Winter, 1989), p.588.

40.   Mitchel, *Jail Journal,* p. 145.

41.   T.F.O. O'Sullivan, *The Young Irelanders* (Tralee: The Kerryman, 1945), p.301.

42.   *United Irishman,* 12 Feb. 1848.

43.   Quinn, *Mitchel,* p. 17.

44.   NLI, O'Brien Papers, MS 438/1882, letter from Mitchel to O'Brien, 24 April 1847.

45.   O'Sullivan, *Young Irelanders,* p.275.

46.   Lalor, *James FintonLalor,*pp120–1.

47.   Ibid.

48.   *United Irishman,* 13 May 1848.

49.   Ibid.,12 Feb. 1848.

50.   Ibid.

51.   Mitchel to Martin, 23 June 1844 in Dillon, *Mitchel,* p. 158.

52.   *United Irishman,* 1 April 1848.

53.   Mitchel, *Last Conquest,* p. 161.

54.   Dillon, *John Mitchel,* pp. 201-2.

55.   NLI, Charles Gavan Duffy papers, MS 5757, letter from Meagher to Duffy, 2 March 1848.

56. Quoted in Richard P. Davis, *The Young Ireland Movement* (Dublin: Gill and Macmillan, 1988), p. 148.

57. *Nation,* 8 Jan 1848.

58. Ibid.,15 Jan 1848.

59. *Newry Examiner and Louth Advertiser,* 10 June 1848.

60. *Ibid.,* 22 Jan. 1848.

61. J. Saville, *1848:The British State and the Chartist Movement* (Cambridge: Cambridge University Press, 1987), p. 128.

62. L. Fenton, 'Young Ireland in Limerick 1848', *Old Limerick Journal,* 43, (Summer 2009), p.38.

63. *Newry Examiner and Louth Advertiser,* 8 Apr. 1848.

64. *United Irishman,* 22 Apr., 1848

65. *Newry Examiner and LouthAdvrtiser,* 26 Apr. 1848.

66. Ibid.., 20 May 1848.

67. W.J. O'Neill Daunt, *Personal Recollections of the Late Daniel O'ConnellM.P. Vol. 2* (London: Chapman & Hall, 1848), p.205.

68. *Newry Examiner and Louth Advertiser,* 22 Apr. 1848.

69. *Ibid.,,* 17 May 1848.

70. NLI, MS 33898, Mitchel to –, 10 Apr. 1848.

71. Mitchel, Jail *Journal,* p. 80.

72. *New York Times,* 8 May1854.

73. Mitchel, *Journal* (enlarged edition with a preface by Arthur Griffith, Dublin, [1913]), Preface.

74. D. Wilson, *Thomas D'Arcy McGee: Passion Reason and Politics* 1815 -1857, *Vol.1* (Montreal: McGill-Queen's University Press, 2008), p.198.

75. *Newry Examinerand Louth Advertiser,* 5 May 1848.

76. *United Irishman,* 6 May 1848.

77. Quoted in D, Gwyn, *Young Ireland and 1848* (Cork: Cork University Press, 1949), pp.174-7.

78. Ibid.

79. R. O'Connor, *Jenny Mitchel Young Irelander A Biography* (Dublin: O'Connor Trust, 1988), p. 73.

80. *Newry Commercial Telegraph,* 15 May 1848.

81. NLI, MS 12B 1049, Pretty Jenny Verner. P. 9.

82. *United Irishman,* 20 May 1848.

83. *Newry Examiner and Louth Advertiser,* 10 June 1848.

84. *Dublin Journal,* 24 May 1848.

85. O'Connor, *Jenny Mitchel,* p. 77.

86. *London Times*, 19 May 1848.

87. Quoted in NLI, MS 12B 1049, Pretty Jenny Verner. p.8.

Dr. Doyle, the Catholic Bishop of Kildare, whom the Confederate Club was called after, died in 1834. He was much admired by Thomas Davis as a leading supporter of Emancipation and for his part in the setting up of the National School system.

88. *United Irishman*, 30 May 1848.

89. Quoted in O'Connor, *Jenny Mitchel,* p. 78

90. *Newry Examiner*, 18 May 1848.

91. Dillon, *John Mitchel*, p. 236.

92. Mitchel, *Jail Journal,* p.449.

93. O'Connor, *Jenny Mitchel*, p. 233.

94. O'Sullivan, The Young Irelanders, p 144.

95. Ibid.

96. Mitchel, *Jail Journal,*p. xivi.

97. *Newry Commercial Telegraph*, 27 May 1848.

98. P.A. Sillard, *Life of John Mitchel*, (Dublin: Duffy, 1908), p. 211.

99. *Newry Examiner and Louth Advertiser,* 12 July 1848.

100. O'Sullivan, *The Young Irelanders*, p.246.

101. Ibid., pp. 237-8.

102. *The LondonTimes*, 27 May 1848.

103. Ibid., 28 May 1848.

104. *Newry Examine and LouthAdvertiserr,* 31 May 1848.

105. Ibid.

106. *London Times*, 28 May 1948.

107. O'Sullivan, *The Young Irelanders*, p.21.

Chapter Three

1. W. Dillon, *Life of John Mitchel, Vol. 1* (Dublin: Kegan Paul Trench & Co.), p.124.

2. *Newry Examiner and Louth Advertiser*, 14, June 1848.

3. Ibid., 12 July 1848.

4. Ibid.

5. Columbia University [hereafter CU], Melony Mitchel Papers, letter from Jane Verner, n.d. 1848.

6. *Newry Examiner and Louth Advertiser,* 2 June 1848.

7. J. Bew, *Castlereagh A Life* (New York: Oxford University Press), p.128

8. *Newry Examinerand Louth Advertiser*, 16 Feb. 1848.

9. Ibid., 24 May 1848.

10. Ibid.

11. J. Mitchel, *Jail Journal, or Five Years in British Prisons* (Dublin: Gill & Son Ltd., 1913), p.4.

12. Ibid., p.13.

13. Ibid.

14. Ibid., p.8.

15. *Newry Examiner and Louth Advertiser*, 12 July 1848.

16. Mitchel, *Jail Journal*, p.17.

17. *Newry Examine and Louth Advertiserr*, 10 June 1848.

18. Question from Lord G. Beninck to the Home Secretary, *Hansard Parlimenatry Debates House of Commons,* Fifth Volume of the Season, p.758.

19. NLI, O'Connor Papers Boxes 1-3 not catalogued, letter from T. Redington to Captain Wingrove, 30 May 1848.

20. Quoted in Rebecca O'Connor, *Jenny Mitchel Young Irelander A Biography (*Dublin: O'Connor Trust, 1988), p.105.

21. Mitchel, *Jail Journal*, p.53.

22. Ibid., p.96.

23. Ibid., p.45.

24. Department of Taoiseacht, website http://www.google.com/cse?cref=http://search.gov.ie/customcse/www.taoiseach.gov.ie&sitesearch=www.taoiseach.gov.ie&q=flag#gsc.tab=0&gsc.q=flag&gsc.page=1 (accessed on 15 August 2013).

25. *Newry Examiner and Louth Advertiser*, 13 July 1848.

26. *Newry Commercial Telegraph,* 3 August 1848.

27. Ibid., 29 July 1848.

28. Public Records Office Northern Ireland [hereafter PRO NI], Harshaw Diaries, Vol 1. NN, 1848, 7/5–11.

29. *Newry Examiner and Loutb Advertiser,* 19 July 1848.

30. Ibid., 12 July 1848.

31. CU, Melony Mitchel Papers, letter from Jane Verner to John Martin, 17 July1848.

32. J.M. Bennett and A. G. Smith, Irvine, 'Sir Wiliam Hill (1858–1943), *Australian Dictionary of Biography*: 9, 1983. website http://adb.anu.edu.au/biography/irvine-sir-william-hill-6801 (accessed 15/08/13).

33. Mitchel, *Jail Journal*, pp.57–8.

34. Ibid., p.66.

35. Ibid., p.47.

36. Ibid., p.49.

37. NLI, Hickey Papers MS 3226, letter from Mitchel to Matilda Mitchel, 5 Mar. 1849.

38. Ibid.

39. Mitchel, *Jail Journal*, p.72.

40. Ibid., p.139.
41. Ibid., p.149.
42. John Mitchel, *Life and Times of Aodh (Hugh) O'Neil. Prince of Ulster* (New York: Haverty, 1868). p.ix.
43. Mitchel, *Jail Journal*, p.154.
44. Ibid., p.170.
45. Ibid., p.171.
46. Ibid., p.172.
47. Ibid., p.183.
48. Ibid., p.207.
49. Ibid. p. 216.
50. Ibid., p.225.
51. Hamish Maxwell-Steward and Susan Hood, *Pack of Thieves 52, Port Arthur Lives* (Port Arthur: Port Arthur Historic Site Management Authority 2001), p. 6.
52. Mitchel, *Jail Journal*, p.226.
53. *The Irish Felon*, 22 July 1848.
54. *Newry Examine and Louth Advertiser*, 19 July 1848.
55. Mitchel, *Jail Journal*, p.228.
56. Martin to Meagher, 11 Apr. 1850 in T.J. Kieran, *The Irish Exiles in Australia*, (Dublin: Clonmore & Reynolds, 1954), p.80.
57. Mitchel to Meagher, 11 April 1850 in T.J. Kieran, *The Irish Exiles,* p.82
58. NLI, Hickey Papers MS 3226, letter from Meagher to Sir Colman, 27 August 1851.
59. Mitchel, *Jail Journal*, p.230.
60. Ibid., p.231.
61. T.J. Kiernan, *The Irish Exiles,* p.86.
62. PRO NI, John Martin's Diary D560/4, 22 Sept. 1850.
63. Mitchel, *Jail Journal*, p.242.
64. T.F.O. O'Sullivan, *The Young Irelanders*, (Dublin: Kerryman, 1945) p.130.
65. Mitchel, *Jail Journal*, p.246.

CHAPTER FOUR

1. Rebecca O'Connor, *Jenny Mitchel Young Irelander: A Biography* (Dublin: O'Connor Trust, 1988), p.120.
2. L. Fogarty, *Father John Kenyon: A Patriot Priest of Forty-Eight* (Dublin: Mahon, 1921), p.120.
3. T.F. O'Sullivan, *The Young Irelanders* (Tralee: Kerryman, 1945), pp. 234–5.
4. Fogarty, *Father John Kenyon*, p.120.

5. J. Mitchel, *Jail Journal, or Five Years in British Prisons* (Dublin: Gill & Son Ltd., 1913), p.255.
6. Ibid.
7. O'Sullivan, *Young Irelanders*, p.208.
8. Mitchel, *Jail Journal*, p.259.
9. Jenny Mitchel to Mary Thompson quoted in Rebecca O'Connor, *Jenny Mitchel Young Irelander: A Biography* (Dublin: O'Connor Trust, 1988), p.125.
10. Mitchel, *Jail Journal*, p. 259.
11. Ibid.
12. NLI, Hickey Papers MS 3226, letter from Meagher l to Sir Colman, 27 Aug. 1851.
13. Mitchel, *Jail Journal*, p. 259.
14. National Library of Ireland, Hickey Papers MS 3226, letter from Martin to O'Doherty, 14 Aug. 1851.
15. NLI, Hickey Papers MS 3226, letter from Mrs. Connell to Martin, 19th Aug 1851.
16. Mitchel, *Jail Journal*, p.260.
17. O'Connor, *Jenny Mitchel*, p.132.
18. Mitchel, *Jail Journal*, p. 260.
19. Ibid,. p.263.
20. Ibid., p.262.
21. Ibid., P.266.
22. Ibid., pp.267-8.
23. Ibid., P.269.
24. Ibid., p.270.
25. Ibid., p.271.
26. Ibid., p.274.
27. Martin to O'Doherty quoted in O'Connor, *Jenny Mitchel*, p.132.
28. New York Public Library [hereafter NYPL], Madigan Collection, letter from Meagher to O'Doherty, n.d. – early 1851.
29. Mitchel, *Jail Journal*, pp.274.
30. Ibid., p. 275.
31. Ibid., p. 276.
32. Ibid., p.274.
33. Ibid., p. 277.
34. Ibid.,p. 278.
35. NLI, O'Connor Papers Boxes 1-3 not catalogued, letter from Jenny Mitchel to Mary Thompson, 6. Dec 1851.
36. Ibid.
37. Ibid.

38. Mitchel, *Jail Journal*, pp.284–5.

39. NLI, MS 392/2, letter from Mitchel to Mary Thompson, 24 April 1854.

40. NLI, O'Connor Papers Boxes 1-3 not catalogued, letter from Jenny Mitchel to Mary Thompson, 11 September 1851.

41. Bothwell Mitchel Library [hereafter BML], AM87/6, letter from Martin to David Martin, 29 November 1852.

42. Quoted in O'Connor, *Jenny Mitchel*, p.142.

43. BML, AM87/6, letter from Martin to David Martin, 29 November 1852.

44. NLI, O'Doherty Papers MS 10/522, letter from Martin to O'Doherty, 17 Nov. 1850.

45. Mitchel, *Jail Journal*, p.278.

46. Ibid., p. 279.

47. Ibid.

48. Ibid., pp.285–6.

49. Hamish Maxwell-Stewart and Susan Hood, *Pack of Thieves,* p. 6.

50. Ibid.

51. Mitchel, *Jail Journal*, p.286.

52. Ibid.

53. Ibid., pp.286–.7

54. Ibid.

55. Ibid., p.292.

56. Ibid., p.298.

57. Ibid., p. 299.

58. G. Rudé, Thomas Francis Meagher, *Australian Dictionary of Biography* (1967) website http://adb.anu.edu.au/biography/meagher-thomas-francis-2440/text3251 (accessed 28 Aug. 2014).

59. NLI, MS 1630. Letter from Mitchel to Miss Thompson, n.d.

CHAPTER FIVE

1. J. Mitchel, *Jail Journal, or Five Years in British Prisons* (Dublin: Gill & Son Ltd., 1913), p.300.

2. Ibid., p.448.

3. University of Tasmania, Young Irelander Exiles in Paradise website http://www.utas. edu.au/young-irelanders/their-story/young-irelanders-in-ireland (accessed 31 Aug. 2014).

4. Ibid., p.304.

5. Ibid.

6. Ibid., p.306.

7.   Ibid., p.309.

8.   Ibid., p.312.

9.   Ibid.

10. Ibid., p.314.

11. Ibid., p.315.

12. Ibid., p.318

13. Ibid., pp325–6

14. Ibid., p.329.

15. Ibid., pp33-4.

16. Mitchel to Mrs. Mitchel, n. d.July1853 in W. Dillon, *Life of John Mitchel, Vol. 2* (London: Kegan Paul, Trench & Co., 1888), p.24.

17. Mitchel, *Jail Journal*, p.335

18. Ibid., p.336.

19. Ibid., p.317.

20. Ibid., p.309.

21. Steven R. Knowlton, 'The Quarrel Between Gavan Duffy and John Mitchel: Implications for Ireland,' *The North American Conference on British Studies,* 21, no. 4 (Winter 1898). p. 581–90.

22. Mitchel to Mrs. Burke, 5 Mar. 1853 (Hickey Papers, NLI, MS 1630)

23. NLI. O'Connor Papers Boxes 1-3 not catalogued, letter from Jenny Mitchel to Mary Thompson, 11 March 1854.

24. Rebecca O'Connor, *Jenny Mitchel Young Irelander: A Biography* (Dublin: O'Connor Trust, 1988), p.162.

25. John Dooley, *John Dooley Confederate Soldier His War Journal* (Georgetown: Georgetown University Prrss, 1945), p.143.

26. *Sydney Empire* reproduced *New York Times*, 18 Nov. 1853.

27. Mitchel, *Jail Journal*, p.341.

28. Ibid., p.342.

29. Ibid., p.349.

30. O'Connor, *Jenny Mitchel*. p.164.

CHAPTER SIX

1.   J. Mitchel, *Jail Journal, or Five Years in British Prisons* (Dublin: Gill & Son Ltd., 1913), p.49.

2.   R. O'Connor, *Jenny Mitchel Young Irelander A Biography* (Dublin: O'Connor Trust,1988), p.66.

3.   Mitchel, *Jail Journal*, p.350.

4. S. U. Bruce, *The Harp and the Eagle: Irish Volunteers and the Union Army 1861 – 1865,* (New York:New York University Press, 2006), p.14

5. Mitchel, *Jail Journal*, p.269

6. Michael Hanaghan in Jackie Smith and Hank Johnston *Globalization and Resistance* (Maryland: Roman and Littlefield, 2002) p.57.

7. Ibid.

8. Bruce, *Harp and Eagle*, p.12.

9. Ibid., p.18.

10. Ibid.

11. Mitchel, *Jail Journal*, p.350.

12. Ibid., pp.350-1.

13. Ibid.

14. Ibid., p.358.

15. Ibid., p. 361.

16. Ibid., p. 362.

17. NLI, Hickey Papers MS 3226, letter from Mitchel to Reid, 18 Feb. 1854.

18. NLI, O'Connor Papers Boxes 1-3 not catalogued, letter form Mitchel to Matilda Dickson 4 Oct. 1848.

19. PRO NI, John Martin's Diary MS D 560/1-630, 30 Nov. 1848.

20. Mitchel, *Jail Journal*, p. 367.

21. Butler Library, Columbia Rare Books and Manuscripts 801, letter from Jenny Mitchel to Mary Thompson, 12 Dec. 1853.

22. Mitchel, Jail Journal, p.373.

23. Ibid., p.369-70.

24. Ibid., p.358.

25. John Goodbye, *Irish Poetry Since 1950 From stillness into history* (Manchester: Manchester University Press, 2000), P.259.

26. Mitchel to Miss Thompson, n. d. 1856 in Dillon, *John Mitchel*, p.82.

27. *Newry Commercial Telegraph*, 7 July 1855.

28. Mitchel, *Jail Journal*, p.375.

29. NLI, MS 1639, Letter from Mitchel to Miss Thompson 26 Aug. 1854.

30. Butler Library, Columbia Rare Books and Manuscripts 801, letter from Jenny Mitchel to Mary Thompson, 20 April 1854.

31. NLI, MS 609/1, letter from Duffy to Mitchel, 13 April 1854.

32. Mitchel, *Jail Journal*, p.376.

33. NLI, O'Connor Papers Boxes 1-3 not catalogued, letter from Jenny Mitchel to Mary Thompson, 25 Jan. 1855.

34. Ibid.

35. NLI, Hickey Papers MS 3226, letter from Mitchel to Reid, 18 Feb. 1854.

36. Samuel C. Williams, 'John Mitchel, the Irish Patriot and resident of Tennessee', *East Tennessee Historical Society's Publications*, 10 (1938).

37. Mitchel, *Jail Journal*, p.396.

38. *The Citizen*, 14 January 1854.

39. *The Citizen*, 2 January 1854.

40. *New York Times* 13 February 1854.

41. *The Citizen*, 2 January 1854

42. Ibid.

43. Ibid.

44. Ibid.

45. NLI, O'Connor Papers Boxes 1-3 not catalogued, letter from Jenny Mitchel to Mary Thompson, 20 April 1854.

46. Quoted in T.F.O. O'Sullivan, *The Young Irelanders* (Kerry: Kerryman Press, 1945), p.161.

47. NLI, MS 1630, letter from Mitchel to Mary Thompson, 24 April 1854.

48. Butler Library, Columbia Rare Books and Manuscripts 801, letter from Jenny Mitchel to Mary Thompson, 20 April 1854.

49. NLI, Hickey Papers MS 3226, letter from Mitchel to Reid, 18 Feb.

50. *Sydney Morning Herald*, 14 June 1854.

51. *The Nation*, 19 June 1847.

52. Ibid.

53. *The Nation*, 12 May 1861.

54. J. M. Heron, *Celts, Catholics and Copperheads: Ireland Views the American Civil War* (Columbus: Ohio State University, 1968), p.66.

55. O'Connor, *Jenny Mitchel*, p.195.

56. Jenny Mitchel to MaryThompson, 20 April 1854 (O'Connor Papers, NLI, not catalogued, Boxes 1-3)

57. Ibid.

58. NLI, Hickey Papers MS 1630, letter from Mitchel to Mary Thompson, 24 April 1854.

59. Ibid.

60. Mitchel, *Jail Journal*, p. 405.

61. NLI, O'Connor Papers Boxes 1-3 not catalogued, letter from Jenny Mitchel to MaryThompson, 11 Mar. 1854.

62. PRO NI, John Martin's Diary D/560/5, 27 July 1858.

63. NLI, MS 27609 (1), letter from McManus to Duffy, 3 June 1854.

64. NLI, MS 1630, letter from Mitchel to Miss Thompson 26 Aug. 1854.

65. Mitchel, *Jail Journal*, p. 405

66. NLI, MS 1630. Letter from Mitchel to Miss Thompson, 11 Nov. 1855.

67. Mitchel, *Jail Journal*, p. 391.

68. Ibid., pp. 392-3.

69. Ibid.

70. Ibid.,p.386.

71. Ibid. p.397.

72. Butler Library, Columbia Rare Books and Manuscripts 801, letter from Jenny Mitchel to Mary Thompson, 25 Jan. 1855

73. Mitchel, *Jail Journal*, pp 405-6.

CHAPTER SEVEN

1. NLI, O'Connor Papers Boxes 1–3 not catalogued, letter Jenny Mitchel to Mary Thompson, 21 Mar. 1855.

2. Ibid.

3. W. Dillon, *Life of John Mitchel, Vol. 2* (Dublin: Kegan, Paul, Trench & Co.), p.69

4. NLI, O'Connor Papers Boxes 1–3 not catalogued, letter from Jenny Mitchel to Mary Thompson, 21 Mar. 1855.

5. NLI, Hickey Papers MS 3226, Mitchel to Matilda Dickson, 5 Mar. 1849.

6. NLI, MS 1630, letter from Mitchel to Mary Thompson, 1 Nov. 1855.

7. *Newry Commercial Telegraph*, 7 July 1855.

8. NLI, Hickey Papers MS 3226, letter from Mitchel to Mrs. Williams, 24 July 1855.

9. Ibid.

10. Ibid.

11. Ibid.

12. NLI, MS 1630, letter from Mitchel to Mary Thompson, 1 Nov. 1855.

13. Mitchel to Henrietta Mitchel, 19 Dec. 1858 in Dillon, *John Mitchel*, p.81

14. NLI, O'Connor Papers Boxes 1–3 not catalogued, letter from Jenny Mitchel to Mary Thompson 21 Mar. 1855.

15. Ibid., p.88.

16. Samuel C. Williams, John Mitchel, 'The Irish Patriot and resident of Tennessee'. *East Tennessee Historical Society's Publications,* 10 (1938) p.52.

17. NLI, O'Connor Papers Boxes 1–3 not catalogued, Jenny Mitchel to Mary Thompson 21 March 1855.

18. NLI, O'Connor Papers Boxes 1–3 not catalogued, Jenny Mitchel to Mary Thompson, 23 Feb. 1857.

19. Ibid.

20. R. O'Connor, *Jenny Mitchel Young Irelander: A Biography* (Dublin: O'Connor Trust, 1988), p.2 25.

21. Mitchel to Mrs.Wiliams, 16 Feb. 1857 in Philip. L. Brown &, George Russell, (eds), *The Clyde Company Papers Vol. 6* (Oxford: Oxford University Press, 1968) p. 503.

22. Mitchel to Miss Thompson in Dillon, *John Mitchel*, p.96.

23. Rebecca O'Connor, *Jenny Mitchel*, p.228.

24. Mitchel quoted in Dillon, *John Mitchel*, p.101.

25. E. Ruffin, *The Diary of Edmund Ruffin Vol1 Towards Independence October 1856, - April 1861* (Baton Rouge: Louisiana State University Press, 1972.) pp. 263-266. website http://books.google.co.uk/books?id=y5rqrgG34JwC&printsec=frontcover&source=gbs_ge_summary_r&cad=0#v=onepage&q&f=false (accessed 19/08/13)

26. B. L. Mitchell, *Edmund Ruffin, a biography* (Bloomingto: Indiana University Press, 1981), p.254.

27. NLI, MS 3226, letter from Mitchel to Mrs. Williams, 16 Feb. 1858.

28. Ibid.

29. *Irishman*, 25 Jan, 1862.

30. Irish Miscellany, 13 Feb. 1858.

31. *New York Times*, 15 Oct. 1857.

32. T.F.O O'Sullivan, *Young Irelanders*, (Tralee: Kerryman, 1945), p.336.

33. James Stephens Diary, 21 Oct. 1858, quoted in NLI, MS 12B 1049, R.H. Moulder, *Pretty Jenny Verner*, p.22.

34. Ibid.

35. Rebecca O'Connor, *Jenny Mitchel,* p.234.

36. Moulder, *Pretty Jenny Verner*, p.22.

37. *Washington Union*, 5 Dec. 1858.

38. NLI, Hickey Papers MS 3226, letter from Mitchel to Mrs. Williams, 1 May 1859.

39. Dillon, *John Mitchel*, p.124.

40. NLI, Hickey Papers MS 3226, letter from Mitchel to Mrs. Williams, 1 May 1859.

41. Ibid.

42. Dillon, *John Mitchel*, p.131.

43. Mitchel to his mother, 30 July1859 in Dillon, *John Mitchel*, p132.

44. Ibid.

CHAPTER EIGHT

1. Mitchel to Mary Mitchel, 2 Dec. 1859 in W. Dillon, *Life of John Mitchel Mitchel Vol. 2* (London: Kegan Paul, Trench & Co., 1888), p.135.

2. Mitchel to Mrs. Dillon 22 Dec. 1859 in Dillon, *John Mitchel*, p.137.

3. Dillon, John Mitchel, p.135.

4. NLI, Hickey Papers MS 3226, letter from PJ Smyth to John Martin, 20 Nov. 1859.

5. *Irishman*, 8 Oct. 1859.

6.   NLI, O'Connor Papers Boxes 1-3 not catalogued, Photocopy of certificate of naturalization.

7.   Quoted in Dillon, *John Mitchel,* p.142.

8.   Mitchel to Mr and Mrs Dillon, 24 Oct. 1860 in Dillon, John Mitchel, p.145.

9.   Mitchel to his Mother, n. d. Nov.1860 in Dillon, *John Mitchel,* p.146.

10. Mitchel to Mrs. Dickson, 18 Dec. 1860 in Dillon, John *Mitchel,* p.147.

11. Mitchel to his mother, n.d. 1861in Dillon, John *Mitchel,* p.148.

12. Ibid.

13. Mitchel to Mary Mitchel, 22 Dec. 1859, quoted in M. J. Onahan, 'John Mitchel's Daughter', *Catholic World,* LXV11:, 406 (Feb., 1899), p.643.

14. Mitchel to Mrs. Dickson quoted in Rebecca O'Connor, *Jenny Mitchel Young Irelander A Biography* (Dublin: O'Connor Truat, 1988), p. 260.

15. Mitchel to Marty Thompson, May 1861 in Dillon, *John Mitche*l, p.151.

16. Dillon, *John Mitchel,* pp 151–2.

17. Ibid.

18. K. O'Grady, *Clear the Confederate Way! The Irish in the Army of the Northern Virginia* (Mason City: Savas, 2000), p.279.

19. *Richmond Dispatch,* 2 July 1861.

20. K. O'Grady, *Confederate Way,* p.256.

21. Dillon, John *Mitchel,* pp.152-153.

22. Smith O'Brien to Mrs. O'Brien, n. d. 1859, quoted in Thomas Keneally, *The Great Shame* (London: Chatto & Windus, 1999), pp 314-5.

23. Mitchel to Henrietta Mitchel, n.d. Nov. 1860 in Dillon, *John Mitchel,* p.149.

24. Ibid.

25. NLI. O'Connor Papers Boxes 1-3, letter from Mitchel to Matilda Mitchel, 28 Dec. 1860.

26. Mitchel to his Mother, n.d. 1861 in Dillon, John *Mitchel,* p.148 and M. J. Onahan, 'John Mitchel's Daughter', *Catholic World,* LXV11:, 406 (Feb., 1899), p.643.

27. PRO NI, d/1078/m/4, Mitchel to Matilda Mitchel, 5 March 1849

28. Mitchel to his sister Mary, n. d. 1862 in Dillon, J*ohn Mitche*l, p.157.

29. Mitchel to M. Esperendieu, Spring 1863 in Dillon, *John Mitche*l, pp. 158-159.

30. *Southern Illustrated News,* 9 March 1864.

31. Ibid., 19 March 1864.

32. Mitchel to his Sister Mary, 14 Aug. 1861 in Dillon, *John Mitchel,* p.156.

33. John Mitchel to Hill Irvine, 9 July 1861 (Australian Manuscripts Collection, Australain Manuscripts Collection, MS 13698, John Mtchel to Hill Irvine, 9 July 1861. website http://www.slv.vic.gov.au/latrobejournal/issue/latrobe-84/t1-g-t5.html (accessed 18/08/13).

34. Ibid.

35. NLI, Hickey Papers MS 3255, Thomas Meagher, 6 Oct. 1861.

36. Quoted in T.F.O. O'Sullivan, *The Young Irelanders* (Tralee: Kerryman, 1945) p. 194.

37. Dillon, *John Mitchel,* p.161.

38. Mitchel to Henrietta Mitchel, 7 Sept. 1862 in Dillon, *John Mitchel*, p. 161.

39. Dillon, *John Mitchel*, p162.

CHAPTER NINE

1. W. Dillon, *Life of John Mitchel Mitchel Vol. 2 (*London: Kegan Paul, Trench & Co., 1888), p.175.

2. K. O'Grady, *Clear the Confederate Way! The Irish in the Army of the Northern Virginia* (Mason City: Savas, 2000), p.9.

3. Ibid., P.7.

4. C.T. Loehr, *Old First Virginia Infantry Regiment* (Richmond: Ellis Jones, 1884), p.6

5. T.G. Rogers, *Irish-American Units in the Civil War* (Oxford; Osprey Publishing, 2008), p.18.

6. John Beauchamp Jones, *A Rebel War Clerk's Diary at the Confederate States Capital* (Philadelphia: Lippencott & Co., 1866), p. 273

7. Dillon, *Mitchel*, p. 177

8. Mitchel to William Mitchel, n.d. March 1863 in Dillon, *John Mitchel*, p.177.

9. Dillon, *John Mitchel,* p.175

10. John Dooley, *John Dooley Confederate Soldier, His War Journal* (Georgetown: Georgetown University Press, 1945), p.71.

11. Ibid.

12. O'Grady, *Confederate Way,* p.207.

13. Mitchel to William Mitchel, n.d. 1862 in Dillon, *John Mitchel*, p.160.

14. Frank Barnes, *Fort Sumter National Monument, South Carolina* (Washington: National Park Service, 1952), p.17.

15. W.H. Russell, *My Diary North and South* (London: 1863), pp449–51.

16. E. Holmes, *The Diary of Emma Holmes, 1861–1866* (Baton Rouge: 1979), p.106.

17. Dillon, *John Mitchel*, p.179.

18. Ibid., p.183-4.

19. Ibid., p.179.

20. Dooley, *Condederate, Soldier*, p.106

21. O'Grady, *Confederate Way*, p.164.

22. Dooley, *Confederate,* p.143.

23. Ibid., p.90.

24. Ibid., p.143.

25. Mitchel to James Mitchel, 29 July 1863 in Dillon, *John Mitchel*, p. 181.

26. Mitchel to John C. Mitchel, 30 Aug. 1863 in ibid., p.182.

27. Ibid,. p.183.

28. Dooley, *Confederate* Soldier, p.217–18.

29. Ibid., p.117.

30. Mitchel to his daughter Minnie, 22 Oct.1863 in Dillon, *John Mitchel*, p.185.

31. R. O'Connor, *Jenny Mitchel Young Irelander A Biography* (Dublin: O'Connor Trust) p.278.

32. *Richmond Daily Dispatch*, 20 Jan. 1864.

33. War of the Rebellion; Series I - Volume 9: 'North Atlantic Blockading Squadron', (May 5, 1863 – May 5, 1864, p.404.

34. Mitchel quoted in Dillon *John Mitchel*, p. 189.

35. Mitchel to John C. Mitchel, c. Sept. 1863 in Dillon, *John Mitchel*, p.183.

36. Mitchel quoted in ibid., p.199.

37. J.E. Peatman, *Virginians Responses to the Gettysburg Address 1863 -1963* (Unpublished Thesis: Virginia Polytechnic Institute and State University, 2006), pp.32–3

38. Mitchel quoted in ibid., p.174.

39. Mitchel quoted in ibid., p.191.

40. Mitchel to William Mitchel, c. July 1864 in Dillon, *John Mitchel*, p.205.

CHAPTER TEN

1. Miss Pegram, later Mrs. Anderson, in written recollections in William Dillon, *The Life of John Mitchel Vol. 2* (London, Kegan Paul, Trench & Co.1888), pp.193–5.

2. J. Anderson, J. & I. Shuttleworth, Sectarian demography, territoriality and policy in Northern, *Political Geography*, 17 (1998), pp.187-208.

The Newsletter of 19 September 1919 provided an example of a generalized view of peoples John Mitchel could have identified with: 'Ireland is inhabited by two distinct nations, or at least two nationalities … the larger is composed of Celts … the others of Saxon descent. The ethnic character of the two races is as violently opposed as is well nigh conceivable.' For Anderson and Shuttleworth such a view was 'grist to the sectarian mill' and they cited significant religious conversions in both directions, the mixing of different groups through intermarriage, and more temporary arrangements, as evidence of the fragile nature of ethnic identity. For them culture, as expressed in language, literature, sport, music, food and shared myths is socially and not genetically transmitted.[2] Ethnicity is an historical construct, capable of transformation. In contrast, for Mitchel the peoples of Britain and Ireland were inherently different.

3.   Quoted in Dillon, *John Mitchel*, p.195.

4.   Miss Constance Carey, later Mrs Burton Harrison in written recollections in Dillon, *John Mitchel,* pp.197–8.

5.   R. O'Connor, *Jenny Mitchel Young Irelander: A Biography* (Dublin: O'Connor Trust, 1988), p.290.

6.   Mitchel to Jenny Mitchel, c. summer 1864 in Dillon, *Life of John Mitchel Vol 2,* (London: Kegan, Paul Trench & Co., 1888), p.203.

7.   Mitchel to William Mitchel, c. Summer 1864 in Dillon, *John Mitchel*, pp.204–5

8.   NLI, Hickey Papers MS 3226, letter from John Martin to Eva, 16 July 1864.

9.   *Richmond Examiner*, 2 August 1864.

10.   P.A. Sillard, *The Life and Letters of John Martin* (Dublin: Duffy, 1901), pp176–7.

11.   Personal communication with James Quinn, Royal Irish Academy, 2 Oct. 2013.

12.   NLI, Hickey Papers MS 3225, telegram, Gen. Jones to John Mitchel, 20 July.

13.   *Charleston Mercury*, 21 July 21 1864.

14.   Courtenay in *Proceedings Special Meeting of the Survivors Association 1890* website https://archive.org/details/proceedingsatspe00surv (accessed 4 Sept. 2014).

15.   The War of the Rebellion: A Compilation of the Official Records of the Union and Confederate Armies (Vol. xiv, P.210), website http://ehistory.osu.edu/osu/sources/recordView.cfm?Content=020/0201 (accessed 4 Sept. 2014).

16.   NLI, O'Connor Papers Boxes 1-3 not catalogued, letter from Maj. General Ripley to Confederate War Office, 20 July 1864. Text also available at website https://markerhunter.wordpress.com/2014/07/20/cpt-john-c-mitchel-dead/ (accessed 4 Sept. 2014).

17.   J. Mitchel, *Journal*, 20 July 1864 quoted in Dillon, John Mitchel, p.205.

18.   Kelly J. O'Grady, *Clear the Confederate Way! The Irish in the Army of Northern Virginia* (Mason City, 2000), p.279.

19.   O'Connor, *Jenny Mitchel*, p.303.
      In February 1850 the vast western territories, including California and New Mexico were seeking statehood. The Senate was divided as to whether the new states would be free or slave owning. Civil War was a possibility but a compromise accepting California as a free state and allowing New Mexico to vote on the topic was accepted. During the debate, in the Senate chamber, Henry S. Foote pulled a gun on Senator Thomas Hart Benson. For further information visit www.senate.gov/vtour/comp1850.htm

20.   P. Bridges, *Pen of Fire* (Kent: Kent State University, 2002) p.220.

21.   Constance Carey quoted in Dillon, *John Mitchel*, p.197.

22.   Mitchel to William Mitchel, c. Summer 1864, Dillon, *John Mitchel*, pp204

23.   Eye Witness, 'The Fall of Richmond', *Harpers New Monthly Magazine:* 193 (June 1866).

24. Samuel J Moore's, *Complete Civil War Guide to Richmond* (Richmond: n. p., 1978), pp. 48–9.

25. Library of Congress, Manuscript Division, Richards S. Ewell Papers, 27-30 March 1865. pp 296–9.

26. Stephen R. Wise, *Gate of Hell: Campaign for Charleston Harbor* (Columbia: University of South Carolina, 1994), P.1

27. Ibid., p.125.

28. J. Quinn, 'Southern Citizen: John Mitchel, the Confederacy and Slavery', *History Ireland* 3:15 (Summer2007). Website http://www.historyireland.com/18th-19th-century-history/southern-citizen-john-mitchel-the-confederacy-and-slavery/ (accessed 4 Sept 2014).

29. Kelly J. O'Grady *Confederate Way*, pp265–6.

30. Quoted in Dillon, *John Mitchel*, p.109.

31. John Mitchel, *Jail Journal, or Five Years in British Prisons* (enlarged edition with a preface by Arthur Griffith, Dublin: Gill & Sons, 1913), pp. xiii–xiv.

32. Dillon, *John Mitchel*, p.110.

33. *Irishman*, 5 Jan. 1862.

34. Eye Witness, 'The Final Victory', *Harpers Weekly Magazine*: 434 (April1865), pp241–2.

35. John Mitchel quoted in Dillon, *John Mitchel*, p.209.

CHAPTER ELEVEN

1. C. Harrisson, *Refugitta of Richmond: The Wartime Recollections, Grave and Gray, of Constance Cary Harrison* (Knoxville: Charles Scribner's Sons, 2011) p.158.

2. S. A. Brock, *Richmond During The War; Four Years Of Personal Observation* (Richmond: G.W. Carlton, 1867) p.365.

3. Library of Congress, C5_20413, Godfrey Weitzel, Entry of the United States Forces into Richmond, 3 Apr.

4. *Richmond News Leader*, 3 Apr. 1935

5. R. O'Connor, *Jenny Mitchel Young Irelander A Biography* (Dublin: O'Connor Trust, 1988), p.315.

6. Mitchel, quoted in, W. Dillon, *Life of John Mitchel Vol 2*, (London: Kegan, Paul Trench & Co., 1888), p.211.

7. Mitchel to Jenny Mitchel, c. summer 1864 in Dillon, *Life of John Mitchel Vol 2*, (London: Kegan, Paul Trench & Co., 1888), p.212.

8. O'Connor, *Jenny Mitchel*, pp313–14.

9. Mitchel to Margaret Mitchel, 3 June 1865 in Dillon, John *Mitchel, pp213-4.*

10. O'Connor, *Jenny Mitchel*, p315.

11. Ibid., pp 313–14.

12. Mitchel to Margaret Mitchel, 3 June 1865 in Dillon, John *Mitchel,* pp213–14.

13. Mitchel quoted in Dillon, *John Mitchel*, p.217.

14. Ibid., p.218.

15. Mitchel quoted in Dillon, *John Mitchel*, p.220.

16. Ibid., p.222.

17. *New York Times*, 14 Aug. 1865

18. Jenny Mitchel to Mitchel, 28 Aug. 1865 (O'Connor, *Jenny Mitchel*, p.318).

19. Mitchel to Jenny Mitchel, 1 Sept. 1865 in Dillon, *John Mitchel*, p.223.

20. *New York Times*, 1 Nov. 1865.

21. *New York Times, 24 Oct. 1865.*

22. J. Mitchel, *Jail Journal, or Five Years in British Prisons* (Dublin: Gill & Son Ltd., 1913), pp410–11.

23. Ibid., p.411.

24. Mitchel quoted in Dillon, *John Mitchel*, p.224.

25. Brevet Major General Nelson, to Assistant Adj. Gen. E.D. Townsend, 11 Aug. 1865 in O'Connor, *Jenny Mitchel*, p.320.

26. New York Times, 2 Nov. 1865.

27. O'Connor, *Jenny Mitchel*, p.322.

28. W. Dillon, *John Mitchel,* pp.252–3.

29. Mitchel, *Jail Journal*, pp.410-1.

30. Copy of Certificate in, NLI, O'Connor Papers Boxes 1–3 not catalogued

31. NLI, O'Connor Papers Boxes 1–3 not catalogued, letter form Jenny Mitchel to James Mitchel, 10 June 1869.

32. Mitchel to John O'Mahony, n.d. March. 1866 in Dillon, *John Mitchel*, p.232.

33. Mitchel, Jail Journal, p.411.

34. John O'Mahony to Mitchel, n.d. Spring1866 in Dillon, John Mitchel, p.230.

35. Mitchel, *Jail Journal,* p.413.

36. Mitchel to James Mitchel, 7 April 1866 (O'Connor Papers, NLI, not Catalogued, Box 2).

37. Mitchel. *Jail Journal*, p.412.

38. NLI, Hickey Papers MS 3226, letter from John Martin to John Kenyon, 19 June 1866.

39. Mitchel. *Jail Journal*, p.414

40. Ibid.

41. Ibid., p.415.

42. Ibid., p.416.

43. Mitchel to William Mitchel, 16 Oct. 1866 in Dillon, *John Mitchel,* p. 235.

44. Mitchel to Matilda Mitchel, 16 Oct. 1886 in ibid., pp 234–5.

45. Mitchel to Miss Thompson, 16 Oct. 1886 in ibid., p.235.

46. Mitchel to Jenny Mitchel, 2 Feb. 1866 in ibid., pp.236-7.

47. Ibid.

48. Mitchel, *Jail Journal*, p.417.

CHAPTER TWELVE

1. James Quinn, *John Mitchel* (Dublin: University College Dublin Press, 2008), p.78. In 1866, the Fenians invaded Canada with an army of several hundred civil war veterans. In the Battle of Ridgeway, 2 June 1866, they defeated a Canadian militia force. The Fenians were well armed and wore civil war tunics and civilian clothes with flashes of green but with their reinforcements and supply lines cut off by U.S. gunboats on the Niagara River the Fenian raids were short lived.

2. J. Mitchel, *The History of Ireland from the Treaty of Limerick to the Present* (London: Duffy, 1869), p.479.

3. Mitchel in William Dillon, *The Life of John Mitchel Vol. 2* (London: Kegan Paul Trench, 1888), pp254–5.

4. *Richmond Times,* 14 Mar. 1867.

5. Mitchel, *History,* p.479.

6. Mitchel to Martin, c. Feb. 1868 Dillon, *John Mitchel* p.256.

7. Ibid., p.255.

8. R. O'Connor, *Jenny Mitchel Young Irelander: A Biography (*Dublin: O'Connor Trust, 1988), pp336.

9. Mitchel to Mrs. Irvine, 3 Oct. 1867 in Dillon, *John Mitchel*, p.260.

10. Meagher quoted in, G.R. Forney, *Thomas Francis Meagher Irish Rebel American Yankee Montana* Pioneer (not given: Xlibris, 2003), p.77.

11. P.R. Wylie, *The Irish General Thomas Francis Meagher* (Oklahoma: University of Oklahoma Press), p.205.

12. S. U. Bruce, *The Harp and the Eagle: Irish Volunteers and the Union Army 1861 – 1865* (New York: New York University Press, 2006), p.89.

13. Mitchel to Mrs. Irvine, 3 Oct. 1867 in Dillon, *John Mitchel*, p.262.

14. Mitchel in Dillon, *John Mitchel,* p.261.

15. *New York Times,* 21 Feb. 1895.

16. F. Douglass, *My Bondage and my Freedom* (New York: Miller, Orton & Mulligan, 1855), p.451.

   As an escaped slave Frederick Douglass visited Ireland on a lecturing tour in 1845 and supported Catholic Emancipation. In September of that year, he shared a platform with Daniel O'Connell, who opposed slavery, and later 'acknowledged O'Connell's influence on his philosophy and world view for the rest of his life.' Further information at http://douglassoconnellmemorial.org/

17. *Irish Citizen*, 4 Jan 1868.

18. Dillon, *Mitchel,* p.265.

19. Ibid.., p.264.

20. Chris Morash, *Writing the Irish Famine* (Oxford, Oxford University Press, 1995), p.69.

21. J.P. Frayne & M. Marchaterre, (eds.) *W.B.Yeats, The Collected Works of W.B. Yeats Vol. IX Early Articles and Reviews* (New York: Scribner, 2004, p.265.

22. J. Barrington, R*ecollections of Jonah Barrington* with an introduction by George Birmingham (Dublin: Talbot Press, 1918]), p.x.

23. William Carleton quoted in B. Kiely, *Poor scholar* (Dublin: Wolfhound, 1947), p.105.

24. Charles Dickens, *Hard Times For These Times* (New York: Hurd & Houghton, 1869). p.7.

25. Martin to Mitchel, 27 March 1869 in L. Fogarty, *Father John Kenyon A Patriot Priest of Forty-Eight* (Dublin: Whelan and Son, 192?), p.179.

26. Dillon, *John Mitchel,* p.266.

27. Martin to Mitchel, 25 April 1868 in P.A. Sillard, *The Life and Letters of John Martin* (Dublin: Duffy, 1901), p.197.

28. Dillon, *John Mitchel*, p.266

29. P. Fennell, M. King (eds.), *John Devoy's Catalpa Expedition* (New York: New York University Press, 2006), p.70.

30. Martin quoted in, A. M. Sullivan, The "Wearing of the Green" or The Prosecuted Funeral Procession (Dublin: n.p. 1868) website http://www.gutenberg.org/files/12853/12853-h/12853-h.htm (accessed 9 Jan. 2015).

31. Letter to William, 30 April 1869 in Dillon, *John Mitchel.* p.267.

32. *Ibid.*

33. Ibid., p.268.

34. Ibid.

35. Mitchel to Matilda Mitchel, 30 April 1869 in Dillon, *John Mitchel* p.269.

36. NLI, Hickey Papers MS 3226, Mitchel to Smyth, 2 Nov. 1871.

37. Ibid.

38. Dillon, John Mitchel, p.271.

39. John Mitchel to John Martin, 1 Jan 1873 in Dillon, *John Mitchel,* p.274.

40. Ibid., p.275.

41. Dillon, John Mitchel, pp. 271-2.

42. Mitchel to Mrs. Dickson, 1 Jan 1873 in Dillon, *John Mitchel,* p.275.

43. *Freeman's Journal*, 22 Jan. 1873.

44. J. Mitchel, *1641 Reply to the Falsification of History by James Anthony Froude Entitled the English in Ireland* (Glasgow: Cameron and Ferguson, 1873), p.7.

45. *United Irishman*, 12 Feb. 1848.

46. Quinn, *John Mitchel*, p.83.

47. P.S. O'Hegarty, *John Mitchel: an appreciation with some account of Young Ireland* (Dublin, Maunsel and Company, 1917), p.95.

48. Mitchel to Mrs. Dickson n. d. Jan.1873 in Dillon, *John Mitchel,* p.276.

49. Ibid.

50. Mitchel to William Mitchel, n.d. Sept. 1873 in Dillon, *John Mitchel,* p.278.

51. Mitchel to William Mitchel, n.d. Nov. 1873 in Dillon, *John Mitchel,* p.278.

52. Dillon, John Mitchel, p.281.

53. Ibid.

54. Quinn, *Mitchel*, p.84.

55. *Nation*, 27 June 1874.

56. F.S.L. Lyons, *John Dillon: A Biography* (London: Routledge & Kegan Paul, 1968), p.16.

57. Reproduced in *Nation, 27* June.

CHAPTER THRITEEN

1. M. Mulvihill, *A County-by-County Exploration of the Mysteries and Marvels of Ingenious Ireland* (Dublin: Townhouse & Countryhouse, 2001), p.129.

2. Mrs Simpson to Martin, 27 July 1874 in W. Dillon, *Life of John Mitchel Vol. 2* (London, Kegan Paul Trench, 1888), p.282.

3. *Freeman's Journal*, 27 July 1874.

4. *Newry Reporter*, 30 July 1874.

5. Ibid.

6. Mitchel to Jenny Mitchel, 3 Sept 1874 in Dillon, *John Mitchel,* pp283–4.

7. NLI, Hickey Papers MS 3266, letter from Mitchel to P.J. Smyth, 3 Sept 1874.

8. Ibid., 1874.

9. Quoted in, T. De Vere White, *The Parents of Oscar Wilde: Sir William and Lady Wilde* (London: Hodder and Stoughton, 1967), p.81.

10. T.F.O. O'Sullivan, *The Young Irelanders* (Tralee: Kerryman, 1945), p.108.

11. Ibid., p.106.

12. Ibid., p.112.

13. O'Sullivan, *Young Irelanders*, P.278.

14. J. Mitchel, James Clarence Mangan His life, Poetry and Death in, *Poems by James Clarence Mangan.* (New York: Sadler & Co., 1866), p. 8.

15. A. Gibson, Thinking Forwards, Turning Back: Joyce's Writings 1898-1903 in J. Nash, (ed.) *James Joyce in the Nineteenth Century* (Cambridge: Cambridge University Press, 2013), p.67.

16. J. Joyce, *James Clarence Mangan* website https://manganpaper.wordpress.com/2012/10/03/joyces-essay-on-mangans-vastation-of-soul/ (accessed on 1/01/15).

17. Malcolm Brown, *The politics of Irish Literature From Thomas Davis to W.B. Yeats* website http://www.astonisher.com/archives/mjb/irishlit/irishlit_ch9.html (accessed on 18/08/13).

18. *Citizen*, 15 July 1854.

19. Stephanie Schwerter, *Northern Irish Poetry and the Russian Turn: Intertextuality in the Work of Seamus Heaney, Tom Paulin and Medbh McGuckian* (London; Palgrave Macmillan, 2013). p.vii.

20. P. Muldoon, *New Selected Poems: 1968–1994* (London: Faber and Faber, 2004).

21. C. Bonner, 'Exciting, Intoxicating and Dangerous: Some Tiger Effects on Ireland and the Culture of Dublin', Canadian Journal of Irish Studies, 37:1 and 2 (2011), p.69.

22. B. Friel, *Translations* (London: Faber and Faber, 2001), p.417.

23. NLI, O'Connor Papers Boxes 1–3 not catalogued, letter from Mitchel to Mrs. Dickson, 30 Sept. 1874.

24. S. McIntire and W. Burns, *Speeches in World History* (New York: Facts on File, 2009), p.300.

25. *Irishman*, 2 Jan. 1874.

26. Quoted in T.D. Sullivan, *Recollections or Troubled Times in Irish Politics* (Dublin: Gill and Son, 1905), p.123.

27. A. B Hamilton, 'John Mitchel'. *The Open Window*, 3 (1901).

28. Gavan Duffy, *Four years of Irish History, 1845–1849: A Sequel to 'Young Ireland'* (Dublin: Cassell Petter Galpin, 1881) pp.778–9.

29. Mitchel to Mrs. Page, 6 Feb. in 1874 Dillon, *John Mitchel*, p.286–7.

30. Ibid.

31. Martin to Kickham, Feb. 1875 in Dillon, *John Mitchel*, p.288.

32. William Dillon, *The Life of John Mitchel, Vol. 2* (London: Kegan Paul and Trench, 1888), p.289.

33. O'Sullivan, *Young Irelanders*, p.348

34. Martin to Kickham in Dillon *John Mitchel*, p.288

35. Martin to Mitchel, 14 February 1875 in P.A. Sillard, *Life and Letters of John Martin* (London: Duffy, 1893), pp265–70.

36. Mitchel election address in Dillon, *John Mitchel,* p.292.

37. NLI, Mahon Papers MS 22 204, letter form Martin to Mahon, 10 March 187.

38. P. Mitchel (descendant of Mitchel), Lecture in Riverside Presbyterian Church, Newry, 22 Nov. 2012. Quoting unknown newspaper, 5 March, 1875.

39. Dillon, *John Mitchel,* p.300.

40. Ibid., p.301.

41. Ibid.

42. R. O'Connor, *Jenny Mitchel Young Irelander: A Biography* (Dublin: O'Connor Trust, 1988), p.364

CHAPTER FOURTEEN

1. T.F.O. O'Sullivan, *The Young Irelanders* (Tralee: Kerryman, 1945) p. 618.

2. *Newry Reporter,* 25 March 1875.

3. NLI, O'Connor Papers,Boxes 1-3 not catalogued, P. Donahoe, *Sketch of Ireland's Late Leaders* (Boston:1875).

4. *Freeman's Journal,* 23 March 1875.

5. *Irish Times,* 20 March 1875.

6. *New York Times,* 21 March 1875.

7. *London Times,*23 March 187.5

8. *London Times,* 24 March 1875.

9. J. Mitchel, *Jail Journal, or Five Years in British Prisons* (Dublin: Gill & Son Ltd., 1913), pp. 55-56.

10. Smith O'Brien to John Martin 14 January 1861 in *Correspondence Between John Martin and William Smith O'Brien, Relative to a French Invasion, 1861* (Dublin: O'Daly, 1861), p. 12.

11. Martin to his Sister, 21 March 1875 in W. Dillon, *The Life of John Mitchel* Vol. 2 (London: Kegan Paul Trench, 1888), p. 304.

12. Ibid., p. 305.

13. R. O'Connor, *Jenny Mitchel, Young Irelander: A Biography* (Dublin: O'Connor Trust, 1998), p. 374.

14. H. B. Bassett, *County Down. A Guide and Directory 1886* (Dublin, 1886), p 8.

15. J.M. Bennett & Ann g. Smith, 'Irvine Sir William (1858-193)', *Australian Dictionary of Biography*: 9 (1983).

16. O'Connor, *Jenny Mitchel,* p.376.

17. The Quinn Charity, *Scheme for the Administration of the Quinn Charity* Newry, p11.

18. O'Connor, *Jenny Mitchel,* p.396.

19. O'Sullivan, *The Young Irelanders,* pp.358-359.

20. O'Connor, *Jenny Mitchel,* p.375.

21. Ibid., p. 378.

22. NLI, O'Connor Papers Boxes 1-3 not catalogued, letter from William Mitchel to Jenny Mitchel, 18 March 1879.

23. O'Connor, *Jenny Mitchel*, p.385.

24. Charles Russell, *Diary of a visit to the United States in the year 1883* (New York: U.S. Catholic Historical Society,1910), pp. 213-215.

25. O'Sullivan, *The Young Irelanders*, p.270.

26. *Freeman*, 20 Dec. 1884.

27. Zimmerman Davis to Jane Mitchel, 26 July 1890 (Procedings of Survivors Association, Charleston), website http://www.ebooksread.com/authors-eng/tarleton-brown/memoirs-of-tarleton-brown-a-captain-of-the-revolutionary-army-wor/page-2-memoirs-of-tarleton-brown-a-captain-of-the-revolutionary-army-wor.shtml (accessed 14/08/14).

28. Ibid.

29. Ibid.

30. NLI, O'Connor Papers Boxes 1-3 mot catalogued, letter from William Mitchel to James Mitchel, 28 Feb. 1885.

31. NLI, O'Connor Papers Boxes 1-3 not catalogued, letter from Jenny Mitchel to Miss Thompson, 21 March 1855.

32. *Boston Pilot*, 3 March 1860.

33. J. E. Mc Clymer, Of "Mornin' Glories" and "Fine Oaks" in R.H. Bayor, T.J. Meagher (eds.), *The New York Irish* (New Yok: John Hopkins Univesity Press,1997), p.378.

34. Ibid..

35. Ibid., p. 376.

36. Ibid.

37. Ibid., P.380.

38. O'Connor, jenny Mitchel, p.195.

39. NLI, O'Connor Papers Boxes 1-3 not catalogued, letter from Jenny Mitchel to Miss Thompson, 20 April 1854.

40. A. J. Tasman, 'The Last of John Mitchel's Children', *Irish Monthly* 38: 445 (July 1910), p.25.

CHAPTER FIFTEEN

1. *Irish Times*, 22 Mar. 1875.

2. *Citizen*, 14 Jan. 1854.

Mr Haughton was an old gentleman who had known the exiled Young Irelanders in Dublin and wanted Mitchel and Meagher's *Citizen* to denounce slavery. His letter prompted Mitchel's often quoted response in the *Citizen*.

3.   W. Dillon, *Life of John Mitchel Mitchel Vol. 2* (London: Kegan Paul, Trench & Co., 1888), p.311

4.   Padraic Pearse, *The Murder Machine and Other Essays* (Dublin: Mercier Press, 1976), p.93.

5.   J. Mitchel, *Jail Journal, or Five Years in British Prisons* (Dublin: Gill & Son Ltd., 1913), pp.69-7.

6.   M. Moynihan, (ed.), Speeches and statements by Eamon De Valera: 1917–1973 (Dublin: Gill & Macmillan, 1980), p.466.

7.   A. Chambers, *T. K. Whitaker Portrait of* a Patriot (London: Doubleday Ireland, 2014), p.124.

8.   James Quinn, *John Mitchel* (Dublin, 2008), p.89.

9.   *Irish Times*, 3 Oct. 2009.

10.   A. Chambers, *T. K. Whitaker,* P112.

11.   Ibid., P.124.

12.   *Irish Independent,* 10 Oct. 2014.

13.   Quinn, *Mitchel*, p.90.

14.   Mitchel to Kenyon, n.d. 1859 in Dillon, *John Mitchel*, p.106.

15.   Emile Montegut, *John Mitchel, A study of Irish Nationalism* (Dublin: Maunsel & Company, 1915) p.23.

16.   Ibid., p.13.

17.   Ibid., p.19.

18.   Ibid., p.13.

19.   Ibid.

20.   Smith O'Brien to Lucy O'Brien, c. Feb. 1859 in T. Keneally, *The Great Shame, A Story of the Irish in the Old World and the New* (London: Chatto & Windus,1998) pp314–15.

21.   PRO NI, D/1078/M/$, letter from Mitchel to Matilda Mitchel, 15 Feb. 186

22.   NLI, MS 329/3, letter from Mitchel to Miss Thompson, 24 Apr. 1854.

23.   Quinn, *Mitchel*, p.82.

24.   W. Dillon, *Life of John Mitchel Mitchel Vol. 2* (London: Kegan Paul, Trench & Co., 1888), p.311.

25.   *The Boston Pilot*, 13 Jan. 1900.

26.   Quinn, *Mitchel,* p.90.

SELECT BIBLIOGRAPHY

Manuscript Sources

Butler Library, Columbia University Rare Books and Manuscript Library

Melony Mitchel Papers

Irish National Archive

Rebellion Papers

National Library of Ireland

Charles Gavan Duffy Papers

Hickey Collection

James Fintan Lalor Papers

O'Connor Papers

William Smith O'Brien Papers

Young Ireland Miscellaneous Letters

New York Public Library

Madigan Collection

Public Records Office Northern Ireland

Harshaw Diaries

Martin Diaries

Mitchel Letters

Royal Irish Academy

Charles Gavan Duffy papers

Trinity College Dublin

John Blake Dillon Papers

Newspapers and Periodicals

Belfast Penny Journal 1845

Boston Pilot 1900

Bible Christian 1840

Charleston Mercury 1864

Citizen [New York] 1854–5

Dublin Mail 1836

Freeman's Journal 1874–5

Harpers New Monthly Magazine 1866

Independent [London] 1997

Irishman 1959–1874

Irish Citizen 1868

Irish Felon 1848

Irish Independent 2014

Irish Times 1875

Journal of Craigavon Historical Society 1992

London Times 1848–75

Nation 1845–54, 1861 1874

Newry Commercial Telegraph 1848–54

Newry Examiner and Louth Advertiser 1848

Newry Reporter 1874–5

New York Times 1853–65

Old Limerick Journal 2009

Punch 1848

Richmond Daily Dispatch 1864

Richmond Times 1867

Southern Illustrated News 1864

Studi Irelandsi 2012

Sydney Morning Herald 1854

United Irishman 1848

Washington Union 1858

Printed and Digital Sources

Bagot, D. *The Trinity A Reply to the Objections to that Doctrine* (Newry: Keene & Sons, 1831).

Barnes, F. *Fort Sumter National Monument, South Carolina* (Washington: National Park Service, 1952).

Barrington, J. *Recollections of Jonah Barrington* with an introduction by George Birmingham (Dublin: Talbot Press, 1918).

Bartlett, T. Ireland: *A History* (Cambridge: Cambridge University Press, 2010).

Bassett, H. B. *County Down. A Guide and Directory 1886* (Dublin, 1886).

Bayor, R. H., Meagher T. J. (eds), *The New York Irish* (New Yok: John Hopkins Univesity Press, 1997).

Bennett J. M. & Smith A.G. 'Irvine Sir William (1858-193)', *Australian Dictionary of Biography*: 9 (1983).

Bew, J. *Castlereagh: A Life* (New York: Oxford University Press , 2011).

Bonner, C. 'Exciting, Intoxicating and Dangerous: Some Tiger Effects on Ireland and the Culture of Dublin', *Canadian Journal of Irish Studies*, 37: 1 and 2 (2011).

Bourke, *I. J. A Genealogical and Heraldic History of the Commoners of Great Britain and Ireland Enjoying Territorial Possessions of High Official Rank; But Uninvested with Heritable Honours, Vol. 4* (London: Colburn, 1838).

Bridges, P. *Pen of Fire* (Kent: Kent State University, 2002).

Brock, S.A. *Richmond During the War; Four Years of Personal Observation* (Richmond: G.W. Carlton, 1867).

Brown, P.L. &, Russell, R. (eds), *The Clyde Company Papers Vol. 6* (Oxford: Oxford University Press, 1968).

Bruce, S.U. *The Harp and the Eagle: Irish Volunteers and the Union Army 1861–1865,* (New York: New York University Press, 2006).

Carlyle, T. and Carlyle, J.W. *Letters and Memorials of Jane Welsh Carlyle* (London: Longman & Green, 1883). p.374.

Clarke, R.S.J. *Old Families of Newry and District* (Belfast: Ulster Historical Foundation, 1998).

Chambers, A.T.K. *Whitaker Portrait of a Patriot* (London: Doubleday Ireland, 2014).

Curtin, N.J. *The Origins of Irish Republicanism: the United Irishmen in Dublin, Vol.1* (Dublin: University of Wisconsin, 1988).

Crozier, J.A. *The Life of the Rev. Henry Montgomery* (Belfast, E.T. Whitfield, 1875).

Davis, R.P. *The Young Ireland Movement* (Dublin: Gill and Macmillan, 1988).

De Vere White, T. *The Parents of Oscar Wilde: Sir William and Lady Wilde* (London: Hodder and Stoughton, 1967).

Dickens, C. *Hard Times For These Times* (New York: Hurd & Houghton, 1869).

Dillon, W. *Life of John Mitchel, Vol. 1* (Dublin: Kegan, Paul, Trench & Co.,1888).

———*Life of John Mitchel, Vol. 2* (Dublin: Kegan, Paul, Trench & Co., 1888).

Dooley, J. *John Dooley Confederate Soldier His War Journal* (Georgetown:Georgetown University Press, 1945).

Douglass, F. *My Bondage and My Freedom* (New York: Miller, Orton & Mulligan, 1855)

Drennan, W. *Glendalloch And Other Poems (With Additional Poems And Memoir By His Sons William Drennan And John Swanwick Drennan)* (Dublin: Robertson, 1859).

Duffy, C.G. *Young Ireland: A Fragment of Irish History 1840–1850, Vol.1* (London: Cassell, Petter, Galpin & Co., 1880).

———*Four Years of Irish History, 1845-1849: A Sequel to "Young Ireland"* (Dublin: Cassell Petter Galpin, 1881).

Eye Witness, 'The Final Victory', *Harpers Weekly Magazine:* 434 (April 1865).

Fennell F. M. King M. (eds), *John Devoy's Catalpa Expedition* (New York: New York University Press, 2006).

Fenton, L. 'Young Ireland in Limerick 1848', *Old Limerick Journal,* 43 (Summer 2009).

Fogarty, L., *Father John Kenyon: a patriot priest of forty-eight* (Dublin: Mahon, 1921).

Forney, G.R., *Thomas Francis Meagher: Irish Rebel American Yankee Montana* Pioneer (not given: Xlibris, 2003).

Friel, B. *Translations* (London: Faber and Faber, 2001).

Frayne J.P. & Marchaterre, M. (eds) *W.B. Yeats, The Collected Works of W.B. Yeats Vol. IX Early Articles and Reviews* (New York: Scribner, 2004).

Garvin, T. *Judging Lemass: The Measure of the Man* (Dublin: Royal Irish Academy, 2009).

Goodbye, J. *Irish Poetry Since 1950 From stillness into history* (Manchester: Manchester University Press, 2000).

Gwynn, D. *Young Ireland and 1848* (Cork: Cork University Press, 1949).

Harrisson, C. *Refugitta of Richmond The Wartime Recollections, Grave and Gray, of Constance Cary Harrison* (Knoxville: Charles Scribner's Sons, 2011).

Heron, J.M. *Celts, Catholics and Copperheads: Ireland Views the American Civil War* (Columbus: Ohio State University, 1968).

Holmes E. *The Diary of Emma Holmes, 1861-1866* (Baton Rouge: 1979).

Huggins, M., 'A Strange Case of Hero-Worship: John Mitchel and Thomas Carlyle', *Studi Irelandsi, A Journal of Irish Studies*: 2 (2012).

Jones, J. B. *A Rebel War Clerk's Diary at the Confederate States Capital* (Philadelphia: Lippencott & Co., 1866).

Keneally, T. *The Great Shame* (London: Chatto & Windus, 1999).

Kerr, J. 'Churchill – Home of the Verners', *Journal of the Craigavon Historical Society* 6: 3 (April, 1992).

Kiely, B. *Poor scholar* (Dublin: Wolfhound, 1947).

Kieran, T.J. *The Irish Exiles in Australia*, (Dublin: Clonmore & Reynolds, 1954).

Kilfeather, S. *Dublin: A Cultural History* (Oxford: Oxford University Press, 2005).

Knowlton, S.R. 'The Quarrel Between John Mitchel and Gavan Duffy: Implications for Ireland', *North American Journal concerned with British Studies*, 21: 4 (Winter, 1989).

Lalor, J.F. *James Finton Lalor: Patriot & Political Essayist 1807-1849* (Dublin: Talbot Press, 1918).

Loehr, C.T. *Old First Virginia Infantry Regiment* (Richmond: Ellis Jones, 1884).p.6

Lyons, F.S.L. *John Dillon A Biography* (London: Routledge & Kegan Paul, 1968).

MacAtasney, G. *The Dreadful Visitation The Famine in Lurgan/Portadown* (Dublin: Beyond the Pale, 1997).

McGovern, B. P. *John Mitchel Irish Nationalist Southern secessionist* (Knoxville: University of Tennessee Press, 1999).

McIntire, S. & Burns, W. *Speeches in World History* (New York: Facts on File, 2009). p.300

Madden, R.R. *The United Irishmen, Their Lives and Times* (Dublin: Duffy, 1846).

Mangan, J.C. *Poems by James Clarence Mangan.* (New York: Sadler & Co., 1866).

Maxwell-Steward H. and Hood, S. *Pack of Thieves 52, Port Arthur Lives* (Port Arthur: Port Arthur Historic Site Management Authority 2001).

Mitchel, J. *Life and Times of Aodh (Hugh) O'Neil. Prince of Ulster* (Dublin: Duffy, 1945).

———*The Last Conquest of Ireland (Perhaps)* (Glasgow: Cameron & Ferguson, 1861).

———*The History of Ireland from the Treaty of Limerick to the Present* (London: Duffy, 1869).

———*1641 Reply to the Falsification of History by James Anthony Froude Entitled the English in Ireland* (Glasgow: Cameron and Ferguson, 1873).

———*Jail Journal, or Five Years in British Prisons* (Dublin: Gill & Son, 1913]).

Rev. Mitchel, J. *Scripture Doctrine of the Divinity of Our Lord Jesus Christ and other subjects connected therewith* (Newry: Greer, 1828).

Mitchell, B.L. *Edmund Ruffin, A Biography* (Bloomingto: Indiana University Press, 1981).

Montegut, E. *John Mitchel, A Study of Irish Nationalism* (Dublin: Maunsel & Company, 1915).

Morash, C. *Writing the Irish Famine* (Oxford, Oxford University Press, 1995).

Moynihan, M. (ed.). Speeches and statements by Eamon De Valera: 1917-1973 (Dublin: Gill & Macmillan, 1980).

Muldoon, P. *New Selected Poems: 1968 – 1994* (London: Faber and Faber, 2004).

Mulvihill, M. *A County-by-County Exploration of the Mysteries and Marvels of Ingenious Ireland* (Dublin: Townhouse & Countryhouse, 2001).

O'Brien W.S. *Correspondence Between John Martin and William Smith O'Brien, Relative to a French Invasion, 1861* (Dublin: O'Daly, 1861).

O'Cathair, B. *John Mitchel* (Dublin: Clodhanna Teoranta, 1978).

O'Connor, R. *Jenny Mitchel Young Irelander: A Biography* (Dublin: O'Connor Trust, 1988).

O'Grady, K. *Clear the Confederate Way! The Irish in the Army of Northern Virginia* (Mason City: Savas, 2000).

O'Hegarty, P S. *John Mitchel: an appreciation with some account of Young Ireland* (Dublin, Maunsel and Company, 1917).

O'Neill Daunt, W.J. *Personal Recollections of the Late Daniel O'Connell M.P. Vol. 2* (London: Chapman & Hall, 1848).

O'Sullivan, T.F. *The Young Irelanders* (Tralee: Kerryman, 1945).

Onahan, M.J. 'John Mitchel's Daughter', *Catholic World*, LXV11:, 406 (Feb., 1899).

Pearse, P. *The Murder Machine and Other Essays* (Dublin: Mercier Press, 1976).

Peatman, J. E. *Virginians Responses to the Gettysburg Address 1863 -1963* (Unpublished Thesis: Virginia Polytechnic Institute and State University, 2006), pp.32-33

Porter, P, 'Obituary, Rev. John Mitchel', *Bible Christian, 2*: 4 (May 1840). p. 105.

Quinn, 'J. Southern Citizen: John Mitchel, the Confederacy and Slavery', *History Ireland* 3:15 (Summer 2007).

———*John Mitchel* (Dublin, University College Dublin Press, 2008).

Rogers, T. G. *Irish-American Units in the Civil War* (Oxford; Osprey Publishing, 2008).

Royal Dublin Show, *Past Membere William Verner* website http://www.rds.ie/cat_historic_member_detail.jsp?itemID=1103426&item_name= (accessed 27 Aug. 2014).

Rude G. Thomas Francis Meagher, *Australian Dictionary of Biography* (1967).website http://adb.anu.edu.au/biography/meagher-thomas-francis-2440/text3251 (accessed 28 Aug. 2014).

Ruffin, E. *The Diary of Edmund Ruffin Vol1 Towards Independence October 1856,–April 1861* (Baton Rouge: Louisiana State University Press, 1972).

Russell, C. *'Diary of a visit to the United States in the year 1883'* (New York: U.S. Catholic Historical Society, 1910).

Saville, J. *1848: The British State and the Chartist Movement* (Cambridge: Cambridge University Press, 1987).

Schwerter, S. *Northern Irish Poetry and the Russian Turn: Intertextuality in the Work of Seamus Heaney, Tom Paulin and Medbh McGuckian* (London; Palgrave Macmillan, 2013).

Sillard, P.A. *The Life and Letters of John Martin* (Dublin: Duffy, 1901).

———*Life of John Mitchel* (Dublin: Duffy, 1908).

Somerville D.C. (ed.). *Selections from Wordsworth* (London: Dent & Sons, 1966).

Sullivan, T.D. *Recollections or Troubled Times in Irish Politics* (Dublin: Gill and Son, 1905).

Smith J. and Johnston H. *Globalization and Resistance* (Maryland: Roman and Littlefield, 2002)

Stewart, AT.Q. *The Narrow Ground: Patterns of Ulster History* (London: Faber and Faber, 1977).

Tasman, A. J. 'The Last of John Mitchel's Children', *Irish Monthly* 38: 445 (July 1910).

Townend, P. (ed.), *Burke's Peerage and Baronetage, 105th edition* (London: Burke's Peerage, 1970).

War of the Rebellion; Series I–Volume 9: 'North Atlantic Blockading Squadron', (May 5, 1863–May 5, 1864.

Wilson, D. *Thomas D'Arcy McGee: Passion Reason and Politics* 1815–1857, *Vol.1* (Montreal: McGill-Queen's University Press, 2008).

Wise, S.R. *Gate of Hell: Campaign for Charleston Harbor* (Columbia: University of South Carolina, 1994).

Wylie, P.R. *The Irish General Thomas Francis Meagher* (Oklahoma: University of Oklahoma Press).

INDEX

Note: Plate entries appear in bold, i.e. the first plate is indicated thus: P1.